ADVANCE PRAISE FOR INSPIRED TO DANCE

"A singer needs a voice coach, an actor needs an acting coach, a dancer needs this book."

—*Lou Paciocco*, *Stage and Film Producer, Creator of* La Cage Aux Folles *and* An Evening at La Cage

"*Inspired to Dance* is truly a bible for any budding dancer as well as any person working their way through the world of dance. It's written with provocative questions that guide and support. This up-beat, honest book will undoubtedly fill a niche in the world of dance. Brava!"

—*Jane Bernard, Author,* Fine Tuning, Connecting with Your Inner Power *and* Intuitive Eating, The 6th Sense Diet

"*Inspired to Dance* is a phenomenal book that will aid dancers in the professional world of dance, whether it be Los Angeles, Las Vegas, New York, or overseas! It will give dancers the tools to guide them on their road to success. Determination and a passion for dance are essential, and *Inspired To Dance* will give you the knowledge of how it all works!"

—*Kristy Boyd, Professional Dancer/Dance Teacher K-12*

"Working with Mande as director/choreographer on several projects was very exciting; she is a truly dedicated professional, and a very passionate, caring soul. Mande has created an incredible, must-have resource for performers: *Inspired to Dance* is filled with a wealth of knowledge, invaluable experience, and answers that will be priceless to anyone pursuing the journey to dance."

—*Larry Brown, CEO, Fisher Island Club Resort*

INSPIRED TO

DANCE

INSPIRED TO

DANCE

EVERYTHING YOU NEED TO KNOW ABOUT BECOMING
A PROFESSIONAL DANCER WITHOUT BREAKING A LEG

———

MANDE DAGENAIS

iUniverse, Inc.
New York   Bloomington

Inspired to Dance
Everything You Need to Know about Becoming a
Professional Dancer without Breaking a Leg

iUniverse books may be ordered through booksellers or by contacting:

iUniverse
1663 Liberty Drive
Bloomington, IN 47403
www.iuniverse.com
1-800-Authors (1-800-288-4677)

Because of the dynamic nature of the Internet, any Web addresses or links
contained in this book may have changed since publication and may no longer be
valid. The views expressed in this work are solely those of the author and do not
necessarily reflect the views of the publisher, and the publisher hereby disclaims
any responsibility for them.

You should not undertake any diet/exercise regimen recommended in this
book before consulting your personal physician. Neither the author nor the
publisher shall be responsible or liable for any loss or damage allegedly arising
as a consequence of your use or application of any information or suggestions
contained in this book.

Chapters 3, 5, 10, & 16 title page photos by Robert Cerri
Remaining photos are from the author's private collection

ISBN: 978-1-4502-0183-4 (sc)
ISBN: 978-1-4502-0185-8 (dj)
ISBN: 978-1-4502-0184-1 (ebk)

Printed in the United States of America
iUniverse rev. date: 02/12/2010

Cover and chapter format design: Dan Fickett/FVR

"Break a Leg"
An idiom used in "showbiz" to wish someone luck before a performance.
You would say "break a leg" before going on stage
but you would *never* say good luck.

In loving memory of my parents: my mother, Emily Dagenais, a constant source of inspiration, and my father, Elzear Dagenais, who taught me about fine detail and perfection.

And, for *my sweetheart,* my husband Alex Marchant, who has taught me to slow down just enough to smell the roses along the way.

Dear Mom,

For all that I have accomplished throughout my dance career, I owe you a huge debt of gratitude. Mom you are the very reason for my career and, therefore, the reason I'm able to write this book and share my experiences with so many today. I have had an exciting and rewarding career as a dancer, choreographer/director and producer. I have traveled extensively for my work and I've seen parts of the world that otherwise I might never have seen, all thanks to your love and devotion. Without all your hard work and determination, I certainly never would have gone to dance lessons, let alone, fulfilled my dreams. I have always known how fortunate I was to be given such a wonderful opportunity, and lucky for me, I have been able to share many of my experiences with you.

I'm sure that when I was nine years old, first starting out, you did not consider that dancing would be my career; you were simply a mother giving your daughter an opportunity to do something that she loved. What you did was encourage me every *step*—and I do mean literally—of the way, and when you saw the talent I had and how much I loved it all, you encouraged me more. You always taught me to do what I loved and to go for all that I wanted in life, truly supporting every dream and empowering me, whether you realized what you were doing or not.

It is said that there is nothing greater than a mother's love for her children—it is unsurpassed. Mothers are our "everyday heroes"; they go to amazing lengths for their children. They are incredible people, capable of great things all in the name of love. Mom, you have been the best role model of all, strong and kind, hard-working and honest, with great morals and virtues. You taught me to believe in myself and to go for what I wanted in life; you have always been a great source of inspiration in my life and I am eternally grateful. You are forever in my heart.

I love you, Armande

Contents

Foreword by Lou Paciocco

In the beginning of my career as a show producer, I did what was expected of me. I tried to hire the best team available to execute my creative concept. I gathered what I thought was necessary to meet my needs. I hired a director, a choreographer, a set designer, a costume designer, lighting and sound designers, and someone to coordinate it all.

Then luckily for me, I met Mande Dagenais, who in fact, *did it all*, and took my shows to an even higher level. Now, lucky for you, she has written this incredible guide for dancers and all performers alike. In her book, Mande teaches what it really takes to be in "the business." If you have ever aspired to dance, or to perform, or if you would simply like to know what *Show Business* is really all about, then this is the book for you. Mande covers it all: how to get in the business, where you can work—from Broadway to LA and everywhere in between, and what to expect when you get there!

Mande's talent is unique; she possesses a vast knowledge of show business, and is an inspiration to all who have the opportunity to work with her. Her experience from both sides of the curtain, as a performer and as a producer, makes her an invaluable source of information to any aspiring artist. After reading her book, you will understand why I wish to all other producers, a Mande Dagenais.

Lou Paciocco—creator of *La Cage Aux Folles* and *An Evening at La Cage;*
celebrity impersonation revues worldwide.

Acknowledgments

First I'd like to thank my family; my mother and father, Emily and Elzear Dagenais; my sisters, Beverly Cascanette, Joanne Sinclair, Lauraine Friskey and Gail Dagenais; my brothers, Gary Dagenais, and Ralph Dagenais; and my sisters and brothers in law for their loving support always. From dance recitals as a kid to driving me to my first audition, and the many opening nights as a professional, they were always there for me! Thanks to all my friends and family who graciously read my first attempts at writing this, my first book, made invaluable suggestions and cheered me on every step of the way. Without those early enthusiasts, this might still be just conversation.

A great big thank you to my husband, Alex Marchant, for his constant help and undying support from the first word to the last word, and the many re-writes in-between. And to my sister Lauraine Friskey for her endless hours and months of reading, advising, suggesting and editing my early manuscript. A huge thank you to my niece Jody Tierney, for reading and re-reading *every single word* I wrote, and for putting up with me through it all. Very special thanks to Lou Paciocco for never tiring of my *one more question*, my *one more addition*, and my *one more proofread*! But, most of all, for 20-years-plus of friendship, mentoring and support in *all* that I do, and for always reminding me of the importance of "being open and flexible" in life.

A very heartfelt thank you to my Aunt Cletis, I have never forgotten that it was she who suggested to Mom that she send me to dance class. For that, I am forever appreciative.

To my mother and father in law, Mum and Dad Marchant, a very warm thank you for their very early suggestions and words of encouragement that gave me the confidence to keep writing, and for always being available for yet another read-through. To Jay and Marilyn Jiggins, for constantly supporting and keeping me accountable. To Diana Platts, John Ciotta, and Michael Gruber for the many check points along the way. To Debbie Brown for "think tanks and writing escapes," and for all of her encouragement, and to Diana Weber for always being there no matter what, and cheering me on throughout my journey.

And to Arlene Uslander, my editor, a very special thank you for her detailed work, for all of her fine-tuning and her teachings through her work; and for holding my hand, and walking me through the process. To Rusty Fisher for his clever contributions—the many sub-titles and wonderful segues—for making the book flow and giving it a sense of timing, and very important, for introducing me to Arlene. Special thanks to Dan Fickett, *artiste extraordinaire,* for all of his creative genius and for gracing the cover of my book with his magnificent design.

A particular thank you to Dr. Spencer Baron for his enormous input to my fitness and health chapters: "Fit to Dance" and "Let's Get Physical." Without his participation and tremendous knowledge, I could never have brought such important information to you. And to Terry Fay for sharing his financial expertise and knowledge in an interview with me, which was the foundation for my chapter "Money Makes the World Go Round." To Libe Halevy for her help and direction early on, to Patrick Wanis for his caring analysis in the beginning stages, and to Jane Bernard in the later stages, for her subliminal guidance through her book *Write-On: the Art of Re-Writing*.

And last, but certainly not least, my assistant choreographers, the women who *danced by my side*, often through the wee hours of the night! For their round-the-clock devotion and stamina, I am forever grateful to Tracy (Kerr) Bianchi, Jemma (Sawyer) Mckeown, Helen (Chadwick) Timpano, Tracy (Luce) Beetham, Samantha (Wyles) Maxwell, Courtney (Newell) Sternick, Stacey Enyart, Alice Billman, and Angeliki (Piliouras) Lapaire. And to the many talented cast members: singers, dancers, and specialty performers, who found their way into my rehearsal studio and made it through opening night; some, opening night after opening night. Thank you for sharing your talent. You are the gems that I have collected along the way.

Once again, a gracious thank you to all who so indulged me. It seems that "the book" has not only consumed my life, but also the lives of many others. It has been without a doubt the ubiquitous topic of conversations for what seemed to be forever, and now, after three-plus long years it has really happened!

Introduction

You may not know it, but your wish (or future wish) is my command! This book was written to fill what I believe to be a void; to answer the many questions that have been asked of me time and time again over the years by hundreds and hundreds of dancers, performers, aspiring performers, aspiring choreographers, teachers, and parents alike. *Inspired to Dance* is intended to be the most comprehensive guide you will ever need, hence the subtitle—*Everything You Need to Know About Becoming a Professional Dancer Without Breaking a Leg.*

There has never been one single book that simply said it all and told it as it is! And so I have looked back over my years, my successes and my failures, and I have attempted to consider all the questions along the way; the identical questions that you might have on your own journey. There are so many things that we all wanted to know back when we were in your very position. I constantly hear from my peers and from the talent that has worked with me, "I wish there had been a book like this when I was first starting out."

My true desire is to give back to an industry that has given so much to me and has brought me so much pleasure over the years, by giving to others who are as passionate about dance and show business as I am. I admire the complete courage and all that it takes to pursue your passion, and I commend you. "Show Business" can be a complete mystery if you are sitting on the wrong side of the gateway. So go ahead, turn the page and take the first step through that gateway. Over the next sixteen chapters you will learn all there is to know about how to *get in* the business, *be in* the business and *stay in* the business. I wish you much success on your journey and aspire to make it a little bit easier for you with my book. Happy Reading!

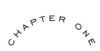

CHAPTER ONE

BORN TO DANCE—TURNING DREAMS INTO GOALS INTO COMMITMENTS

My First Communion, age 7. I already had stars in my eyes—
and a swing in my hips. Check out my left foot!

> *"I don't want people who* want *to dance; I want people who* have *to dance."* —*George Balanchine*

So, you want to be a dancer! Let me ask you something: *Why* do you want to dance? What is it about dance that attracts you? Its beauty, grace and elegance? The excitement, the glamour, the stage, the lights, the music, the applause? Do you dream of being on stage, do you fantasize about being famous, or do you simply want to dance because you love how you feel when you're lost in the motion?

How about *all* of it?

Why not? Dancing is all that and so much more.

I ask these questions not merely for the sake of it, but because the teacher in me wants to make sure your eyes are squarely on the prize. I've seen so many dancers with big dreams and plans, with bright hopes and shiny fantasies, but it's the dancers who turn their dreams into goals—and their goals into commitments—who truly succeed.

Goals and dreams are the energy of life; commitment is the outlet through which that electricity turns into reality. It is tremendously important to have goals and dreams. They help fulfill us, they fuel us and drive us to great accomplishments, and they can relax and comfort us by providing our very own private sanctuary within—a sanctuary where all dreams are possible, limited only by our own imagination.

Throughout my career, people have asked me such questions as:

- How do I become a dancer, a performer, an entertainer?
- How do I get into the business?
- What should I expect?
- How can I ace that big audition?
- How do I know if I'm ready?

Now here's a question for all of you: What if I told you that within you, lies the key to your own success? It does, you know. Within you, lies the road map to your own bright success; you simply have to know how to tap into it. Fortunately, that's what this chapter—what this entire book—is all about.

Together, we are going to go through the entire process of becoming a dancer: from dream to goal to commitment; from audition to getting the part; from fantasy to reality. The first thing I want you to know, however, is that it all starts with *you*.

I firmly believe that when you want something badly enough, very little can stand in your way and, even more importantly, when you know *why* you want it so badly, you will be truly empowered! Simply knowing why you want to dance is a huge secret to your success. And that's why this first chapter is so important. First we'll discover your "why"; then we'll find your "way."

Encore:
Goals and dreams are the energy of life; commitment is the
outlet through which that electricity turns into reality.

Find Your "Why" and You Will Find Your "Way"

You may have heard this before (I've personally heard it repeated over the years by many great teachers), but it's so helpful—and central to our goals together—that I wanted to repeat it one more time: Find your why and you will find your way!

So many of us skip the why in favor of the how. We just want to know how to get the part, how to be a star, that we lose sight of *why* we want to get the part or be a star in the first place. So do we really need to know the "why" in the first place?

Short answer? Yes, it really is that important.

Longer answer? Knowing why you want to dance can truly determine your outcome. When you know why, and that why is big enough, and when you know exactly what you want from the business, "how" you get there will be revealed. Your path will become undoubtedly clear.

So, take a moment and think about it: Why do you want to dance?

What are your goals and dreams? Be specific! What passion burns inside you? One thing is certain—dancers know about passion and burning desire, and if they don't, they shouldn't be in the business. If you don't have passion, then I ask you, what is the point? After all, there are certainly much easier ways to earn a living.

Dance is all about passion. Dance is art, art is passion, and all artists express their passion through their work. The musician plays an instrument, the fine artist uses paint and canvas, and a dancer tells a story through expression and movement.

A dancer is like a canvas that has come to life. The passion of dancers is witnessed and experienced by their every move; their body is their instrument. What an incredible way to be able to express oneself—and one's passion: through his or her entire body, with every gesture, no matter how subtle. A dance void of passion is like a life without purpose.

When you have passion, everything else falls into place. Everything that is required seamlessly comes together. They all go hand in hand: hard work, dedication, and commitment all come effortlessly when you know where you are going. Nothing is too difficult when you want something badly enough. When you know what you want and why you want it, there is only one thing left to do, and that is to *just go for it*!

Encore:
When you know why, and that why is big enough,
and when you know exactly what you want from the
business, "how" you get there will be revealed.

Getting to Know You

So you say that all you want to do is dance. Well then, let me tell you about what it takes to be in the business:

- Talent—of course!
- The right attitude—a must.
- Commitment—you won't get anywhere without it.
- Hard work—till your toes bleed!
- Dedication, desire, extreme passion and vision—yes, they are all necessary.

Still interested? Of course you are; you love to dance, and it's all you ever wanted to do, but it doesn't stop there—the list goes on. How about tough skin and staying power? How many times can you take "no" before you get a "yes"? The answer had better be as many as it takes! Fall down seven times, get up eight. You love it, so enjoy the journey because the process can be amazing; this can be one of the most exciting rides of your life.

I'm sure you've heard the many proverbial sayings. Two of my favorites are "Where there's a will, there's a way," and "If you believe it, then you can achieve it." Another one of my personal favorites is the Japanese proverb I just mentioned above, "Fall down seven times; get up eight." No matter how many times you fall down, the only way to make it is to get straight back up again—and again and again. Mountain climbers also say that the only way to reach the summit is to take one step for every two you get knocked back.

The bottom line is this: if you want something strongly enough, you will never take *no* for an answer. Rejection is not an option. Now, that doesn't mean there won't be any rejections along the way. On the contrary; there could be many, and at the very least, most likely several.

Rejection is simply a fact of life in our business. You just can't take it personally. Another way to look at it might be, "Take it seriously, just don't take it personally." In many cases, it's not you they were rejecting; not your style or your shape or your form or your commitment. You simply were not what they were looking for on that particular day.

How can that possibly have anything to do with *you*? It's purely the nature of the business, and you can't be right for every part or be everything to everyone. Once you learn to accept this, the rest is a piece of cake.

In the big picture, it's all just part of the process. The sooner you understand and accept certain realities about this business you have chosen, the better equipped you will be to set out on your journey. How interesting would this journey be if it was all just handed to you on a silver platter, and at the end of the day, you had no war stories to tell?

You know as well as I do that everyone loves a little drama—particularly entertainers—and it's much more fun for the performer in you to re-enact the story. So enjoy the journey and the many stories that you will gather and tell along the way. On the other hand, I'm not saying that it never comes easy; it's simply a fact that more often than not, you're going to take several knocks before you land on your feet.

Some people moan and groan every step of the way; they look at every hiccup as a stumbling block or, even worse, a roadblock. I prefer to think of these hiccups as building blocks—and suggest that you do the same. The choice is yours. You can make this really hard on yourself by taking every knock and every blow and allowing them to slowly crush you along the way, or you can set out on your path to success by standing firm in your conviction and thereby enjoying this incredible journey. (And, yes, that does mean taking the bad with the good.)

Encore:
The bottom line is this: if you want something strongly enough, you will never take no for an answer. Rejection is not an option.

Two Questions to Unlock Your Secret Desire

With the right attitude, clear-set goals, and total commitment, this can be the most amazing journey you will ever take. Ask yourself these two questions:

1. What are your aspirations? This is where I want you to be totally honest with yourself and as specific as you can be. Be very clear about where you want to end up. What is your ultimate destination? Don't worry about how you are going to get there; just define what that final destination is, how it looks, and how it feels. The clearer your picture is, the more specific your goals can be.
2. Are you willing to break down walls to get to where you want to be? If you have talent and the kind of passion and conviction that it takes to persist, even when rejection is staring you in the face, then you *will* succeed. We can't all star in our own Broadway show or be the next pop idol or film icon, but with all those ingredients, you not only will find your way within the industry; you will find your place—a place where you can shine.

In order to help you define your process, I will address some of the various opportunities for building blocks and how you can utilize them to your advantage. Remember, a dream alone is great, but it's not enough. We must add goals and commitment to the recipe to make our dreams become reality.

Opportunity is all around you; even when something seems like a failure, it can really be success in disguise. Don't believe me? I want you to take into account every single class, every audition, every rejection (and every success), every compliment, every correction, every criticism and every accomplishment. By utilizing all these various opportunities in a positive way, you will be building a strong character and stamina with a great attitude, all-around good habits—all of which contribute to building a solid foundation for your career.

The truth is, they can all be accomplishments, every single one; it just depends on how you look at them. At the end of the day, it's all about perception. We can sit in our lonely rooms and dwell on the negative all day long, but where would that get us? Worry, regret, and negativity are three of life's biggest time wasters. Just imagine how positive, uplifting, and hopeful your life could be if you got rid of all three.

You *can* get rid of them, you know. Think of a polishing stone; the more you rub it—the more you polish it—the shinier and more beautiful it becomes. It simply continues to get better and better, closer and closer to perfection with every loving touch. Sure, I can hear those negative little voices already: "That's easier said than done." But the truth is, no one ever said it was going to be easy. However, with the right outlook and a good game plan, the road will keep getting smoother every step of the way.

I remind you, it is absolutely essential to set goals; they are the building blocks of our dreams. As Lewis Carroll (author of *Alice in Wonderland* and *Through The Looking Glass*) said, "If you don't know where you are going, any road will get you there." I love that expression! To that I will add, "If you don't know where you are going, you certainly don't know where you are going to end up—and you may not like it once you get there!"

So remember to set clear goals. Again, I ask you, what is your ultimate destination? Setting goals will get you through the rough patches, and your commitment to those goals is what will get you to your final destination. Never take your eye off the prize, and one step at a time, you will just keep getting closer and the big picture will become clearer and clearer. I've said it before and I will say it again: it's your dream; how much do you want it? This is your journey; do you want a smooth path or a rocky road? You choose.

I will guarantee you this: if you choose a positive and nurturing approach, you will have a much healthier and happier journey. Along the way, you will make your path smoother by simply having the right outlook, and that in itself is a huge success. And no matter how big or small, make it a habit to acknowledge your successes, each and every one of them. Never underestimate the power that comes with each little success. Sometimes it's the exact push you need to get you to the next step, which could then catapult you to your ultimate goal. Besides which, life is simply a better and happier place if you acknowledge yourself for a job well-done.

As I keep saying, the truth is, it all comes right back down to your outlook. You can walk out of an audition and say to yourself, "*Wow!* What a great audition! I learned a fabulous routine, did a great job of performing it, and I made some new contacts, which might bring future possibilities." Or you can walk out of that same audition discouraged and berating yourself, saying "How could I blow it so badly? I completely messed up the routine… they hated me… I'll never get this gig."

Once again, the bottom line is this; you will have a much more positive experience if you simply look for the good in every situation. It truly is that simple. Look for everything that you did great in each situation, be it a class, an audition or a meeting.

Don't dwell on your failures; dwell on your successes. You will feel so much better about yourself, which, in turn, will build self-esteem and confidence, both of which are absolute necessities in this business—not to mention in life.

Encore:
Opportunity is all around you. Even when something seems like a failure— it can really be success in disguise.

The (Not So) Impossible Dream

When commencing rehearsals of a new production, or working with a new cast for the first time, I start out with an orientation. This is a great opportunity for everyone to meet each other and for the cast to know what they can expect and what will be expected of them. This interaction could be the most important interaction I will ever have with a cast; I always look forward to it.

One of the first things that I talk about and a subject that I feel so strongly about is the fact that we are such a privileged group of people. As dancers, singers, actors and performers, we get to do what many of us have dreamt of our whole lives. How many people never get to fulfill their dreams? How many people go through their entire lives settling because they were too fearful to follow their dreams?

Take a look around you. How many people do you know in your own life who have either been stuck in that fear, just didn't believe in themselves enough to go for it or, even worse, had others discourage them from pursuing their dreams? How many people don't even know that the power to fulfill their dreams is really within them? They wouldn't even know where or how to begin. Some even forget how to dream because their goal or passion has been suppressed within them for so long.

The mere fact that you had a dream and you went for it makes you very special indeed. Many of the world's great motivational speakers and authors would say that this decision alone separates you from about 90 percent of the population. Take heart and be grateful for the fact that actually going for those desires and dreams puts you in a very small, unique group that represents only 10 percent of the population. The fact that you can take your dreams and turn them into goals, and commit to the journey, is an incredible achievement. In fact, turning your dream into a goal *creates* your commitment. Once committed, it is a one-way street, with no U-turns and no turning back.

Remember: stay the course; your commitment is what will get you there. Your talent is a gift, something so unique and so special that you must never lose sight of it or take it for granted. As one dancer to another, I ask that you please nurture your talent, respect your talent, and respect the business and the people in it. This business is full of very special people and once-in-a-lifetime moments just waiting to happen. Always be grateful for this life; although it is sometimes difficult, it is, in fact, a very extraordinary life.

Encore:
Your talent is a gift, something so unique and so special that you must never lose sight of it or take it for granted.

Inspiration—Trusting Personal Heroes and Mentors

I'd like to say it was all fun and games! Production Team, Umbro Licensing Show, Montreal, Canada

"Great dancers are not great because of their technique; they are great because of their passion." —*Martha Graham*

This book is called *Inspired to Dance* for a reason, and that simple reason is this: dancing is inspiration; inspiration is dancing. It may take blood, sweat and tears to train ourselves to perform at peak physical perfection onstage, in front of an audience, but inspiration is the fuel that drives our dreams.

To be truly inspired requires a lot of soul-searching and asking of very personal questions, such as: What inspires you? What inspired you to dance as a young child? What magical moment created in you this most incredible desire to dance?

Then think back to a time when you were very young, and remember: Was it one particular performance? A big sister or brother who danced? A famous dancer or choreographer who knocked you off your feet? (Or "onto your feet," as the case may be?) A movie musical? A Broadway show? Or was it simply an innate need to express yourself through the creative outlet of dance?

Whatever that inspiration was, it was obviously strong enough to keep you dancing, or interested in dance, and to find yourself reading this book. Whatever that initial inspiration was, it created your love for dance and your desire to dance. It is so important to remember that; to keep in mind how incredibly inspired you were, and what you've accomplished so far *because* of that inspiration.

They say that when the student is ready, the teacher will appear; inspiration can teach us many things, but only if we are ready to be moved by it. If you look back over your years of training, you probably will find that there were different inspirations at different times of your life, each one of them fulfilling a purpose and often times taking you to the next level. So where are you today? Are you first starting out in your professional career? Are you training and dreaming of a career in dance? Or are you already well on your way in your performing career?

Regardless of whether you are just starting out or you are a seasoned professional, inspiration plays a big role in the key to your success. Go ahead and look back into your own life and training and bear in mind why you started and why you continued. Chances are you'll find that your greatest accomplishments were in those very moments in which you were most inspired.

First, though, let's define inspiration so you and I are both on the same page:

> *Inspiration (noun): The action or power of*
> *moving the intellect or emotions.*

I love this definition because it's so specific: *moving the intellect or emotions.* Isn't that a great phrase? How often have we watched a wonderful dance routine, listened to a beautiful musical score, or felt the dancer's emotions ring through their footwork and were "moved"?

The beauty of inspiration is that it works on two levels: our intellect and our emotions. When it comes to our intellect, we can be inspired to be rational and logical about planning our success. We can watch a dancer or dance, be inspired and think, rationally or logically, "I can do that; with training and persistence, I can be up there doing that."

Emotionally, we can be inspired to provoke our feelings of passion and intensity, both of which are so desperately needed on our long road to success. In the first chapter, I talked about setting goals and meeting them; in this chapter, I will talk about what inspires you and how to tap into that inspiration to sustain your desire long enough to reach your goals.

So, what moves you today? Where are you at this very moment? What is it that you want more than anything else in the world, and what is it that inspires you to set that goal and actually reach it?

The answers to these questions are just as important as asking the questions themselves; find your inspiration and you will find your way. Most people don't ever give this step any thought, but very often, inspiration is the overriding force behind one's motivation to do most anything in life.

That's why I've dedicated an entire chapter to it.

Encore:
This book is called Inspired to Dance for a reason, and that simple reason is this: dancing is inspiration; inspiration is dancing.

Mentors + Trust = Inspiration

Mentors are synonymous with inspiration. And when you look up to your mentors and trust them to guide you with experience and wisdom, you can be doubly inspired to achieve all your dancing goals. That's because being inspired follows a simple formula: Mentors + Trust = Inspiration.

- Whom do you look up to?
- Who are your personal, everyday life heroes?
- Who are your mentors?

I would like to take this opportunity to tell you about some of my own mentors, the importance of having them in our lives, and the significance of recognizing them. As I mentioned in my dedication, I always knew how fortunate I was in my life and along my own path to dancing. Specifically, so much of that has to do with the people who have touched my life and helped me along the way.

When I was very young, I remember thinking to myself that if I could have just the right balance of my mother's strength and my father's sensitivity, I would have a great start in life. And guess what? Here I am many years later to say that I pretty much got what I asked for. Had I known back then how truly powerful those thoughts were to become in reaching my goals, the list might have been a bit longer!

I'm sure you've heard the saying, "Be careful of what you ask for in life because you're liable to get it." And to that I add what a very dear girlfriend of mine always said, "when doing the asking, make sure that you are very specific and *ask for exactly what you want.*" Don't leave out any details; make sure the list is complete. Keep in mind that this is your list and you can change it or add to it whenever—or whatever—you want. For me, it all started way back, with my mother and father, as I would guess it does for many of us.

My parents were both wonderful, hardworking, honest people with high morals and values. They were great role models, each in their own way and in their own specific areas. My mother was very strong, proud, and extremely devoted to her family. She was the rock, the foundation. My father was somewhat complex, as he was a very quiet, but sensitive, man with an "all or nothing" sort of approach to things. If he was going to do something, it was a firm commitment which he saw through to the end or he didn't do it at all. Dad was definitely the risk taker; an entrepreneur in his own right.

They inadvertently taught me to be independent while instilling the importance of family values and integrity. In a large family, one learns the importance of sharing and being a team player. Being independent and yet knowing how to be a team player are both extremely important traits to possess in the entertainment industry. When it comes to creative genes, I have both my parents to thank. My mother was an excellent seamstress and costume designer. She made all, or most of, our clothing growing up, and when I went to dance class, she designed and sewed costumes for our company. My father was exceptional at carpentry and fine finishing. They were both perfectionists in all that they did. As a kid, I remember thinking about qualities in each of my parents that I would like to take on as my own, and how they might affect me in life. This seemed a pretty solid foundation from which to start. If life is, in fact, about the choices we make, then who better to emulate than two people I respected and loved so dearly?

Next were my siblings: my four big sisters, Beverly, Joanne, Lauraine, Gail, and two big brothers, Gary and Ralph. I thought I was the luckiest little girl ever to have all those big brothers and sisters of my very own. I was the baby, and a surprise at that, but Mom always assured me that I was a wanted surprise. As I was a "change of life baby," I was much younger than my siblings. My brothers were six and seven when I was born and my four sisters were nine, ten, twelve, and thirteen years old.

In my earliest memories, my sisters were either married, had moved away from home or were teenagers. It was almost like two separate families and, although my brothers and I were so much closer in age, by the time I was eleven or twelve, they had moved away as well. Inevitably, this made me somewhat of an "only child."

My sisters, being so much older than I, were a strong influence in my upbringing. When I was about five or six, my oldest sister was already an adult; I thought this was pretty cool. At such a young age, I got to take part in their adult and teenage lives, so my conscious lessons started early, and I had so many varied examples right there in my own family.

As a result, I learned about influences and making choices at a young age. You can imagine growing up at the tail end of all those kids; there were some great life lessons to be learned. It was a bit like being handed my own personal manual on the *do's* and *don'ts* and how to survive just about anything. I won't go into all the details of growing up in such a large family, but I will say that I was very fortunate to have been raised in one; I wouldn't change a single minute of it.

In life, we have choices, and the choices we make along the way help determine and mold our life and who we become. With six siblings before me, and growing up in the sixties and seventies, to boot, the lessons were invaluable. I would have had to be catatonic not to learn the importance of making your own choices. This lively and caring cast of characters quickly became my early-life personal heroes—and remains so today.

They also became my own personal audience! Before I ever had a single lesson, I was making up dance routines and performing them for my relatives. Formally or informally, I was always dancing around everywhere we went.

The summer that I was nine years old, my Aunt Cletus recommended to my mother that she send me to dance class. So that very September, it was official; off I went to dance school. This was a really big deal! You see with seven children in our family, five being girls, my parents could never have afforded dance lessons, let alone any kind of lessons for all of us. I, being the baby and so much younger than the rest, got lucky. By this time, the others were all grown up and I was the only one left at home. This was an opportunity for Mom to do for me what she would have loved to, but was never able to do, for all the others. Who could know that this decision would have such an impact on the rest of my life?

The next nine years or so brought some of the best experiences a child, and then teenager, could ever hope for. Luckily for me, my second oldest sister Joanne was a good friend of the wife of one of the owners of a dance school close to where I grew up. The fact that this school was so renowned, combined with my sister's personal association with an owner's wife made our search for the perfect school very easy. I still remember that first day, walking up the big wide stairwell to the second floor of the school of performing arts. I was so incredibly excited! Mom signed me up, bought me a pair of tap shoes, and another of the owners, "Mrs. G," whisked me off to my first tap and jazz class.

It was the beginning of one very long, and satisfying, love affair with dance...

Encore:
Mentors are synonymous with inspiration. And when you look up to your mentors and trust them to guide you with experience and wisdom, you can be doubly inspired to achieve all your dancing goals.

"You'll Never Walk Alone"

Who will your mentors be? Let me start out by saying that owners of dance studios, dance teachers and directors can be a huge influence—and have a great impact—on your career, as well as your life. If there are any parents reading this book to help guide your young aspiring talent, please remember how important it is to choose studios wisely.

Do your research: know who these people are, know their reputation, their background and their experience. Inquire about the possibilities of viewing a class or two. If taking up dance is something that you have been thinking about for some time, try planning far enough in advance so that you can see recitals or performances of the schools you may be considering.

Although most schools hold recitals near the end of the school year, from May through June, some studios may have local events that they perform at throughout the year. A quick phone call to the schools that you are interested in can get you that information.

My first year of dance classes was very exciting and what I thought to be a great experience. Aside from my regular weekly class, I had been chosen to participate in a semi-private class and a choreography competition, in which I would perform my own dance at the end of year dance recital.

My mother and I were invited to the annual showcase, a spectacular performance of the school's dance and performing arts company. In order to get into the company, one had to audition—or be chosen. This was a wonderful opportunity for any young, aspiring talent as the company had such an excellent reputation and was known for its travel and performances throughout the country and abroad. Formed in the '60s, this performing arts company was quite innovative for its time, from its artistic presentations and the creativity demonstrated in performances, to its company philosophy and structure. There was nothing like it around, definitely not for children, and not in an amateur arena, and certainly not in Sudbury, Ontario. For that matter, I don't imagine many professional companies could boast performances to such foreign audiences. But least likely of all, this small company of young amateur dancers from Northern Ontario.

The opportunity to see this performance was so very exciting for me; I had never been to a show like this before. Off we went, Mom and I, and to this day, I remember that performance like it was yesterday. I swear that my mother could barely keep me from standing and dancing in my seat. I was so taken by their performances and thought to myself, "*Wow!* These dancers are fabulous." All I wanted was to be up there on that stage with them. If I wasn't already hooked, by the opening number, I was a goner. I knew my destiny now; this was it and there was no turning back.

A week or so after the company's showcase, my dance recital took place. It was now my turn to be on stage and I couldn't wait. This was my first recital and I was ten years old. I performed my class routines and then, finally, the jazz routine that I had choreographed. As I was exiting the stage, the director of the company was standing in the wings. Unbeknownst to me, I had just auditioned for his company! Suddenly, he shook my hand and congratulated me; I had just been accepted in Training School (this was the youngest student body of the company). To me, it was all so grown-up and professional, as though I had just been offered a role in some great big Broadway show.

That evening, I received the Dancer of the Year Award and a scholarship for the following year in the company. This was huge for me, as my parents certainly didn't have the kind of money to afford all that was involved in taking company classes. Yet, as I mentioned earlier, my mother would, and did, over the years to come, everything she could in order for me to dance. She made costumes for the dance company, and she even cleaned the dance studio at night to help pay for my lessons. Between my mother's relentless energy, all her hard work, and the many scholarships given to me by my studio, I was able to have the experience that some kids only dream about. In fact, it was the professionalism of the studio and the experience that I gained through my director and teachers that aroused in me the desire to pursue my career in dance.

Encore:
I knew my destiny; this was it and there was no turning back.

You Should Be Dancin'

If I were to recount one single moment that solidified that desire, I would have to say that it was the night I went to see Bob Fosse's *Dancin'* on Broadway. To me, Bob Fosse was and will go down in history as one of the all-time greats; his choreography and direction have been a huge influence on my own career. That night, as I sat in the audience of this incredibly inspiring show, I remember thinking to myself, *I can do that. I can be that dancer. I know I can. I know that I have what it takes!* And that evening was in fact a turning point in my career, it was that night that I decided that if I was going to pursue this career, I would have to leave my home town and move to the city, where there would be opportunity. The lesson here is simple: first there's the passion, then the conviction, and finally, the commitment. Within a few short years, I was living in Toronto earning a living as a professional dancer and choreographer.

Years later, when I was working in Los Angeles as choreographer of *La Cage Aux Folles*, a famous "LA" dinner theatre, and place to be seen, Bob Fosse, himself, my all-time favorite choreographer, came in to see the show. Unfortunately I was not there to meet him in person, of all times for me to not be at the show. Apparently, he came in all dressed in black, just as he was so well known for, on his own, and asked to be seated alone. We often had celebrity guests at *La Cage,* and we always respected their privacy. Upon leaving, he told my producer that he thoroughly enjoyed himself, and he thought the show was great. Wow… my hero, Bob Fosse, thought our show was great! That is certainly one of those once-in-a-lifetime moments!

Go Toward the Light!

These moments have such significance to us as children, and I share mine with you because I know that each one of you reading this book has their own "Mrs. G.," a "Gerry", a "Miss Suzie" or a "Len"—that teacher or mentor in your life, whether past or present, who above all the rest made an impact on you. Mentors are like lighthouses along our journey, guiding and gently lighting the way. Sometimes, when just the right light is shed, it can reveal an unknown path; a new path we may otherwise never have discovered. It is very important for our own personal growth to recognize these people and all that they have to offer or teach us along the way.

I believe that it keeps us humble and it keeps us in tune. In our world, the world of performing arts, it's only natural to have these mentors as young children. Most of you, I would imagine, have at least one teacher who is (or was) a personal hero. Not only do I think it is so important to recognize personal heroes and mentors from our youth, but I also want to emphasize the importance of having such a presence throughout our lifetime.

The roles that mentors play in our lives can be enormous; they can influence us in such positive ways and teach us through their own experiences. They can be an incredible wealth of information for you to draw from and can help make your path a lot easier—*if* you are willing to be open and learn by their examples and from their know-how. Although there is nothing quite like personal experience to solidify a life lesson, there is nothing wrong with making your life that tiny bit easier by learning from those who have been there before you.

After all, why reinvent the wheel?

As a young adult, there was yet another teacher, an amazing teacher who taught me lessons far beyond dance steps. That teacher was a gentleman by the name of Len Gibson. In my opinion, he was one of the best. During a short time studying with him, I learned lessons about the business that have helped carry me through my career. When I had first arrived in Toronto, I immediately looked him up. I knew of his reputation and studio, and I was extremely eager to meet him. I called the studio and spoke with him directly. I introduced myself, told him I had just moved to the city, and would love the opportunity to study with him. He invited me to audit one of his classes; it was the last class of the evening and we could speak afterwards, he said. I, of course, arrived nice and early and was very excited, but rather nervous about meeting him. I observed an excellent class! Talk about inspiring—this man did not miss a trick. In a class of fifty or more dancers, you could be in the last row and if your pinky was out of place, he saw it. There I was about to embark on the first step of my dance career away from home and I was ready to take on the dance world! At the end of class, Mr. Gibson tore into a male dancer like nothing I had personally witnessed before. He went up one side and down the other; I was horrified for this poor guy. Talk about intimidating… I was shaking in my boots, and now I had to go introduce myself and say hello. *Do I leave now? Maybe he didn't notice me and he'll never know I was here?* I thought to myself. But no, rather than slipping out, I went up to him and introduced myself as the young girl who had called earlier, we shook hands, and he immediately addressed what had just happened. He said to me, "You see that young man, I believe that he has talent, but he needs to get his act together. It's a tough business out there, and if this is the career he wants, then he has to work much harder than what he just did. He has to prove himself. He doesn't know it yet, but I just did him a huge favor. You see, one of two things will come of this: one he'll never dance again, or two, he'll be in class again tomorrow ready to work and he will become one of the finest dancers you've ever seen. It takes so much to be in this business and he needs to learn now if he is going to succeed." This was certainly an event that made an impression on me, one I never forgot.

I went on to study with Len for the next few years, and I really loved him. He was tough on us, his dancers, but he certainly made me want to work hard for him. He was already an older gentleman at this time, but that never stopped him; he was in amazing physical condition. He demonstrated everything first; didn't matter what it was—turns, leaps, falls—he did it all. I don't believe he ever asked anything of a dancer that he did not first execute himself. He was extremely inspiring, I only wish I had had the opportunity to work with him from the time I was younger, and for longer. It's always such a reward when a teacher that you love so dearly, and respect so much, reciprocates, and commends you on your work. He was never short of a correction or afraid to rake you over the coals when necessary, but at the same time, if he thought you were talented, he wasn't afraid to praise you. His praise meant the world to me. A real highlight for me was a few years later when I had my own dance studio and Mr. Len Gibson accepted my invitation to come regularly to teach master classes to my students. My studio was a couple of hours away, and as he didn't drive, he would take the train in every two weeks. What an honor this was for me to have this man whom I respected so much give of himself to teach at my school.

Throughout my adult career, I have been blessed with a handful of great mentors. Some were friends from various walks of life, both in and out of the business, while others were teachers like Len, or employers, producers and promoters whom I first worked with and, from there, developed longstanding friendships with.

When a Left Turn becomes the *Right* Turn

I would like to share with you a story that truly depicts *the* turning point in my own career. One day while on a promotional job with a dancer friend of mine, she told me of an audition that was being held on that very day. Apparently, there was an American show from Los Angeles, Las Vegas, Atlantic City, and Miami coming to Toronto to hold auditions for dancers, as they were opening a production in Toronto in the near future. Although the lead roles would be played by Americans, the chorus would be all Canadian. It was always a big deal when an American company came to Canada to open a show. Back then, around the same time that Toronto was just developing its theatre district, there were not many opportunities like this; American productions in Canada were still quite unheard of.

How we managed it, I'm still not quite sure, but somehow we scheduled our lunch break to coincide with us getting to this audition; we were not going to miss this one. Once at the audition, we were taken through the paces, and taught a challenging and well-choreographed routine. Always a good sign of what is to come! We met several of the key players that day: the production and company manager, the set designer, the director, and, of course, the choreographer. I had a great audition and landed the gig! How exciting, as it always is when you get that awaited phone call or offer. As fate would have it, I was exactly where I was supposed to be on that day. This "lunch break audition" would become the most major turning point of all in my career. Once in rehearsals, I met Lou Paciocco, the creator of the show, and producer from Los Angeles. He was in town and came to rehearsals to meet the cast, and check on how things were progressing. No sooner had he arrived when the rumors were already spreading that he was looking for, and interviewing, choreographers for his Los Angeles revue. Always being pretty attentive, that kind of information did not need to be given to me twice. I immediately inquired and was told that yes; in fact, he was seeing quite a few people in town about the newly available position. I thought to myself, and expressed to him, that if he was considering different local choreographers, then he should also see my resume and demo reel of my work as a choreographer. I certainly thought *if there was a position up for grabs, I should be considered, as well as any other choreographer.* After all, my work was very good and I had a fair bit of experience. Of course, he would never have known this, as I had auditioned for and taken the position of a dancer. You may recall me mentioning earlier that since I was a young girl, my love for choreography was as strong as my love for performing, and from the moment I set out on my own career quest, I actively pursued both. Lou showed interest in seeing my work and knowing more about the dance studio that I owned at the time. So no sooner had I expressed interest in this position, but here I was preparing my promotional material to submit to him, and off to dinner and a meeting I went with demo reel and resume in hand. Looking back on that, I'm sure he must have thought this was rather ambitious of me as I was quite a bit younger than some of the more experienced choreographers who were also vying for the position.

About one week after Lou Paciocco had returned to Los Angeles, I received a phone call inviting me to come out there. I would have the opportunity to meet the cast and to discuss the position of resident choreographer of this highly successful musical revue, *La Cage Aux Folles.* I was thrilled and terrified all at the same time. For one thing, I had never been to Los Angeles and it was miles away from my family and the life that I knew so well, and two, it was a very exciting opportunity that could, and did change my life completely. That trip to Los Angeles was twenty something years ago and I never looked back. Not only did I choreograph the Los Angeles show, but I went on to direct and open more than a dozen *La Cage* productions around the world. To this day, I continue to work with one of my best friends and mentor, Lou Paciocco.

For me, there was never an important decision to be made without running it by one of my mentors, if not all of them, and to this day I still make those few important phone calls first. Having left home at quite a young age, to pursue my career in dance, and coming from such a large family, being on my own was somewhat difficult for me; I missed my family so much! I was fortunate enough to have a few "big sisters" on the road; they were always a shoulder to lean on for strength; a pep talk for encouragement, or a sounding board if I was blue, and to these women and my real big sisters, I am forever grateful.

There are many significant lessons and great memories from my childhood and early career days that have, to a great extent, influenced me and still go on to be some of the best lessons of all, many of which I continue to draw on for inspiration today. And so, although some of these mentors may not be directly involved in my life today, the memories and the lessons they carry will always be with me.

Encore:
Mentors are like lighthouses along our journey;
guiding and gently lighting the way.

Accentuate the Positive!

When you are young, it is very important to pay close attention to those lessons that shape us; this isn't always easy. In fact, sometimes it can be downright difficult to decipher the advice and information you are given. You may very well receive conflicting advice from various sources and, therefore, all decisions should be weighed carefully and discussed with trusted sources.

As a side note for parents, I do encourage you to be involved and present in your child's training and/or career. My only caveat is to suggest that you do so without becoming a stereotypical "Stage Mother." It is so important to encourage and support children while ensuring that they are always in good hands. You want to be there and be in the know without being pushy, as you don't want to hinder their careers, only help them make their own wisest decisions. Fortunately for me, my mother was very involved in all that I did. And as she always said, she knew exactly what was going on without ever having to interfere. Just as I tell the talent to have "the right attitude," so must the parents; it simply makes for a better experience all around.

There are many wonderful and talented people who surround us every day in our personal lives and in business; you have absolutely nothing to lose—and everything to gain—by embracing and aligning yourself with these people. You could be meeting them every day, at class, at auditions, working, performing, and through friends of friends. Be aware of your surroundings; the more you put yourself out there, the more opportunities you are creating.

We should constantly be growing; without growth, we become idle and stagnant, which is like a death-sentence to creative people. There is so much to learn every day if you just remain flexible, open and aware. I know this sounds very basic and simple, and the truth is, it is. Unfortunately, so many people walk through life with blinders on; they have no peripheral vision—none of that extrasensory ability that allows them to tap into all the many side trips and journeys life has to offer "off the beaten path."

As an artist and performer, you cannot afford this habit. I am going to suggest that if you don't have any mentors in your life at present, you start looking. These mentors could be people that you already know, or new acquaintances that you seek out. Look for lifestyles, qualities and accomplishments that you yourself aspire to. A mentor is someone whom you look up to and respect; someone who will help inspire and motivate you to accomplish your goals and dreams. You may be fortunate enough to have certain mentors all through your life, while others will come and go, staying only as long as you need them. Various circumstances in your life will dictate certain needs.

I remind you of the old African proverb that says, "When the student is ready, the teacher shall appear." I know from personal experience that they do appear, as if out of nowhere. It seems that often, a mere realization of the need is enough to fulfill the request. Trust, ask, and you shall receive.

You want to make sure that you are open enough to recognize these golden opportunities and not miss them when they are right in front of you. Once again, I reiterate the importance of being aware and being open—and choosing wisely. The right mentor can make all the difference in the world.

Encore:
You may well receive conflicting advice from various sources and therefore all decisions should be weighed carefully and discussed with trusted sources.

Triple Threat—Training + Versatility = Options

Bringing it…all together! Cast of Arbitron Corporate Event—Toga Party, Miami Beach, Florida

---

*"And my goal in life is to give to the world what
I was lucky to receive: the ecstasy of divine union through
my music and dance."*   —Michael Jackson

A dancer's training is absolutely crucial to his or her overall career and performance. Training never ends; a dancer is constantly in training. In this ever-changing industry, it is absolutely imperative that dancers continue their education throughout their career. The business is far too demanding and competitive to sit back on your laurels or think that training doesn't apply to you; you must constantly be growing and developing your talents, continuously ensuring your versatility and depth as a performer.

This is not to say that only the most trained or talented work in the industry; it's not just about talent. In fact, it's just as often about a specific look or a specialty. We all know a dancer or two with natural gifts who either had no formal training or was incredibly stylized in one specific area only and still succeeded in finding work.

Absolutely, this can and does happen very often. However, these careers may inevitably be somewhat limited. It's like anything else in life: you *can* get by in life being a "one-trick pony," but what happens when not knowing that second or third trick limits your career?

The hip-hop dancer, the ballerina, or the "hoofer" who chooses not to train in other areas will be limited, working within a very small and specific area of the business. Even within their area of expertise, they still limit themselves, as there are so many incredibly versatile dancers out there today. What's more, these dancers not only do what dancers with only one specialty do, as well or better, but they also come with everything else to complete "the whole package."

This may have little significance to you if you have already determined that you want to be that specialty performer or the next prima ballerina. You may have your plan laid out and you don't see the need for any study outside of your forte.

But even if this is the route you are taking, I still strongly suggest that you explore training in other areas as it will only enrich you as a performer in your own specialty. In business, as in life, we can never have too much knowledge and, the more we have, the more we have to offer.

Encore:
Training never ends; a dancer is constantly in training.

Are You A Quadruple Threat?

This chapter is called "Triple Threat," but perhaps we should update that familiar old saying to something more modern: being a "quadruple threat." We talk about being a triple threat like it's something new. However, the truth is that if we go back to the Golden Era of movie musicals and studio contracts (1930s to 1950s), all actors had to be triple threats.

In other words, they all had to sing, dance and act.

Of course, within the industry, there has always been the need for the chorus dancer (otherwise known as "the single threat"). Throughout the decades, there has always been some work in film and television for dancers, whether it be in variety shows, award shows, pageants or commercials, not to mention the big dance feature film every so many years. The fact is that there simply isn't a great deal of that type of work—and certainly not enough to go around. This means, it just may not be enough to sustain you.

There are certainly plenty of stage shows, revues and variety-type shows for specific venues that do not require dancers to sing, but once again, let me remind you of how limited that area will be. For some of you, that may be just what you are looking for and there's absolutely nothing wrong with you wanting to work strictly as a dancer. On the other hand, I just want you to understand the parameters and limitations that this can mean for you.

Let me just add this food for thought: Although you may very well work consistently as a dancer, at some point, you will probably decide that it is time to hang up your dance shoes. When this time comes, your versatility as a triple threat will leave you with many more options. I really do want to drive home the importance of being that triple threat. As a director, choreographer and a producer who has spent a great deal of my career auditioning and hiring talent, let me tell you that versatility is a key factor in my decision-making.

I look for well-rounded dancers, those who can handle anything I throw at them. I can only speak for myself, but I can certainly tell you that many of my friends and acquaintances in the business, who do what I do, will tell you the exact same thing.

So what does this mean? This should give you an indication of how important it is to be well trained in all areas of dance: ballet, jazz, modern, contemporary, lyrical, hip-hop, tap and then some.

Encore:
At some point you probably will decide that it is time to hang up your dance shoes. When this time comes, your versatility as a triple threat will leave you with many more options.

A Well-rounded Dancer

A well-rounded dancer will have training in as many styles as possible. I understand that your schedule or budget may not always allow for all of that, and I'm not suggesting that you have to be in all of those classes all of the time—or even all at the same time.

What I am suggesting is that if someone is first starting out, either as a young child or an adult, that individual should, at the very minimum, get into ballet and jazz. As you or your child progress, and if your budget allows, you can add various styles and different classes, all in the effort of becoming a more versatile dancer.

There are many performing arts schools and dance studios today that have dance and performing arts companies within; these are a great vehicle in which to maximize your learning opportunities. Most often, dance and performing arts companies will teach several of the above styles of dance as part of the company class curriculum.

Once again, I do advise that you do your homework. Know all that you need to know about the school and its faculty: who they are, and what their background, training and experience is. Ask yourself some pertinent questions before you commit, not the least of which should be: Will you be studying with several teachers, each specializing in their own particular area or style of dance, or will you be studying many styles with one teacher?

In either case, you will want to be sure that they have the experience and versatility that you seek. If you are fortunate enough to be involved in a performing arts school or company, then you may have the added bonus of studying acting or singing, or both, as part of the company's curriculum.

Encore:
There are many performing arts schools and dance studios today that have companies within; these are a great vehicle in which to maximize your learning opportunities.

"Everything Old Is New Again"

Let's talk strictly dance for a moment. The first mentioned is ballet, ah! The importance of ballet cannot be debated, while the passion of it often leaves readers debating; some of you love it and some of you love to hate it.

I know the story well; I've heard it all too often. I'm here to tell you, if you don't know this already, that you had best find something about it that you can like and appreciate, or at the very least, learn to endure. Ballet is your core foundation; it is the basis for all that you do as a dancer. It gives you your technique, strength and power, your center, alignment, grace and poise.

Many young dancers often ask me what they can do to help prepare for their careers. One of the first things I ask them is if they are studying ballet. If not, I suggest that they immediately begin taking classes. If you are a young adult, first setting out in your career as a professional, and you have not had any ballet training, then I suggest you get yourself into ballet class *now*.

The technique and strength that you develop will support you in all areas of dance. I'm not saying that dancers of other disciplines cannot be equally as strong or technical; I am simply saying that where technique and strength are necessary as a dancer, you can be certain to get them from good ballet training.

Jazz dance, which is often the favorite with so many young dancers, also offers you a strong technique, as well as style and much versatility. One of the great things about studying jazz dance is that you will cover a wide variety of music and styles. Specifically, if you train with some excellent and stylistically versatile teachers, you can then cover an incredible amount of dance styles within a strong jazz syllabus.

The more variety there is in choreography and style, the more stylized and versatile the dancer will be. These are all things to take into consideration when you are choosing a school, a studio, teachers and/or coaches. Hip-hop, which may include street, funk, popping or locking, or b-boying ("breaking," as it is commonly known), is also a very popular class, and once again offers great variety and versatility of style, not to mention some pretty impressive tricks.

Tap speaks for itself and is always an asset. Not every show will require it, but many will have the one token tap number in it. Modern and contemporary, once again, offer strength and technique, captivated with intense emotion while lyrical offers a more graceful, lingering emotive style of dance. Latin, ballroom, belly dance and other ethnic styles of dance simply add to your versatility. Any-and-all different types of dance you can study will only help to enhance your abilities and your performance.

For me, it's all about style, technique, and performance—plus the perfect combination and blend of the three. Versatility, versatility, and more versatility; this is the strength of any well-rounded dancer. If musical comedy is not a part of the dance curriculum within your company, or within a particular class that you are already taking, make sure to get yourself into a few classes, at the very least.

Encore:
Ballet is your core foundation; it is the basis for all that you do as a dancer.

Finding Your Voice

Next, let's talk about the dreaded (for so many dancers, that is) vocal audition and the importance of singing for a dancer. If you are out there auditioning, or first starting out in your career, and you have not had any vocal lessons as part of your training, find yourself a vocal teacher and start taking some private lessons *ASAP*. Trust me; I do speak from personal experience, both as a dancer who wasn't a strong singer and as a choreographer who has seen many talented dancers not get a gig due to lack of vocal ability.

At twenty-two, I auditioned for the musical *Cats*. I was living in Toronto at the time and this was the first-ever Broadway musical to be produced in Canada, so you can imagine the stir and excitement amongst the industry. They auditioned in several cities, and at the Toronto audition alone, there were over one thousand dancers, both equity and non-equity. (Actors Equity Association is a union which is often referred to as "Equity." You will learn more about this union and others in Chapter Fourteen: United We Stand.)

This was so very exciting and I loved every minute of it. I felt so confident and I did a great audition.

Cut after cut, we were narrowed down to eight dancers and I was so thrilled to be one of the eight. How exciting to have gone from so many down to such a small group; the realization that I had made the cut felt pretty amazing. But, suddenly, I heard those dreadful words, "We are going to have you sing one at a time; please wait in the hallway for your turn."

Although I knew I would have to sing and came prepared with sheet music and all, I guess there was a part of me that thought surely there must be one cat that doesn't have to sing (or at least I hoped so). I knew in my gut, even though I tried to convince myself otherwise, that it was all over. When my turn came around, dreading every note, I went in to sing, and to make matters worse, I had prepared the song "Home" from *The Wiz*. Hello, is anybody home? What was I thinking? I'm sure the performance was stellar; it was just the sounds that came out that weren't. Needless to say, I took up private vocals immediately after that audition. By the way, the jury is still out as to whether or not those vocal lessons actually helped!

I told you all that to point out: It can be absolutely heartbreaking to be up for a part in your dream show and lose out because you can't carry a tune, or even worse, hold a note. You spent the entire day there, you got through the "cattle call," they've cut and they've cut again and again, you're down to the last few, and now the moment you have either been waiting for—or dreading—is about to determine your fate.

Don't be afraid of it; just prepare for it! If you lack confidence in your singing ability, do not allow this to keep you from getting the training that you need.

Singing, especially in a private lesson situation, can be very intimidating to one who lacks the vocal confidence, and many dancers, unfortunately, are notorious for their fear of singing. If you are already confident in this area as either a dancer-singer (or a full-on singer), then you can certainly understand the importance of your vocal training and development. So as I mentioned earlier, if you haven't done so, you absolutely must take singing lessons. Find yourself a private singing coach. Even if you do not have the most amazing voice, you must still do all that you can to train your ear and develop your voice. At the very least, you want to learn to carry a tune. If money holds you back, as it often can when first starting out, consider the most affordable options first. If private lessons are not an option initially, then try to find a choir that you can join. At the very least you might have a friend who is a strong enough singer to help with some vocal exercises and coaching tips to help get you started.

Of course, as we discuss throughout this book, there is a great deal of disappointment in our business. What I hope to accomplish—and help you prevent—is experiencing disappointment based on your lack of preparation. And so I continue to emphasize the importance of ensuring yourself the best shot at every opportunity, which you can accomplish by grasping the importance of—and acting on—the advice given in this chapter.

Encore:
If you are out there auditioning, or first starting out in your career, and you have not had any vocal lessons, find yourself a vocal teacher ASAP.

They Don't Call it ACT-ion for Nothing!

Dancing? Check.
Singing? Check.
Acting? Check it out: If you have any dreams or aspirations of performing in musical theatre, whether you are Broadway or West End bound, or you would like to perform in community, dinner or regional theatre, you absolutely must *sing* and *act*. Before I segue to the acting portion of our training, I would like to remind you that musical theatre is not the only market that casts dancers who sing. Many variety shows, musical revues, cruise ships, theme parks, and corporate events also hire dancers who sing.

When it comes to acting, it's not only in musical theatre that these skills will be put to the test. How about film and television? How about commercials? Certainly, if you are sent on an audition, a casting call, or a reading for any of the above, there are going to be acting skills required. As a dancer, you could be cast in any number of commercials where movement is a prerequisite.

With the recent rise in popularity of dance, over the last several years because of such television shows as *Dancing With the Stars* and *So You Think You Can Dance*, even the most unlikely products have dancers in their commercials. Gap, of course, set the trend some time ago, which propelled so many others to follow suit. This is a great time for the dance world. *So You Think You Can Dance* continues to grow in popularity. Canada, Australia, and the U.K. all have their own versions, and the American show added an additional season in the fall of 2009. This was the first time the show aired two seasons back to back, and, in the same year.

Okay, back to where we were, acting for commercials. It's not always a choreographed dance routine that you may be asked to perform. You may be required to assume the role of a "young mom" dancing around your kitchen as you prepare the children's lunch or while doing your laundry. Perhaps they are looking for a "dad" to do a little "break-dance" while repairing his son's bicycle or picking up his new car. What I'm trying to point out here is simply the fact that there will *always* be some acting—and often improvisation—involved and I want you to be ready for it. I don't believe that there is any kind of performance that would not benefit from acting training.

If you are not already in an acting class, I highly recommend it. At the very least, you want to have a few acting or commercial workshops under your belt. Unfortunately, the truth is that just a few isn't always enough, but it's better than none, so do all that you can to get yourself as much training as possible. Do what you have to do to be ready for it, whatever it takes. Many famous film stars or recording artists either first started out in the business as dancers, or studied dance as children.

Think of Madonna, Sarah Jessica Parker, Shirley MacLaine or Patrick Swayze, for example. Madonna moved to New York City to pursue a career in dance. Who could ever have foretold the life, career and legendary status that this young girl was about to create for herself? Sarah Jessica Parker's family relocated to New Jersey after she was cast in the Broadway production of *The Innocents*. This was only the beginning. Although she is famous for her role in the hit television show *Sex and the City*, which is only one of her many television and film credits, she was first a child star on Broadway. Shirley MacLaine's biography is one to be greatly envied. She also began by studying ballet as a young girl. She then moved from Virginia to New York City straight out of high school to pursue her career. Her first roll on Broadway was in *Pajama Game*, where she understudied the second lead. One evening while performing as understudy, legendary producer, Hal Wallis, was in the audience and spotted her. This was the catalyst for her incredible film career. Important to note, one never knows who could be in that audience. Patrick Swayze was introduced to dance at a young age by his mother, who was a dance teacher, choreographer, and dance studio owner in Houston, Texas. At the age of 20, he moved to New York City to pursue his career as a dancer. He studied with the Harkness Ballet School and Joffrey Ballet School. His first professional performance was with *Disney on Parade*, and he debuted on Broadway in *Grease* before going on to Hollywood.

These actors are all so multi-talented; it is hard to put them in any one category: actor, singer, dancer, etc. In short, they are all truly triple threats!

Speaking of triple threats, here is an actor who continues to personify these words. John Travolta, the youngest of six children in an entertainment family, grew up in Englewood, New Jersey. He dropped out of school and moved to New York City at the age of sixteen, to pursue his acting career. Having already studied voice, dancing, and acting at drama school, he went on to win many roles that featured all of those talents. He gave the characters he portrayed in such movie musicals as *Saturday Night Fever* and *Grease* their definition. If you haven't already seen *Hairspray*, be sure to do so. He gives yet another outstanding performance as Edna Turnblad.

This next star may not have started out as a dancer, but when it comes to triple threats, "Queen Latifah" says it all. And although her biography may not have "dancer" next to singer/actor, she certainly has all the moves. Her performances in the movie musicals *Chicago* and *Hairspray* are, in my opinion, unrivaled. These are two of my favorites, but only two specific performances in a long list of her fabulous credits.

The simple truth of this business is: if you get that bug for entertaining, there is usually no denying it, whether you get it from a dance class, a play that you've been to or singing for Mom and Dad.

So, back to where I started with all of this. Even if you are not aspiring to pursue film and television, what I am pointing out is simply the fact that you never know where your love for dance might take you. And so, if you have a desire to perform, then you must consider all training possible. Any and all classes or workshops that offer you yet another skill or help to develop existing or hidden talent, or even stir interest, are all excellent vehicles to help further create the performer and "triple threat" in you.

Encore:
*How many famous film stars or recording artists do
we know of today who either first started out in the
business as dancers, or studied dance as children?*

Don't Wait for Opportunity to Come to You

As we wrap up this chapter on becoming a more multi-layered performer, I would like to take a moment to address a few questions that have come up time-and-time-again; these are predominately from young talent first looking to pursue their interest in show business. If you find yourself living in an area that doesn't offer much in the way of training and lessons, then what do you do? First things first: find out what is available to you in the town or city that you live in. Next, find out what is available to you that might be close by.

Some of you may find yourself with an incredible desire and natural talent, but with few options available in the way of training. First and foremost, get yourself enrolled in the best available classes and then start considering all the various options outside of formal training that may be right at your fingertips. You are after all an artist and, therefore, have special abilities, one of which is the ability to improvise. So be innovative by creating your own tools and activities and establishing your own practices; study music videos, movie musicals, and dance movies.

Try to find yourself a good, reputable series of instructional dance DVD's. Check with the most trusted sources first. Some of the most well-known studios carry their own line of instructional DVD's, which can often be purchased on line. I would start by checking out Broadway Dance Center in New York City. They produce and sell their own line of instructional DVD's, which they seem to be adding to all the time. How about forming a dance troupe or theatre group with friends who have these same interests? Read everything you can get your hands on that relates to your talent, your interest, and the industry, and the people who have made it in the industry. Who are some of your favorite performers? Find out where they studied and whom they studied with?

Create your own commercial practice ritual by tearing advertisements from magazines and even recording television commercials. All magazines, from beauty and fashion to business and homemaking, contain ads which, along with your recordings, can be turned into a mini-commercial workshop.

Don't forget your local library and book stores! There are hundreds of books on monologues, cold readings, and on scene study available from a variety of sources. In today's world, you have a wealth of information readily available, thanks to the luxury of the Internet. Web surfing allows you to locate and purchase an abundance of information in the form of books and videos, and lets you indulge—for free—in a tremendous amount of educational information in the form of articles, write-ups or reviews on just about every facet of the business.

As for vocals, I would be willing to bet that you will have no problem finding yourself a private singing teacher or coach. Start by inquiring with your neighborhood school's music department or your local church choir. So, while you may not have Broadway Dance Center or Screen Actors Studio right down the street, there are certainly plenty of things you can do to help yourself along the way, at least until you reach the point when you have greater access to the right learning institutions.

I hope that in this chapter, I have clearly conveyed to you not only the importance of being a triple threat, but also the importance of choosing wisely when considering all your training needs. As well as the many affordable and creative ways in which you can help yourself. I leave you with this thought: If the choice is yours to make, why would you *not* choose to have *everything* you need?

Don't cut yourself short; go for it all! You can always find a way!

"I don't see my dancing or acting as two separate things.
More than anything I love being on stage and performing."
*~ **Bebe Neuwirth** (TV & film actress, and singer/dancer)*

CHAPTER FOUR

DANCING FOR A DEGREE—TO COLLEGE OR NOT TO COLLEGE?

It's not just about the steps. Script and vocal study, Opryland Productions, Nashville, Tennessee

---

"I was under the impression that I could do anything."
—Alvin Ailey

For those of you who are currently in high school and have decided that you do, in fact, want to pursue a professional career in dance, you are now facing some very important decisions: decisions about college, decisions about your career, and, of course, the age-old question: should one go to college for dance? How does that question apply to you?

Throughout my book, I explore the many possibilities within the dance and entertainment industry, from where to work to how to get the gig. You may already have decided in what capacity and specific area within the dance world you would like to work, and some of these areas will benefit greatly from a college degree in dance, while others may not necessarily. I, personally believe that you will always benefit from a college degree; it's more a matter of whether or not it will benefit your chosen career path. After all, a degree in dance won't necessarily land you the lead in a Broadway show; however, if you are looking to teach dance within the school system, whether at an elementary, middle, or high school, or at the college or university level, a degree will not only be of tremendous benefit; in some cases, it will be mandatory.

As a young dancer, I was taught that one did not go to college for dance. It was somewhat ridiculed by my dance director at the time, so it was embedded in my brain that the two just didn't go together.

When it was time for me to decide about furthering my education, I sat down with my high school guidance counselor to discuss my options. My dilemma was simply whether to go to college at all, or to just get out there and work at my career as a dancer/choreographer, which was ultimately my dream. Some people believe it's best to follow your dream wholeheartedly without any deviation; this, of course, is my school of thought. However, others believe it's important to have a back-up plan. Ultimately, this is your decision and only you can make that choice. My guidance counselor's advice to me, as someone who was fully aware of my already young career—as a dancer, teacher and choreographer—was this. He said: "We are very fortunate here in North America. You can always go to school any time. You have a great talent in dance and it can be a short-lived career. I suggest you get out there and pursue your career first. You can always go to school later."

My father desperately wanted me to go to University and the thought of me trading in a university education for a career as a dancer was absolutely ludicrous to him. "What will you do when you can no longer dance? What if you become injured and your career ends prematurely?" He would say, "Get a university degree as insurance for your future." This was all excellent, sound advice, but in the end, the desire to dance seemed to me the only choice. Dance was my true passion and I couldn't deny it, nor did I want to put it on hold. And, as I've already mentioned, the idea of going to college for dance was not even a conversation, or so I had been convinced.

On that note, I will say this: college programs in dance have come a long way in the past several decades. Twenty-five or thirty years ago, going to college for dance was relatively unheard of. Today, there are over six hundred college and university dance degree programs to consider, and yet, it is still a topic that brings out all the skeptics, or should I say, often invites a debate? Some topics evoke much emotion, and this is certainly one of them, at least within the dance circle: do dance and a college degree go hand-in-hand? Ask the question and you will get an abundance of opinions, all different, yet equally valid. The simple truth is that this is a very personal and individual decision, and at the end of the day, what's right for one may not be for another. There is a great deal to consider and you want to make the best choice for you.

A college degree is a wonderful advantage to have and to fall back on; it can benefit you in your present career path and in any future career transitions. Although it may or may not make a difference at your audition, or for that matter, be the deciding factor as to whether or not you get that gig, it certainly won't inhibit you and it will definitely be an asset to you in your career and in life in general. There are obvious career paths that you can take where a dance degree will make all the difference in the world; others where it will not make a bit of difference. In order to make the right decision for yourself, you will want to consider closely where and how you see yourself working in the industry. This will be important in helping you to decide whether or not a dance degree is right for you, and if so, what program will be best suited to you. Following is a work sheet that you can use to help you in your career path decisions.

Encore:
A college degree is a wonderful advantage to have and to fall back on; it can benefit you in your present career path and in any future career transitions.

The Dance of Self Discovery

Goals and Aspirations
- List all your dreams and desires—everything and anything you ever imagined being. As far back as you can remember.
- When you were a child, did you dream of becoming famous? If yes, how did you see yourself being famous? Please describe briefly.
- If there was no possibility of rejection or failure, what would you most want to do or be today? No limits; no holds barred.
- What do you think you most need to work on to achieve such goals and dreams?

- If you could make your mark in the world, what would it be?
- Does your dance training assist you with that goal?
- List ten things you most want to do in your lifetime.

Evaluation

- What do you like most about yourself?
- What do you dislike most about yourself?
- What are your strongest assets as a dancer? (i.e., technique, style, passion, creativity, performance ability, musicality, retention, etc.)
- What are your weaknesses as a dancer?
- What are your personal strengths?
- What are your personal weaknesses?
- What other strengths or skills do you possess that could help you in your career, or in business?
- What disadvantages do you have that might work against you, and how can you transform them into advantages?
- What would your teachers, parents, fellow dancers say are your strengths in dance, in business, and on a personal level?
- What natural talents do you possess that you may have discovered along the way? Not things that you've been taught, but rather, abilities that just came naturally to you. For example, you might be a natural born leader, a great organizer, you might hear music and envision the steps, or maybe you have a great imagination and can instantly create a story-line.
- Are you a natural born teacher, creator or performer?
- Do you see yourself as a business owner? (This could be a dance studio, a talent agency, or production company, etc.)
- Do you like to help others, and if so, what areas could someone call on you to help out with?

Personal Interests

- What makes you happy?
- What are your favorite pastimes, hobbies or activities?
- Whom do you most like to spend time with?
- What activities did you most enjoy as a young child?
- If you could travel anywhere in the world, where would it be and why?

Personal Inspirations
- What first inspired you to dance?
- What show, book or movie most inspires you?
- Who are your heroes or idols?
- Whom do you most admire or respect in the entertainment industry and why?
- Who are the people who most influenced you in a positive way in your training or in your career, and how? (This could be a parent, teacher, coach, employer etc.)

Now that you have taken this time to ponder the above questions, and reflect on your needs, your desires, your strengths, and your weaknesses, I ask you to complete one final and very important task. Go ahead and write down a brief paragraph—a summary of what you see in your answers. Is there a set pattern that you see repeating itself? Do the same desires keep coming up time and time again, and do the same key words find themselves in various areas? Are there weaknesses that might inhibit you, or that you feel could benefit from study at college or other modes of additional training? You get the idea! Careful consideration of the above questions and your summary, thereof, will allow you to take a closer look at the decision you must make, and will help you create a road map or action plan. Now, if, in fact, college has an immediate place in your future, you will want to pay close attention to the next section.

College or Bust

Once you have made the decision to go off to college, there will be much more for you to think about and to explore. You will want to be meticulous with your research, considering all your needs, interests, talents, strengths, weaknesses, and, of course, finances. The above questionnaire will already have addressed some of these very important considerations.

Where to study, and what program will be best suited to you, will be your first and most difficult choices as there are numerous and varied programs available today. I will give you much too think about in the next pages; however, I will only skim the surface as there is much more than a chapter needed to assist you in your ultimate decision. This will be an excellent introduction, but there are books specifically devoted to college programs for dance and other performing arts. These books will not only give you very detailed information about the various programs and degrees, their areas of concentration, and whether they are performance or education oriented, but will also give you contact details, the do's, don'ts, and great advice on the "how to" process.

I suggest that you learn all that you can about the different colleges and universities that you are interested in, and the dance programs they offer. College for dance can be a wonderful arena to grow and experiment in, to make contacts, and to help you determine your place, both in your early career, and for what lies ahead, should a career transition be necessary. The right choice is paramount. Here are a few additional things to keep in mind as you make your decision.

- Is it important to be close to home or not?
- What is your main interest? Once again consider your strengths and weaknesses. Are the programs offered in line with your needs?
- What diplomas or degrees are offered?
- What is the program curriculum and what is its focus and objective?
- Who are on the faculty, and what are their backgrounds?
- What are the studio facilities like?
- Are there any performance opportunities?
- Are there any affiliations with dance companies?
- What famous alumni went through their program?
- What have any of their alumni gone on to accomplish?

Careful research and consideration of these above questions will be very helpful in assisting you in your quest to compile your preliminary list of colleges. This list should be consistent with your ultimate career goals, having considered both future and immediate future career paths. Especially if you are interested in performing, as I've already mentioned, and I'm sure you've heard before, a performance career can be short-lived, so it is a good idea to look ahead as to what you will want to do if a career change is necessary.

The range of Bachelor of Arts Degrees and Masters Degrees is endless, and the only way you can really get to the bottom of this decision is through careful consideration of exactly what the various programs have to offer. The differences are so varied, you will want to take everything into account—your academic likes and dislikes and your personal needs. Be honest as you evaluate the many pieces of the puzzle. If you're not one who likes to write essays or if there are certain studies that you just never want to have to be subjected to again, be certain that you are not wasting your time with programs that may require exactly that very thing you want to avoid. Be mindful of what is required within the programs themselves. All your in-depth research from various institutions' websites, any additional information you may have requested from them directly, and all that we have touched on in this chapter will help you in narrowing your choices. The recommended college guides in the following section "Where do I begin? The College Search" will be invaluable tools for you from the get-go and will be very useful in helping you to compare those Colleges and Universities you are considering, at a quick glance, all in one book.

You will find similar questions to the ones above in other chapters. After all, whether you are deciding on college, or a move away from home to pursue a career in dance, you will want to ask the same questions of yourself. A combination of all these considerations will help you in your final determination.

Follow Your Heart

Following your heart is key to being happy and feeling fulfilled in your life and career. If you do not follow your heart, you will never be truly happy. Ask yourself these two very important questions: "Is dance the one thing that I absolutely want to do more than anything in life? Is there anything else that I would be happier doing?" And there you have it—your answer. That, by the way, applies to dance in college or dance as a profession. I mentioned earlier in Chapter One: Born to Dance, that if you don't have passion, what is the point? There are much easier ways to earn a living than a career in dance or show business. Essentially, asking yourself this one question can help you to determine where your true passion lies, and if it's not 100 percent in dance, you should save yourself the heartache. Now, if in fact, there is only one path for you and there is no turning back, please read on!

Encore:
There is so much to consider, take everything into account—your academic likes and dislikes and your personal needs.

Where Do I begin? The College Search

One of the first things I recommend is to pick up one of the following college guides. These books will offer you a concise list of the various programs available, all in one location, and therefore facilitate you in creating your initial list of Colleges to consider and to compare to each other. *Dance Magazine's College Guide*, published and updated yearly, lists the various college dance programs and also features articles about the topic of college for dance. You can visit their website at www.dancemagazine.com. *Peterson's College Guide for Performing Arts Majors* is very comprehensive, and also an excellent choice. It includes a selected listing of dance programs broken down into the following categories: Most Highly Recommended Programs, Recommended Programs, and Other Noteworthy Programs. Peterson's also has a website loaded with information and wonderful articles which will answer so many of your questions. I'm sure that you will find it very useful, www.petersons.com. Both guides can be purchased on line at their respective websites, and at some of the on line book stores, such as Amazon.com and Borders.com. Some of the major book stores will carry them on their shelves; if not, they may be able to special order them for you. I have found that *Dance Magazine's College Guide* is more difficult to find and your best bet may be ordering it directly from their website. You can always check at your local library as well.

Next, you will want to visit the various college websites. There is an abundance of information available on line, from entire catalogs to virtual tours. Be sure to take full advantage of the many different marketing tools available from the Colleges and Universities such as their websites, viewbooks, and videos, all of which are helpful and should be utilized. You can also request additional information from the school directly, either on line or by writing to the Director of Admissions. If you write, be sure to give your name, address, date of birth, and main interest or area of concentration. They may also require your social security number as this will later be used as a way of identifying you. For obvious safety issues, check first whether or not to include your social security number in your correspondence. With over six hundred different degree programs available, it can seem a daunting task.

Keeping yourself organized—much like the advice and tips I give in Chapter Thirteen: No More Starving Artist, it will be very important for you to create a college organizer for yourself. Just as you would with any task to be organized, you will first want to create a plan. I recommend a "to do" list and a "check list" to keep track of your progress. You will also want different sections to record details of your emails and letters; any telephone conversations, when and with whom you spoke; any important information you may have been given; and your first impressions of the school. This is very important to reflect back on. After several conversations or inquiries, you will appreciate this journal to help keep the abundance of information straight.

Careful reading of the school catalogs will give you detailed information about the different programs, which will, in turn, help you to narrow your list. Campus visits, if possible, are undisputedly the best means to get a full picture, but that's not until you've narrowed your list to your few final choices. This is a huge decision and you want to give yourself the most complete picture in order to make the best decision possible.

Narrowing the Search

Once you've gathered and read through the catalogs or visited the various websites of those Colleges that you have serious interest in, you can begin to narrow down the list. Your list should include a "wish list"—this will be a list of your ultimate dream colleges; a "safe list"—those colleges you feel pretty certain you will be accepted at, and a "possibly list"—those colleges you would also love to attend and feel you have a good shot at. Ultimately, you want to give yourself options.

As I've previously mentioned, mentors can play an extremely important role in our decision process, and this would be an excellent opportunity to take advantage of these advisors. Speak to your dance teachers, mentors, and guidance counselors; they often will present just the right food for thought. Sometimes, when we are too close to the subject, a mentor can show us a different angle or way of viewing our options. A combination of their advice, your own heart, and careful examination of the information you've gathered, will be a good way to filter your process. Speaking to other students from your high school, your area, or your dance studio who have been, or are presently in college for dance, and asking them about their process of elimination and their final decision, offers yet another form of tried-and-tested advice. Better yet, if there are any students from your studio who are attending the various colleges that you are considering applying to, try to get as much information from them as you possibly can. One very important question to ask them is whether or not they are happy with their choice, and in hind sight, would they have chosen the same college.

Lastly, I recommend that you find out about upcoming college fairs. This information can be acquired through NACAC (The National Association of College Admissions Counselors). You can visit their website www.nacacnet.org for a complete list of upcoming fairs. This is a perfect time for you to learn about educational opportunities, admission and financial aid, and audition and entrance requirements. When you visit the fairs, you can speak with the admissions representatives. This is a great time to ask questions, so having done your initial research, go prepared, with questions in hand. You will gain a real sense of what the colleges and specific programs you are interested in are like.

Campus Visits

Once you've narrowed your search to your final choices, you may want to visit a campus or two, depending on what is realistic. If an interview is required, you should be prepared and try to plan it in advance, thereby combining your visit and interview. This will prove to be very efficient, from both a time and financial viewpoint. The opportunity to visit gives you a sneak preview of life on campus. You will be able to meet other students and audit classes. This is an excellent time to gain feedback from those living in the environment, and lastly, the occasion to see if, in fact, this is where you envision yourself.

Be sure to plan your campus visit before the application deadline; this way, if you absolutely fall in love, and decide that this is where you ultimately want to be, you will not have missed your window of opportunity. If you are unable to visit due to financial restrictions, contact the Admissions Department and find out if there are any alumni or students from your area whom you might be able to contact and meet. If you have not already looked into the College Fairs schedule, ask the Admissions Department if they have any Admissions reps coming through your area for any College Fairs or presentations.

How to Plan Your Visit

In order to get the most out of your visit, be sure to find out what is happening on campus. You want to make sure that your visit is not at a time when there is so much going on that you cannot meet with the appropriate people and/or accomplish what you went there for. At the same time, you will want to know the class schedule and any possible concerts or rehearsals that you can attend. Is staying overnight an option? This is a fine way to maximize your visit. Make sure that the time you choose is favorable for the school; make sure that the Admissions Department is not inundated with placement so that you can benefit from meeting them and asking questions.

Prepare a list of all questions. Think about everything you want to know about the school, about their studio facilities, the faculty backgrounds and experience, the student body and the social life. Consider all questions as you would with any first move away from home—questions that relate to living arrangements and the neighborhood. Is the campus safe, and what are the crime statistics, etc? You can never ask too many questions and you must consider everything that could be a concern to you. After all, you intend to spend the next several years living in this environment, and you want to make sure up front that this is going be a comfortable place for you.

Just as with the advice I gave about auditioning for jobs in the professional scene, be certain to use the same respect and thoughtful gestures with all personal contact, especially once you have made your visit. Make sure to send a thank you note to your interviewer and to your host if you stayed over. This small gesture will be appreciated and will not go unnoticed; it may very well become part of your file.

How to Best Prepare and Shine at Your Interview: The Do's and Don'ts

First of all, find out if interviews are required or optional. Often you will find that the interview process will be optional due to staff restrictions, and travel or financial difficulties. If you are planning a visit to a campus, I believe it would be in your best interest to set up an interview even when it is optional. Nothing makes as important an impression as a face-to-face meeting. Do not confuse the interview with the audition, which is a completely different matter. An audition will almost always be required. Some institutions will hold live auditions, while some will accept video submissions. Audition requirements will be different for each institution, and this you should learn about in the admissions information when doing your research.

I will not proceed to list all the "do not's" as some are simply common sense; i.e., don't chew gum, don't use inappropriate language, don't speak in a negative manner, etc. This is your opportunity to make a good first impression, so you want to present yourself in the best possible light; you want to be someone whom this establishment would be proud to have in its student body. When it comes to attire you will want to dress appropriately. Just as I suggested earlier, you want to appeal to your audience and not offend anyone. You can still be fashionable and current while in good taste. I suggest that you check with the individual colleges for their specific dress requirements and recommendations.

During your interview, take this opportunity to share information about yourself, your family, your background, your interests and experiences. This is your moment to sell yourself in a positive way without being too boastful or coming off as arrogant. It is also not a time to be overly modest; it is a perfect time to share with your interviewer any special accomplishments or interests you may have.

Application Requirements

Application requirements could include the following: high school transcripts for freshmen, or college transcripts if you are transferring, a personal profile which could include extra-curricular activities, recommendations from teachers or guidance counselors, and essays. An essay is a good opportunity for you to let the admissions office get to know you. Even if it is optional, write one. And, of course, last, but certainly not least, your audition. College auditions will differ somewhat from professional auditions. You will want to consider everything there is to learn from Chapter Seven: The Audition, but keep in mind that the attire will be considerably different. Check with the establishment you're auditioning for on restrictions, guidelines, etc. As with all advice I give, I will reiterate that you want to be fully prepared for your audition; so again, make sure that you know exactly what to expect by reading the audition guidelines thoroughly. Where live auditions are concerned, some establishments will teach a class or two, whereas others will ask you to prepare an audition piece. Some will do both, teach class and ask you to present an audition piece. Whether you choreograph your routine or have someone choreograph it for you, be prepared to introduce yourself and speak about the piece that you will be performing. Composure, courtesy, and respect should always be standard behavior in any presentation.

If you are performing a set audition piece, make sure that you are well rehearsed. Set up a mock audition in which you perform your piece before an audience: invite your teachers, guidance counselors, and a few family members or friends. Ask your teacher to critique your performance, and then plan to perform it for them again at a later date a little closer to your actual audition. Be sure to video tape these trial runs so that you can view your performance and critique yourself. This is an excellent learning tool, so take advantage in order to best prepare yourself. The more rehearsed you are, the more confident you will be, and the less chance for your nerves to interfere. You want to exude a certain self-confidence and poise and allow your talent to shine through. Very important, remember to begin the application process well in advance of audition and interview dates. These take place months before the courses start and you want to ensure that you have plenty of time to prepare fully.

Financial Aid

When it comes to financial assistance, you will want to check all avenues. Several books are available, which will help guide you. There are various grants, stipends, scholarships, and awards available. The first thing you will do is fill out your Free Application for Federal Student Aid (FAFSA). The U.S. Department of Education will determine your eligibility based on your answers. FAFSA is the form used by virtually all two and four-year colleges, universities and career schools for the awarding of federal student aid, and most state and college aid. Please make sure to visit their website at http://studentaid.ed.gov.

This website will assist you in so many ways. First and foremost is your FAFSA; however, you will also find tons of information on the long list of scholarships available to you. There are so many avenues you must consider; colleges and universities will also offer scholarships for certain *specific* programs. There are scholarships offered through various organizations, including state government, the federal government, and private associations. As you have heard repeatedly, do not leave any stone unturned. Check with your local religious groups, professional associations, private companies, employers, and last, but not least, individuals. There are individuals who like to support the arts, and, will allocate certain monies to assist young artists to pay for their college education. You never know who is offering what, and if you don't ask, you don't get. You may be surprised at the sources that are willing to support individuals looking to better themselves and further their education. Many people who have a passion in these specific areas look to help new fresh talent along. Sometimes, it's a way of giving back and sometimes it's simply a passion that they get to fulfill. Explore all avenues. What could you possibly have to lose?

In Closing

As I mentioned at the beginning of this chapter, my intention for this section was to introduce the idea of college for dance, and to give you an overview of what you will need to consider in making this decision. In closing, I would like to remind you of something that I have repeatedly driven home, and that is not to throw anything away. Treat your education as you would your professional career. Every experience is an opportunity to learn something that you will carry with you throughout your lifetime and career as a dancer. There will be many challenges along the way. It is an extremely competitive field and in college, just as in the professional world, you will have to earn your place and work hard to *keep* your place. This is a wonderful arena in which to experiment and grow, so take full advantage and don't be afraid to put yourself out there. Go for it and grow from it!

Gain as much outside experience as possible, bearing in mind that each establishment will have its own set of rules about extra curricular activities, such as classes and auditions. When and where it is allowed, be sure to attend as many shows and classes as possible, observe as many auditions as you can, and attend any that do not interfere with your college program. These are fine learning opportunities and a great way to keep current and informed about what is going on in the industry. So take full advantage; you can only gain greater knowledge from these experiences.

If you do decide to go to college, go with an optimistic attitude about all the wonders that await you, take hold of all that is in your path, and give every single thing that you go for 100 percent. Don't miss one single opportunity. As the Latin saying goes "Carpe diem!" (Seize the day!)

Encore:
Every experience is an opportunity to learn something that you will carry with you throughout your lifetime and career as a dancer.

LEAVE YOUR ATTITUDE WHERE IT BELONGS: AT THE DOOR!

If you're going to do it, do it 100 percent! "Think," La Cage Opening Night at the Blue Angel, New York City

"The one important thing that I have learned over the years is the difference between taking one's work seriously and taking one's self seriously. The first is imperative and the second is disastrous." —Margot Fonteyn

What kind of attitude do you need to make it in the field of entertainment, in general, and dancing, in particular? The right attitude—a positive outlook, that is—is the only kind of attitude to have in this industry. You might think it's a big industry, but it's a small world, and it is, therefore, very important to create good, strong, and lasting relationships.

Since there is so much more talent than there is work, who do you think are getting the gigs? Could it be the pleasant and consummate pros who are grateful to have the work? Or do you believe it's the divas who think that you should feel lucky just to have them working for you? Be the kind of performer that a producer, director, or choreographer wants to spend hours on end with. Be that person; the one they want to call in for their next gig.

We've all known what I charitably call "big personalities," who are more about the drama and the demands than they are the performance and the professionalism. While some of these dancers are talented enough to be forgiven their egos, the rest of us simply can't get away with that. Burn enough bridges in an industry like ours and soon enough, you'll have nowhere left to audition.

I've been in this business a long time. I love what I do and I give 100 percent plus, to every production, to every client, and to the talent that work with me. If I have one pet peeve, it is a person with a bad attitude. It is the one thing that completely puts me off, and it is the one thing that I will not accept from anyone. Whenever I am starting rehearsals with a new cast, I make my expectations clear from the get-go. I look at it this way: at the very least, I expect my cast and production team to give me as much as I give them. I am extremely passionate about my creative work.

There is so much that goes on behind the scenes; so much that the cast is not needed for and oftentimes, they don't get to see. As a choreographer, I prepare the majority of my work in advance in order not to waste any precious rehearsal time. Sometimes, when the cast is first arriving to rehearsal, I have already been there for several hours, so it is extremely important to me to get the most out of the time that I have with a cast during rehearsal.

Work ethics and morals are at the top of my list. I want everyone to work hard and I want everyone to enjoy themselves. When it comes to the gig, I like to keep it simple; I have *three* rules:

1. Always be on time;
2. Check your attitude at the door;
3. Give me 100 percent, *100 percent* of the time.

If the talent working with me respects these three simple rules, we will *never* have a problem. I want to see a great performance; I want to know what I have before me. I want to know what my cast is made of, and I want to know that on opening night, they will deliver the goods. Is that so much to ask?

It is my position as an artist—and my mission as a producer or director/ choreographer—to deliver a fabulous show on opening night. I want to know that it's all going to be there. I may be considered by some to be a bit of a taskmaster; however, my intention is never to overtax anyone in rehearsal; it's simply to prepare the best talent and the best shows and, in the end, that will be to everyone's benefit.

If you give me *100 percent*, then I know exactly where we are, what we have to do, and what it will take to get there. I will always keep your best interest at heart, I will give you all that it takes to make you shine on opening night, and all I expect in return is that you do the same.

Does that sound like the right attitude to you?

Encore:
The right attitude—a positive outlook, that is—is the only kind of attitude to have in this industry.

Attitude Adjustment

So, let's get back to attitude and asking you to check it at the door. My reason for this is simple; there is no room for it in my rehearsal and I have neither the time nor the patience for bad attitudes and prima donnas. I personally will not tolerate it. Depending on the size of the production, we could end up living together for the next several weeks or months and I value my time and life way too much to spend it in bad company.

The rehearsal period and opening of a production are extremely intense processes; which are very involved and can be both physically and emotionally exhausting. We spend many long hours together; therefore, it is absolutely essential to have the right blend of personalities in order to form a cohesive group and make for a harmonious time together.

As far as I'm concerned, everyone in the cast is an equal. I don't have time for negativity or for any moaning and groaning. If someone is not up to the task, they shouldn't waste my time—or anyone else's, for that matter. We must all have one common goal, and that is to work together to mount the most amazing production possible; one that we can all feel proud of and the cast will love to perform.

What we do is very intimate and specialized; we should be able to enjoy the process. I don't know about you, but I certainly did not go into this business to have a miserable time. I trust that you also chose to go into this business because you wanted to work at something you love.

I don't know too many producers, directors or choreographers who would want anything less considering the amount of time involved, not to mention the time we spend together in such close quarters. The only people you may spend as much time with, or you may be as intimate with, is a spouse or your family.

I often tell young dancers who work with me that the friendships they make today may be friendships that last a lifetime. Some of my dearest friends are people whom I met through dancing. To this day, one of my best girlfriends' is a woman whom I danced with when we were first starting out in the business.

So attitude is clearly something that transcends both our personal and professional lives. In other words, a positive attitude helps both, while a negative attitude robs one from the other.

"Best Foot Forward"

It's easy for us to lose our good attitudes in a challenging profession, but it's imperative that if you've lost your positivity, you get it back. I've known many a dancer who started out as cheerily optimistic, only to be rejected one too many times and ended up pessimistic and bitter. Maybe that never happened to you, or maybe you're somewhere in the middle.

Either way, I would like you to think back to the very beginning and how this all started. What were your reasons for choosing this profession? I would imagine that it was an undeniable love for dancing, for performing and being on stage. So how to keep that positivity even when times get tough and jobs are hard to find?

Let me put it in a few words that might help you further on down the line: do all that you can; do everything within your power to ensure a positive journey. In spite of its ups and downs and complexities, this is a great profession, so be intelligent about your choices and how you handle yourself. Have some fun and enjoy the ride. Your ride is the process, and the process is an integral part of the big picture. Well traveled, the process can be as great as the final destination.

Of course, there will be times that try your patience, and even worse, there will be people who push your buttons. There may be days when you wonder why you do it at all, or whether you really have it in you. And that's positively okay; it's normal. It's life and "stuff happens," as they say; just always consider the outcome first.

The truth is that life can and sometimes does deal us what we would consider an unfair hand. It is almost certain that you will have some serious difficulties along the way, so what you must try to do is ease those rough times with a little preventative known as a positive attitude. This way, at least you can be ready for, or better equipped to, make the most of all that comes your way.

You have the ability to choose how you react in any given situation; make it the right outcome for yourself—and your career. Fast-forward the movie and look ahead at the various possible endings: if I react or behave in a certain manner, this will happen. What are the possible endings? Play the tape through all the way to the end and pick your ending; don't leave it to the audience or, even worse, to chance.

If you don't like the outcome, then make a different choice; make a better choice—one with a happier ending. This is not to say that if you are in a bad situation, you should just accept it and adjust your attitude. No, of course not. Should you ever find yourself in a compromising situation, then you need to take a closer look at the reality of the circumstances and determine what is right for you.

Accept only what you can commit to and will fulfill. Don't ever compromise your integrity; once you *do* commit, be true to your word. Your word is the one thing that no one can ever take away from you. All you can do is have the best outlook possible and go in with great energy and a positive attitude. That, in itself, will always help you make the best choices.

There will be so many choices for you to make along the way—whether it's how you react to a potentially negative situation, or whether it's a decision on what move to make next. This is all part of life; more importantly, this is *your* life. How do you want your role in it to play out? Perhaps you've heard the expression, "It's a small business, don't burn any bridges." I cannot emphasize this strongly enough.

Life is a journey, but don't be afraid to ask for directions. Specifically, if at times you're just not sure what's correct or acceptable, don't be afraid to ask. We are constantly learning throughout our lives; always remain open to the lessons. Be a sponge; learn from everyone and every situation. Take what's good and throw away what's not. Be aware of everything around you, turn on your extrasensory potential, and be in touch. You are constantly fine-tuning.

A very dear friend and mentor always told me, "It is important in life to be flexible." You mustn't be so rigid in your ways that it interferes with your growth. If you stay flexible, your chances of gaining the most from every experience are much greater. Sometimes, the greatest gifts of all come from those moments that might otherwise be overlooked; fall in love with the surprises along the way. There are often those moments in life when we just can't understand why we are going through something, only to find that, in the end, the outcome is fabulous after all.

You never know what's waiting for you just ahead; positivity opens you up to seeing the good in the bad and knowing the difference between the two. There have been situations in my own career that may not have felt the most pleasant or rewarding at the time. However, I look back on them now and am grateful for the experiences because of the gifts that came with them, often in the form of life-long relationships.

Don't miss out on an amazing opportunity because of your short-sightedness. Your life will be so much more fruitful, so much more balanced, so much more fulfilled, if you always keep a positive attitude and remain open and flexible.

> *"Life is what we make it,*
> *always has been, always will be."*
> **~ Grandma Moses**

CHAPTER SIX

MARKETS & VENUES—WHERE AND HOW TO FIND A GIG

Picture Perfect! Cast of Swing Train, Celebrity Cruise Lines' Mercury

---

"What success I achieved in the theater is due to the fact that I have always worked just as hard when there were ten people in the house as when there were thousands. Just as hard in Springfield, Illinois as on Broadway."
—Bill "Bojangles" Robinson

For some of you, this chapter will be a complete revelation; a discovery of what this profession really has to offer you, while others will already be familiar with its content and will have given the industry and its offerings a great deal of thought. You may already know exactly what market or type of venue you want to work in.

You may have your heart set on being in a dance company or on Broadway or in the West End. You may choose Hollywood for the movies, while others will prefer pop videos and tours, not to mention some of the other desirable markets, such as Las Vegas, cruise ships, theme parks and last, but not least, corporate entertainment. Then again, some of you may not want to wander too far from home; you may have aspirations of owning your own studio or you may be excited at the potential of creating additional opportunities for yourself, right there in your local market.

In this chapter, I will touch on all of these markets and some of the situations you might encounter when working in them. As I said before, show business truly is a great business. It's also a huge industry; but I do believe there is room for anyone who has the passion and determination. It's definitely not the easiest business to be in, but I'm sure you've heard that from other sources as well. The good news is that there are many different markets and venues and various capacities within the industry in which one can work. It's just a matter of finding your place within it.

Not all dancers solely want to perform; some of you may prefer to be behind the scenes—you may aspire to be a producer, director, or choreographer. Your passion may be in teaching, coaching, or developing talent. Or for some of you, it could be all about production support. You may start out with a strong desire to perform, yet for various reasons, find a new direction or passion along the way. One never knows what hidden talent can be developed or what feelings can be stirred up from the magic of being around show business.

I personally am a Gypsy at heart and always have been. I absolutely love to dance, but I love to choreograph even more. As far back as I can remember, I believed I was destined to be in show business. I adored performing as a young dancer, and as much as I loved being on stage, I had an equal affinity with the creative and cherished the responsibility of putting it all together. Before I even knew what the word "choreography" meant, I was making up routines at home; a true choreographer in the making. By the time I was twelve years old and training regularly, I was already experimenting with my choreography on other dancers. My forte is musical revues, musical theatre and variety. My background and training, as for most dancers, is in all styles of dance.

A male teacher once told me that women do not make good choreographers. Today, with professional choreography credits representing over seventy Production Revues, hundreds of corporate events, and a smattering of television and film, I say to you, *do not let anyone*, I don't care who they are, take your dreams from you. Was his an attempt to shatter my hopes and dreams or merely a test to see if I had what it takes? It could have been either. The truth is, not everyone you meet will be well wishers or cheerleaders, but sometimes that opposition or lack of encouragement and support is just what you need to turn things upside down.

> **Encore:**
> *I trust that you also chose to go into this business because*
> *you wanted to work at something you love.*

The Work is Out There—You Just Have to Find It

So, do you know where you are heading, or are you looking for some guidance? Is this something you've given a lot of thought to or are you still searching and not sure what options are really available to you? Following is a list which will help clarify some of your questions.

This list of markets and venues will help you to identify areas in which you can find work as a dancer. I suggest you look it over and give some thought to where you see yourself. What is your forte? What area of performance do you feel most passionate about? Once you've looked over the list, take a moment and create a new list of your own.

Write down the areas that are of interest to you, and notate what you like most about each of these areas. In doing so, this list can become a useful tool in helping you to make decisions about your career path.

- Broadway and The West End
- Broadway touring companies
- Cabaret
- Community and Regional Theatre
- Corporate entertainment (conventions, conferences and trade shows)
- Cruise ships
- Dance companies
- Dinner Theatre
- Film and television
- Hotels and resorts
- Las Vegas and other casino or entertainment cities
- Musical revues and variety shows
- Pop and/or other music videos
- Pop and/or other music concert tours
- Theme Parks

Many young dancers with stars in their eyes have their sights set on the likes of Broadway and Hollywood, and why shouldn't they? Both are huge entertainment capitals and exciting cities. These two markets, along with professional dance companies, are probably by far the most popular and most obvious aspirations for young dancers in the United States. However, as promised, I will introduce you to a plethora of other markets and venues and hopefully, create excitement about the many possibilities available to you within this industry. With all of this new-found information and knowledge, you will be able to make informed choices about where you might want to live, the business, and your place within it.

New York Versus Los Angeles:

A Tale of Two Cities

New York City and Los Angeles are two very exciting cities and incredible markets for dancers, both buzzing with mind-boggling energy and more than enough to satiate any performer's appetite. However exciting they both are, New York City and Los Angeles are extremely different from each other. First of all they have two very different main entertainment markets, i.e. stage in New York City versus film and television in Los Angeles. Secondly the lifestyles are as opposite as "chalk and cheese." A.L. Gordon, *of The New York Sun,* said, "New Yorkers revel in good works and historic institutions. In Los Angeles, people revel in the beauty, clothing, love affairs, and talent of the entertainment industry." This common belief translates into the dance world as well; some teachers tend to encourage their students to choose New York City over Los Angeles, intimating that New York City has more to offer the serious dancer, while Los Angeles is about trends, glamour and glitz. For this very reason I will compare the two, and I will also follow this with a third entertainment city which is often overlooked when making career choices, "Las Vegas." Having worked and lived in all three cities, I can tell you that they all have much to offer. At the end of the day, it all comes down to your personal tastes, needs and desires. What are your career goals, what are your personal goals, and what does each city have to offer you in relationship to those goals? What your heart longs for first and foremost is ultimately what you must pursue.

New York City

New York City and Broadway are synonymous. Loaded with culture and diversity, New York (city) is a fabulous destination plain and simple, but for a singer, dancer or actor, it can be the ultimate destination. Why is it that the Broadway stage always beckons even the most accomplished and highly sought after Hollywood movie stars? "Home sweet home," and just as the stage is home to actors, it is also home to dancers. It's where we started out and it's where we gained our first experiences. I believe that there is no greater sensation or more gratifying recognition than the applause or ovation of an audience. Nothing can truly replace the exhilaration of a live performance, especially on *Broadway!*

As I am completing this book, there are currently forty Broadway theatres and forty-one off-Broadway theatres. Now playing on Broadway, there are twenty-two musicals and fourteen plays, with approximately another dozen new shows expected to open this year. Off-Broadway and off-off Broadway will present well over one hundred different productions, some with short runs, ranging from two weeks to six weeks, and a few with longer runs, ranging from three months to twelve months. The Broadway League is the trade association of the Broadway industry. Its members consist of theatre owners and operators, producers, presenters, and general managers of Broadway and Touring Broadway productions as well as suppliers to this industry. To learn more about The Broadway League you can visit their website at www.broadwayleague.com. According to the league's end-of-season statistics for the 2008-2009 Broadway season (which began May 26, 2008 and ended May 24, 2009), forty-three new productions opened on Broadway during 2008-2009. Ten new musicals, four musical revivals, eight new plays, and sixteen play revivals.

Los Angeles

Hollywood, with its celebrities and all the glamour, can be very enticing; the idea of rubbing elbows with "the who's who—the cream of the crop" can be rather alluring. One most often chooses Los Angeles when his or her interests lean more towards film and television or pop music videos and concert tours. In today's market with the whole world having a newfound love affair with dance, thanks to those shows I mentioned earlier; *So You Think You Can Dance* and *Dancing with the Stars*, Los Angeles is certainly an exciting place to be. Not only have we seen so many dance-related reality TV shows over the last few years, but many advertisers are featuring dancers in their television commercials. Just as live work brings great exhilaration and a sense of accomplishment, so does seeing yourself on the big screen. Let's face it; most people would love the opportunity. For many it would be a dream come true.

Encore:
New York City and Los Angeles are two very exciting cities and incredible markets for dancers, both buzzing with mind-boggling energy and more than enough to satiate any performer's appetite.

Las Vegas

When you think of Las Vegas, you might think of casinos and variety shows or hundreds of showgirls in larger-than-life musical extravaganzas. Las Vegas is all that and more. It is a huge entertainment city with a great market for all types of performers; a place that aspiring performers relocate to all the time. (Though other gambling cities may also have live entertainment, they simply do not have as much work to offer. Dancers don't usually relocate to these smaller centers in the hopes of finding work, but rather, move there for a particular contract.)

Las Vegas is home to forty-plus headliners and approximately fifty production shows, including several *Cirque du Soleil* style shows. However, it doesn't stop there; Vegas has also been the West Coast home to several Broadway shows. There have been many attempts to bring Broadway to the Las Vegas Strip, some of which have been more successful than others. *Avenue Q*, Steve Wynn's first big attempt at bringing the Broadway musical to Vegas, opened at Wynn Las Vegas and closed after a nine-month run. Steve Wynn is one of the world's most famous casino and resort developers, credited with spearheading the expansion of the Las Vegas Strip back in the 1990s. Next, *Hairspray* ran only four months at the Luxor in 2007. *MaMa Mia* however, holds the record as the longest running Broadway show in Vegas. It ran almost six years at the Mandalay Bay and closed at the end of summer, 2008. Now there's a new "King" in town and his name is Simba. *Disney's The Lion King*, a true phenomenon on stage, is currently playing at the Mandalay Bay. *Phantom* has been reconceived for the Las Vegas Strip and is playing at The Venetian in a forty million dollar custom built theatre. It opened in 2006. *The Jersey Boys* took up residency at the Palazzo, and is enjoying great success. Last, but certainly not least, Broadway's award winning, smash hit, *Spamalot*, had a very successful fifteen month run at the Wynn Las Vegas and closed July 13th, 2008. Also in the line-up are a few Off Broadway hits, *Stomp Out Loud*, a newer, bigger version than its original *Stomp*, *Blue Man Group* and *Menopause the Musical*. Although the complete fate of Broadway shows in Las Vegas has not yet been determined, the attempts to give theatre its place out West persist.

There are currently five *Cirque du Soleil* shows playing: *O, Mystère, Zumantiy, Love* and *Ka*, plus the *Cirque* style show, *Le Rêve*. These are all extravagant productions performed in multi-million dollar theatres built to specification. A certain extent of *Cirque's* popularity was brought on, in part, by a need for something new and innovative, and it is absolutely fabulous what they have done. The intense demand and interest that has been created is absolutely genius.

With so many *Cirque*-style shows in town, there may not be quite as much work for dancers right now, but no one can dispute that Las Vegas certainly still offers it all. From showgirls to trapeze artists, magicians to comedians, impressionists to impersonators, and musical theatre to huge celebrities, such as Elton John, Cher, Prince, Janet Jackson, Tim McGraw and Gwen Stefanni, to name just a few. Dancers who choose to pursue work in either musical theatre or revue type of work can find themselves equally at home. If you love the excitement of a city built around entertainment, Las Vegas could be just the city for you.

Where Will You Land?

Regardless of whether you are deciding between New York City and Los Angeles, or considering any other city, I want to point out some very real concerns that you must address when planning any potential relocation. Since there is no guarantee that you'll get the first Broadway show, musical revue, feature film or pop video you audition for, you must consider the following:

1. How will you live while waiting for the perfect gig to come along? and
2. How will you survive in between gigs?

Let's face it; the glamour of show business will fade quite quickly if you are consistently re-defining the "starving artist" role. We will discuss more on that topic a little later in our "No More Starving Artist" chapter.

You may want to have your pen and paper handy; here are a few more key questions you should ask yourself:

- Do you have any friends or relatives living in the city or cities that you are considering, which could help make your transition a little easier?
- How much money will you need to make the move?
- How much money will you need to survive until you find steady work?
- What job skills other than dance do you possess?
- What is the average cost of living and what can you anticipate spending on an apartment?
- Will you live on your own or share an apartment with fellow performers?
- Where will you study? Do you have your heart set on studying with any specific teachers or at any particular studios? There is certainly no shortage of great teachers on either coast; many are even bi-coastal.
- What will your monthly training costs be? Consider all classes— dance, acting and vocal.
- What will transportation to and from auditions and classes cost?

Obviously, these are all good considerations whenever relocating from home. Not all aspiring talent is lucky enough to grow up in a city let alone an entertainment city! Many aspiring performers must relocate in order to pursue their dreams. It is important to have a solid plan, and considering the above questions carefully can help you to strategize how you will get there and how you will survive. This pre-planning will give you the optimal shot at success.

Encore:
Let's face it; the glamour of show business will fade quite quickly if you are consistently re-defining the "starving artist" role.

City Lights

Having grown up in Northern Ontario, I decided to move to Toronto at nineteen years of age to pursue my career in dance. I knew that in order to fulfill my dreams of working as a professional dancer and choreographer, I had to leave my home town, and move to the "City." My goals had been long determined; I was excited for the adventure, but sad to be leaving my family. Once in Toronto, the first thing I did was get myself into dance classes at the best and most popular studios in town. This was great; I immediately started meeting other dancers and finding out who was who. Who were the working choreographers, and who were the best local production companies? I would constantly check the audition postings at the studios as well as the weekly entertainment columns in the various newspapers. I quickly learned which magazine was the Number One place to find audition notices, and between word of mouth and these notices, I was soon off on every audition that had the word dance in it.

Now as you make your final decision, I remind you, be honest with yourself. No one knows you better than you, and it is you who must consider what positions you can slot into most comfortably and most naturally based on your talent type and your goals. One of the big differences between New York City and Los Angeles is the different type of work that each city has to offer and, consequently, the different types of talent recruited for that work.

If you haven't already done so, it would be a good idea to subscribe in advance to several of the "industry rags" or periodicals. This can help you to identify and learn about prospective agents, studios, dance companies and various production companies, in addition to the obvious: "What is happening in the industry?" "Who is holding auditions?" and "What new shows are coming to town?" *Backstage* has been the New York Actors' resource for over forty five years and has two different publications, *Backstage East* (New York City) and *Backstage West* (Los Angeles). Once known as *Dirt Alert, Call Back News* covers the industry happenings in Las Vegas. And a newer on line service called VegasAuditions.com is well-regarded by industry professionals. For any of you living in Europe, *The Stage* publication, which covers the industry throughout Europe and predominantly London, has long been the number one resource for dancers. *Dance* magazine, for the young dancer and professional dancer, has been an industry leader since 1927, and *Dance Spirit,* their newer addition, is known as the young dancer's resource. Both offer an excess of educational and informative articles to help keep you in the know. These industry resources can also be accessed on line. Additionally, there are numerous Internet-only resources which are also great ways to find out what is going on in the industry.

These materials, along with an honest and fair consideration of the above questions, should give you a reasonably clear indication of the market you are best suited for and which one will offer you the most longevity. Keep in mind some of what we discussed in earlier chapters on the importance of being a triple threat. Clearly, as a triple threat, you not only create more diversity and, therefore, broaden your markets, but you also increase your career opportunities. Think about whom you see on Broadway and whom you see doing the latest pop tours and videos. Are you that type? Do you see yourself working in that market? These are important questions, and you need to consider all of this when making your decisions.

Although much emphasis has been placed on New York City and Los Angeles, these are by no means the only significant markets; as prefaced earlier, they are simply the two largest and most popularized dance markets. There is an entire dance and performing arts world waiting for you to discover, you need only read on!

Encore:
No one knows you better than you, and it is you who must consider what positions you can slot into most comfortably and most naturally based on your talent type and your goals. Be completely honest with yourself.

Give Me Somebody to Dance For

When it comes to seeking employment with specific venues or independent production companies, do your homework first, as you should in any situation. Some venues that have on-going or long-running shows will hire independent production companies to produce their shows, while others will produce them in-house. More often than not, when holding open auditions, such venues and/or production companies will post their audition notices at various dance studios as well as advertise in trade papers, magazines, and on various casting or audition websites. Some may choose to go through casting directors or call on talent and dance agents directly.

Today there are many sites that post auditions; you can find them by simply doing a search on line for castings, auditions or dance jobs. Keep in mind that the various publications mentioned previously will often have an Internet presence, as well, and it is always good to go with those most trusted sources first: those that have been around for many years and/or those who are endorsed by trusted sources and sponsors. When considering a new website, if there is a contact number call to find out how they verify the accuracy of such postings and their advertisers.

Many production companies will accept photos and resumes throughout the year. They may also accept video/DVD submissions to have on hand in the event of a need for a sudden replacement. Some companies have been known to handle their entire casting needs via snail mail or email, hence cutting the costs of live auditions.

Prior to sending out a promo package or photo and resume, it is always a good idea to make a phone call to introduce yourself first. A dancer would normally be expected to send out a photo and resume. A choreographer, a director, a specialty act, a performing group, or a production company are a few examples of those who would send out promotional packages, when soliciting new clients or business. Such promo packages might include a DVD and bio, press reviews, and any special promo pieces. This would normally be packaged in a press kit folder, with a cover letter to introduce the act, the group or the company.

When calling to introduce yourself, you should ask if there is an entertainment director, a head choreographer, or an in-house person in charge of casting with whom you can speak. Find out if they accept talent submissions via mail, and if so, whom your submission should be addressed to. This call will give you the opportunity to establish personal contact and identify a secretary or administrative assistant should you be unable to speak directly to the person in charge. For future calls, an established contact can go a long way; you will be able to address the person directly and remind her or him of your initial call, thereby creating some affinity. My advice to you is to be polite, courteous, and respectful at all times when dealing with people and to always be appreciative of any assistance given to you. You always want to make a good impression, especially on the person answering the telephone. Our business is so personable and first impressions are very important. Your attitude can make it or break it; it can be the deciding factor as to whether your call gets put through to the person in charge, or whether you come up against a roadblock. And, of course, this last bit of advice applies to any and all contacts you make, regardless of the market or venue. You must always present yourself in the most professional manner. On that note, I would like to add a side note—do not allow your professionalism to be influenced or altered negatively by the lack of respect that we see so often on television today in certain reality TV shows. Although the over-the-top auditions in the early stages of many of these shows may sell air time, the truth is, if anyone ever spoke to a producer that way (the cursing, talking back and belligerence as so many of these contestants are encouraged to do), they not only would get themselves thrown out of the audition, but there is a great chance that they would *never* work in the industry. Sensationalism may get John Q Public interested from season to season, but it just doesn't cut it in the real world, so don't believe for one second that this demeaning and often ridiculous behavior you see in the early stages of some of these shows is normal or acceptable.

Encore:
When it comes to seeking employment with specific venues or independent production companies, always do your homework first.

Dance Agents and Talent Agents

Although we will discuss agents in further detail in our "No More Starving Artist" chapter I would like to take this opportunity to mention the tremendous role that agents can play in your career. As they relate to markets and venues, there is no greater resource than an agent to find you work. Yes, many auditions are advertised, and open calls are exactly that—open to the public; but there are a great number of castings that go on every day that a dancer without agency representation would not be privy to.

Plain and simple is the fact that some production companies have no interest in going outside the inner circle. Therefore, dance agents and talent agents play an important role in our industry and can play an important role in you landing many of the jobs we are discussing in this very chapter.

As you will see throughout this chapter, the topic of markets and venues is very much intertwined. Most large entertainment cities will have an assortment of venues, all with varied entertainment needs. What follows is an overview of the most often pursued commercial markets, in addition to the cities outlined earlier.

Encore:
There is no greater resource than an agent to find you work.

Corporate Entertainment

Most large cities, especially tourist and convention destinations, have a vast corporate entertainment market. Las Vegas, Nevada, and Orlando, Florida, are great examples of such cities, as they both thrive on their tourism and their convention business. Therefore, there is a need for corporate entertainment which can be a very lucrative market for you, the performer. For those of you who are not familiar with corporate entertainment companies, these are production companies that provide entertainment to various corporate clients.

This could mean anything from a new product launch to business theatre, or an awards presentation and a gala evening. The clients can be as diverse as a group of doctors, to an automobile company or a chain of grocery stores, to a software company. Your job as a performer might involve introducing new products through song and dance, meeting and greeting guests, presenting awards, or performing in a full-blown musical revue for a company's or an organization's final gala celebration. You may be involved in only one aspect of the convention, conference, or trade show; or you may be involved in various activities throughout its weeklong meetings, seminars, or sessions. The shows are often fun and always upbeat. They may not always be the most challenging artistically, but they will usually be enjoyable. And, obviously, the better the production company, the better the production. Rehearsals and the performances can run from as little as a few days to a few weeks, depending on the client, the size of the show, and the nature of the presentation.

As a young dancer, I did a great deal of corporate entertainment work in between long-running shows. Some corporate work was during daytime hours, which was a bonus as I was often able to do both, the corporate gig and my evening show. When a contract was coming to an end, I would start planning ahead. I would contact the various corporate entertainment companies to let them know that I would be available for work or, to find out if there were any auditions coming up. I first contacted those companies by telephone that I had already been working with, and then sent out promotional materials to new companies I had not yet worked for. This way, I was not only securing work through my usual channels, but I was also making new contacts for future opportunities. I have always enjoyed working in corporate entertainment. As a dancer, there were always new shows to learn, which made it interesting, and it kept me busy performing when I didn't have a steady show. As a choreographer, they kept me busy creating a variety of new material.

Unfortunately, there is no one industry resource that will list all corporate entertainment production companies. So put on your thinking caps; this is where you get to be creative net-workers and promoters. Your best bet is always to learn of these companies from fellow dancers, choreographers, and through the studios. This will allow you to learn more about them and verify their reputations through tried and true experiences of others.

As I'm sure you know, the Internet has become the number one resource for information world-wide; once again, you just need to be creative with your searches. Especially if you don't know anyone in the industry, this is a great place to start. There is no limit to what you can access; you can even search the Yellow Pages on line. Such companies can be found under different headings: production companies, entertainment production companies, entertainment agencies and bureaus, talent agencies, and several other entertainment-related headings. Although this is a very good starting point, I must warn you that you will need to check them out through other reputable sources in the business. At the very least, you will want to call the companies in order to determine what type of work they do, and whether or not they even employ performers, specifically dancers. If they hire dancers, make sure you are clear on what kind of dancers they hire.

I learned that lesson very early on, and although my example comes from having answered an ad in the local newspaper, the point of the lesson is nevertheless the same. Having just arrived in the city and eager to get to work, I responded to an audition notice looking for dancers. However when I arrived at the venue and was greeted by a cocktail server wearing a thong and a couple of pasties, I quickly gathered that they were looking for a *different* type of dancer. Needless to say, I hightailed it out of there. At that moment, I promised myself to do my homework and to check things out before wasting my time going to every call that said "dancers wanted."

FYI—The title "Production Company" can mean everything from stage builders to video production, while the title "Entertainment Company" or "Entertainment Agency" can mean anything from show producers to escort services. So be sure to check them out. Some production companies that do use dancers in their presentations may often refer to outside sources for hiring this talent; i.e. casting agents, dance agents and managers, and/or dance companies and studios. So again, do your homework thoroughly.

Production guides, which are known predominantly as resources for film, television and commercial work, will sometimes list corporate entertainment producers under their "Production Companies" category with different sub-headings, such as live events or corporate events. You may also find some production companies listed under meeting planners and party planners.

Most important, if you are new to a city, pick up the local industry paper, see what auditions are going on, get yourself to class and start meeting other dancers. This method alone can be the most valuable means of getting to know the business. It will be a wonderful network for you to tap into immediately and get to know your new market, as well as make some friends. From there, you should find out which choreographers are doing most of the work and see if they are teaching any classes or workshops; then attend them.

Encore:
*Don't get caught up with the paycheck unless it
comes with happiness and fulfillment.*

Musical Revues and Variety Shows

Musical revues and variety shows represent a very large market as there are so many different venues in which these shows can be presented. This genre is a personal favorite of mine. I've spent the last twenty-five years choreographing and directing musical revues throughout the United States and abroad. I love this genre of production because of its variety and the versatility of the material. If you enjoy a wide range of music and styles of dance, then these shows can be great fun and might just be perfect for you.

In any one revue, you could find yourself covering material from your favorite Broadway show to your favorite pop star's repertoire. And the markets and venues are often just as varied. Some contracts will offer great travel opportunities and exciting experiences; i.e., a touring company, a cruise ship or an engagement abroad. Each venue or production company will have its own contract standards and lengths of runs. Often, you will be hired as an employee, rather than an independent contractor, when signing on with a large corporation for a long-running show. When dealing with major corporations such as some of the big hotel chains or theme parks, you may also receive employee benefits. The following is a list of some of the types of venues in which you will find musical revues and/or variety shows:

Resorts, Hotels and Showrooms

Many hotels and resorts, especially those in tourist destinations, have showrooms and theatres that present long-running, ongoing musical revues or variety shows. These venues can be found all over the world.

In the United States, you have several gambling or entertainment cities, the Mecca, of course, being Las Vegas with over one hundred casinos. Other popular gambling cities that are also known for their entertainment are: Atlantic City, New Jersey; So. Lake Tahoe, California; Reno, Nevada; Laughlin, Nevada; and Mashantuchket, Connecticut (home of Foxwood Resort and Casino).

There are over seven hundred cities in the United States with casinos; now that's not to say that every casino will have a show, but you can be sure that a great percentage will have some form of entertainment. This should give you an idea of how vast the employment opportunities truly are.

The city of Branson, Missouri, is a huge entertainment market with over sixty shows in town—everything from magic shows to country-western style productions, and celebrity artists to musical revues. Branson is all about the entertainment; there is no gambling.

Myrtle beach, South Carolina, and Pigeon Forge, Tennessee, are also great destination cities. Myrtle Beach is full of golf resorts and numerous entertainment venues, while Pigeon Forge is more of a family vacation destination with several theatres dedicated to family entertainment.

Theme Parks

In this section, I will mention a few of the largest and most popular theme parks. Many dancers who have worked for me have spent years working in these establishments. The reviews are often mixed; some dancers absolutely love it. These are the dancers who stay on for years, while others may do one contract and not care to return. Working in a theme park can be a fabulous ongoing-gig. However, it can also be very demanding. You probably will work long days doing several shows per day, often outdoors, in very hot temperatures. But looking on the brighter side, this can be an incredible way to earn a steady livelihood and a terrific experience living somewhere new and exciting, and meeting people from all over the world. You will be performing daily while gaining invaluable experience that you will take with you throughout your career. What great fun to be able to do what you love and get paid for it! For some, these gigs will be a stepping stone, and for others, a place they are happy to settle into and call home. As you can see, working in a theme park can be very rewarding for many reasons.

You are generally hired as an employee, not as an independent contractor. As an employee, you are most likely eligible for a benefits package. These benefits will vary and can be determined by the number of hours in a work-week or the amount of time you have worked for the company. There are usually different levels with different packages.

In the United States, the opposite of being hired as an employee (W2 tax form) is to be hired as an independent contractor (1099 tax form). There are certain guidelines that dictate this classification. If you meet these guidelines and are hired as an independent contractor, you are responsible for yourself. You will be responsible for filing and paying your own taxes, and very often, you will also be responsible for your own health insurance. As an independent contractor, you have the ability to act as your own company, and you will have many deductions that can help reduce the amount of taxes you pay. Deductions such as the cost of travel to and from work, make-up, dancewear, and classes are just a few. I discuss the advantages of working as an independent contractor in greater detail in Chapter Thirteen: No More Starving Artist, and Chapter Fifteen: Money Makes the World Go Round.

Some theme parks will allow you to swing out of shows as long as your track (your position or part) is covered. Some companies promote this as a way to keep cast members long-term. They understand that a little flexibility keeps things interesting and fresh. As long as the show does not suffer and your position is adequately filled, they encourage a little moonlighting. Some will even allow you to take a leave of absence. This is a very nice bonus in the event that another great opportunity were to come along. What a wonderful incentive to know that you can always come back to steady work!

Don't lose sight of the fact that you are doing what you love and that you have steady employment, which is not too shabby in this business. But don't get caught up with the paycheck unless it comes with happiness and fulfillment. Always remember why you went into this business. I find nothing more heartbreaking than seeing talent wasted or turned bitter. I am not saying that you shouldn't take a job for the steady paycheck and wonderful perks that it offers; on the contrary, these are all excellent reasons to take the job. What you mustn't do is grow tired, stale or bitter. I believe that as long as you keep your attitude in check, always look for the good in every situation, and create an excitement for yourself with every new performance, you can have the best of both worlds: doing what you love and earning a steady paycheck. And for the record, that goes for any job you take. After all, there's so much to love about what you do. Never compromise your integrity, your employer, the business, or the audience by putting yourself in a situation in which you cannot fulfill your obligations.

Here is a list of theme parks you may want to consider researching and learning more about. As you will see, some of them have several locations, and I have listed them with the name of the group or corporation in bold type.

- **Busch Gardens:**
  - Tampa, Florida
  - Williamsburg, Virginia
- **Cedar Fair, L.P. & Paramount Parks:**
  - California's Great America—Santa Clara, California
  - Carowinds—Charlotte, North Carolina
  - Cedar Point—Sandusky, Ohio
  - Dorney Park and Wild Water Kingdom—Allentown, Pennsylvania
  - Kings Dominion—Doswell, Virginia
  - Kings Island—Kings Mill, Ohio

        Knott's Berry Farms—Buena Park, California
        Michigan's Adventures—Muskegon, Michigan
        Valley Fair—Shakoppe, Minnesota
        Worlds of Fun and Oceans of Fun—Kansas City, Missouri

- **Cedar Fair International**:
  Canada's Wonderland—just outside of Toronto, Ontario
- **Disney Parks:**
  Disneyland Resort—Anaheim, California
      Disneyland
      California Adventures
  Walt Disney World Resort—Lake Buena Vista, Florida
      Magic Kingdom
      Epcot Center
      Disney-MGM Studios
      Disney's Animal Kingdom
  Tokyo Disney Resort—Urayasu, Chiba
      Disneyland
      Disney Sea
  Disneyland Resort Paris—Marne La Valle, France
      Disneyland
      Walt Disney Studios
  Hong Kong Disneyland—Penny's Bay, Lantau Island
- **Dollywood:**
  Pigeon Forge, Tennessee
- **Hershey Park:**
  Hershey, Pennsylvania
- **Sea World:**
  Orlando, Florida
  San Antonio, Texas
  San Diego, California
- **Six Flags:**
  Six Flags America—Baltimore, Maryland
  Six Flags Discovery Kingdom—Vallejo, California
  Six Flags Fiesta Texas—San Antonio, Texas
  Six Flags Great Adventure—Jackson, New Jersey
  Six Flags Great America—Gurnee, Illinois
  Six Flags Kentucky Kingdom—Louisville, Kentucky
  Six Flags Magic Mountain—Los Angeles, California

Six Flags New England—Springfield, Massachusetts
Six Flags over Georgia—Atlanta, Georgia
Six Flags over Texas—Arlington, Texas
Six Flags St Louis—St Louis, Missouri
The Great Escape and Splash Water Kingdom—Lake George, New York
- **Six Flags International:**
  La Ronde, Montreal, Quebec
  Six Flags Mexico, Mexico City
- **Universal studios:**
  Orlando, Florida
  Universal City, California

As you can see, the list is endless. There are theme parks throughout the United States, some larger than others, all offering multiple shows. Aside from Disney, Paramount, and Six Flags, I haven't even touched on the international market of theme parks. The bottom line is that there is no shortage of theme parks for anyone interested in opportunities in this type of venue.

Cruise Lines

Cruise lines employ staff from around the world and, therefore, are accustomed to all that it takes to obtain any necessary visas or work permits. Should you need a visa or work permit, depending on your citizenship, the ship's country of origin, or your travel itinerary, the cruise line will be able to guide you and assist you with any process necessary.

The cruise ship industry is one of the fastest growing industries today. Over the past fifteen years, I have done a great deal of work with the cruise industry. I have worked for several lines and watched the industry grow. In the past ten to twelve years, it has grown by leaps and bounds, with every cruise line trying to outdo the other. It's a bit like keeping up with the Joneses: who will have the latest and the greatest? Each new ship is more luxurious and spectacular than the last. The entertainment facilities on board some of these ships are not to be believed. The theatres are state-of-the-art with every special effect and gimmick available today, from hydraulic stages to intelligent lighting. The scenic elements even rival some of the grandest Disney productions and Broadway stages.

Having said this, you should be aware that not all ships are equal. There are some smaller ships that also have lovely showrooms and theatres, but they may not be on as grand a scale as the newer, larger ships. Then you have some of the more luxurious cruise liners which are, in fact, known for their smaller ships. There are older ships, both small and large, which will normally have more standard showrooms. All ships and contracts offer different experiences. Some staff members much prefer the smaller lines or ships as there is a comfortable and often considered friendlier atmosphere. Others will prefer the larger or more lavish ships for their size and grand showrooms.

As always, you must do your homework and get to know your ships and cruise lines. The industry is so huge today; if you are interested in auditioning for, or have been offered a contract with a cruise line, it is very easy for you to access information about the company and even the ship itself. Chances are, if you don't know someone who has worked on board, someone you know will. So ask around, and make sure you speak to several people. You want as much feedback as possible on individual experiences with a variety of cruise lines. As a mentor once told me, one person can be wrong but an audience never is.

From a performer's viewpoint, working on a cruise ship can be a very enticing prospect with all that ships have to offer: steady work with contracts that range anywhere from six to nine months, free food and accommodations, very few expenses, travel with exciting itineraries to foreign and exotic places, and a variety of shows from Broadway style to Rock and Roll and everything in between. As with theme parks, theatres, and some showrooms, you have the opportunity to do multiple contracts, though not necessarily always back-to-back. Life on board can be very demanding and most cruise lines understand the importance of having a break from life at sea. If you enjoy the work and you do a great job, you can always have future work. For some people, working on a cruise ship is an ideal situation; they do a six-month contract, take a break, and come back again. Some performers choose to stay with one cruise line and will move around from ship to ship and itinerary to itinerary, while others will work for a variety of cruise lines. Just as all ships are not created equal nor are their contracts.

Some cruise ship companies are better than others to work for. They can be as different as night and day. Some produce their own shows in-house, while others contract independent production companies. As a result of the numerous variables, not all shows are of the same standard. From what I have seen, some on board productions, whether produced in-house or by outside producers, can be fabulous, while others can be mediocre. Of course, this does not apply to the cruise ship industry alone; it applies to show business, in general.

Most important, remember to do your homework; I cannot emphasize this enough. Learn about the business you want to be in. Who are the top producers and the best cruise lines to work for? A lot of what I am pointing out here applies to the industry at large. Who are the best cruise lines, the best Las Vegas showrooms, the best theatres, the best theme parks and the best corporate entertainment companies? *Who are they?* Ask around; read the reviews and company profiles; get to know who is producing what and where. Who are the people you want to work for? The more you know about this industry, the better equipped you will be to make intelligent choices, which will allow you to improve your overall performance and to gain the best experiences.

I will tell you exactly what I have told countless numbers of dancers and singers who have worked for me on board various ships. Working on a cruise ship is a completely different venue than any other venue you will work in. Life on board is not for everyone. Some people love it and make entire careers out of performing from one ship to the next, while others simply cannot adhere to the conformity of on board life or handle the confinement of a ship. A ship that appears overwhelming in size when you first step on board will, over time, become smaller and smaller. Then there is always the consideration of motion sickness. Not everyone is a good sailor; not everyone can handle the motion of the ocean. I have had some people work for me who just never got used to it, while others were never affected by it.

If you are not one who likes rules and regulations, you probably will not appreciate the military structure and attitude of the cruise ship. Since life at sea is not to be taken lightly, there are many safety rules and regulations, as well as training and responsibilities that could be a mandatory part of your contract. Some cruise lines may include cruise staff duties in your contract; some companies pay you extra for these additional duties, while others don't. Some companies do not require cruise staff duties at all, from any of their performers. The bottom line is, if you are offered a contract, make sure to read it thoroughly, ask questions and clarify: know and understand what you are getting into.

I've had some wonderful experiences working at sea; I've also had some not so wonderful. But as you're about to find out, some of my greatest memories and life-changing moments are all thanks to ships. After all this is how I met my husband! So, as I've said on many occasions, be grateful for all experiences, for you never know what gifts they bear or what lies just ahead. I've been very fortunate to have produced, directed and choreographed my work on some incredible ships, with some exceptional theatres and showrooms. I have also had the great pleasure of working with some fabulous creative people and some extremely talented performers. I've enjoyed many fantastic moments, both in and out of rehearsals, while putting on these various productions. Some of my favorite people and memories are from my time in the cruise ship industry. As I've told countless performers, I do think that working on ships can be an excellent experience. Aside from the steady work and travel opportunities, one of the best aspects of all is the family-like ties that you create. It's your home away from home and you will build friendships that can last a lifetime. To this day, many performers who have worked for me are still the best of friends with each other ten and fifteen years later. It's always such a pleasure to hear that one of them is coming through town and the old gang is planning a get-together. Whenever I travel back to New York City, Los Angeles, England or Canada to hold auditions, I always manage a get together with those same special friends of mine who live there.

One thing that I haven't mentioned yet is rehearsals, and in the case of cruise ships, just how grueling they can sometimes be. Then again, I don't want to put you off entirely. After all, the purpose of this information is to enlighten you as to the many wonderful opportunities. I will say this though: just be prepared to work hard. The rehearsals can seem endless, especially when you are rehearsing on board, and every day you arrive in a new port only to watch the passengers disembark as you head to the showroom. This is sometimes the only opportunity you have to work on the stage as rehearsal space and time can be limited. There is a ship full of passengers needing to be entertained, as well as other artists who must also rehearse. Keep in mind that once the shows are up and running, you will have plenty of time to enjoy these lovely ports of call.

Always remember this; you get out of life what you put in, and the same applies to your work. If you are going to perform a show night after night, I am certain that you want it to be a fabulous show, one that you can be proud to be a part of. As the saying goes, "Practice, or in our case, rehearsal, makes perfect" and a well-rehearsed show and timely opening make for a smooth run and a very happy choreographer.

The following is a list of several (but not all) of the most popular Cruise Lines:

- Carnival Cruise Lines
- Celebrity Cruises
- Costa Cruises
- Cunard Line
- Crystal Cruises
- Disney Cruise Line
- Holland America Line
- Norwegian Cruise Line (NCL)
- Princess Cruises
- Radisson Seven Seas Cruises
- Royal Caribbean Cruise Lines (RCCL)
- Silversea Cruises

Encore:
If you are offered a contract, make sure to read it thoroughly, ask questions and clarify, know and understand what you are getting into.

Crossover in Markets and Venues

Many of the same types of shows that you could be hired for will cross over into different markets and venues. For example, the many musical revues, or Las Vegas style revues as they are sometimes referred to, will be found in various markets and venues, from gambling cities to tourist destinations around the world, whether in a small cabaret-style room or a large several thousand-seat theatre.

When it comes to theatre, other than the obvious markets of Broadway, the West End in London, and, of course, the theatre districts in some of the larger cities across the United States and Canada, there are additional opportunities in local dinner theatre and regional theatre.

Film, television and commercials are not only produced in Hollywood, although it certainly is the Mecca. There are many other major cities in which you can pursue this genre of work; it's just that there won't be as much work produced. Chances are, there won't be as large a pool of talent vying for the same roles, either. I'm sure that by now you get the idea of the crossover in both markets and venues available to you.

Last, but certainly not least, I will touch lightly on the various types of jobs in which one can work within our industry. After all, not everyone who is captured by the industry's magic grows up wanting to be on the stage. You may have aspirations of becoming a director, choreographer or producer, teacher, agent or manager. You may have additional talents and creative abilities in other areas of the business, such as costume design, make up artistry, music, writing, lighting design or scenic design. Each of these departments offers yet another list of possibilities, from assistants to all of these various positions mentioned above, to stage managers, dressers and various stylists.

The world of entertainment and show business is such a fascinating business to be involved in that I want all of you who have a love for it to be aware of all the opportunities that it holds. And very important is to know how truly wonderful these opportunities can be, and how significant your role will be, whether you choose to be on stage or off stage, in production support, or the producer. No production can come to realization and be a spectacular work of art without the team. And every team player is of equal importance.

Las Vegas, Los Angeles, Hollywood and New York City have all, at various times, gained the distinction of being known as "The Entertainment Capital of the World." Where will your dreams take you? Wherever your passion lies, whichever genre or specialty you choose, do it for all of the right reasons and chances are you will have a fabulous experience.

THE AUDITION—WHAT IT TAKES TO GET THE GIG

It's all about teamwork. Dancers rehearsing their vocals off to the side, Opryland Productions, Nashville, Tennessee

"The more auditions you go on, the more you will learn not to take it personally." —Paula Abdul

It is my sincere desire to help educate and prepare you for the audition process and the career possibilities that lie ahead. I aspire to teach the do's and don'ts, what to expect, how to present yourself, and how to have the best shot at a career in dance. We've all been there; we've all been in your shoes before.

We know how scary the other side of that table can be, all the while having to contend with your own fan club or not-so fan club, the cheering, heckling, bashing and berating, as you stand there trying desperately to remain calm, cool, and collected while not letting them see you sweat.

You know the fan club I'm talking about—those thousands of little voices in your head telling you: "They love me." "They hate me." "Why did

I come here?" "What do they think of me?" "What are they saying?" And so on and so on.

I believe one of the first and most important things you need to know and remember is that "We want you to succeed." It is our utmost desire as producers, directors and choreographers to find talent. So in essence, we need you. Keep in mind that we are on your side. We want you to dance your backside off and perform as if it's your last performance. If you have the talent and are the person we need, then show us. If you do your job and let us see this, then we all walk away successful. It is in both our best interests for you to be your best. As bad as you want the gig, we want to find the right talent.

Now I do realize that no two auditions are exactly alike. We all have our own way and style of handling different situations, and no two people will handle their audition in the exact same manner. However I feel quite certain in saying that for the most part, they are truly on your side. So if you go into the audition *confident* and *deliver* the goods, chances are you will walk away feeling great about your performance. I often take the time during my own auditions to remind the talent of why I'm there and to let them know that I am routing for them. I want to see the performance of a lifetime, and it is their job to give me the most incredible performance, both from a technical standpoint and as a showman. They have to prove to me that they are, in fact, that talent I went in there looking for. I personally will not settle for anything less. It is your job at an audition to sell yourself to the people auditioning you. If you give one of those "I can't be bothered performances," then you will walk away disappointed. Could you possibly expect anything else? If you do not give it everything that you're made of, then you don't deserve the gig. You have spent so much time training, taking a variety of classes, and perhaps even performing—some of you professionally and some of you in local productions or school recitals, and now you stand before a panel of people who can make it or break it for you. Don't waste their time, or yours, for that matter. Whether it's your first audition or your one hundredth, don't sell yourself short; don't deprive yourself of this opportunity to be anything but your very best; don't give less than 100 percent ever! After everything you have worked towards, everything you have been preparing for, here you are! This is your moment; you have only one shot at this job, don't blow it.

Let's start at the beginning: how did you hear about the audition? Was it an ad? If so, what did it say? Did it specify attire, shoes, make up?

What are they looking for? Who is the production company? Who will be holding the audition? Do your homework; do your research; know what you are auditioning for; know whom you are auditioning for. Is this a pop video, a Broadway show or tour, a theme park or cruise ship, a commercial, a feature film or a Las Vegas revue? You need this key information in order to determine how to dress, what your overall look should be and what shoes to wear. As for the shoes, bring them all: heels, dance sneakers, tap shoes, ballet slippers, point shoes, and jazz shoes; you want to be prepared for it all. You may even want to have your roller blades in the trunk of your car; you just never know, so expect the unexpected and be ready for it.

Encore:
Whether it's your first audition or your one hundredth, don't sell yourself short; don't deprive yourself of this opportunity to be anything but your very best; don't give less than 100 percent ever!

Dress to Impress

Okay, you've done your research the best you possibly can and hopefully you now have a general idea of what to expect. When it comes to attire, unless a specific look is asked for, keep it simple; dress nice and look your best. Dance attire of course is always best. Wear something fitted, something body-conscious and flattering. We want to see you move. You may want to add something different and unique that will make you stand out, whether it's a bright color, a bandanna, a special belt or something in your hair—you don't want to simply blend into a sea of dancers.

If the audition is more specific; for example, a particular role in a Broadway show, then once again, do your homework: find out what the character is like. How would he or she dress or wear their hair? Take on that roll and let the audition team see you as that person. If it is a chorus position, then stick to dance attire, let them see your movement and your lines—all things important to a dancer and the choreography. Be sensible in your choice of outfits. You want to impress them and you don't want to offend anyone. As I said in the beginning, no two auditions are identical, and no two audition teams will have the same view. So when I say be sensible, consider the wide range of people you could be auditioning for and try to appeal to the masses. You want to look your best, have your hair done and makeup on. Choose dancewear that you like, that you feel good in; something that is a bit fun and stylish, yet fitting. Remember, we want to see you dance. It is so important for us to see those lines. If you're wearing real big baggy clothing or layers upon layers, how will I as a choreographer, be able to see what I need to see? Don't forget to add that little something special to help you stand out.

If you are auditioning for a pop video or pop tour, then we're talking about a whole different subject matter. Consider the group or artist, consider their style, and choose appropriately. Find out all that you can about the look that they are looking for. *Girls*, as for makeup, in this case, less may be more. Eyes and lips—let them see your natural beauty; let them see what they have to work with. Accentuate your eyes with a little liner and mascara, and by choosing a light and natural color for your lips, you can't go wrong.

If you are in Las Vegas auditioning as a showgirl, then you had better pull out the old high-cut body suit or trunks. Although high-cut isn't exactly the *style-du-jour* today, show some leg. You know what I mean: get out your fishnet stockings, and heels. Oh, and while you are at it, you may want to put on your false eyelashes. Talk to other dancers to find out if anyone you know has ever auditioned for this particular venue, artist or show. Maybe they know the production company; maybe they know the choreographer. Don't be afraid to ask. Someone may be able to give you a head's up, and the exact information or advice you need to help you best prepare.

Encore:
Choose dancewear that you like, that you feel good in; something that is a bit fun and stylish, yet fitting. Remember, we want to see you dance. It is so important for us to see those lines.

Location, Location, Location

Next, the location. As part of your research, you should have mapped out where you're going and how long it will take you to get there. Very important: always be sure you have enough time to get there, taking into account the time of day, rush hour, etc. Always arrive early. Give yourself plenty of time for a thorough warm-up, which means time to prepare both mentally and physically for your audition. As you approach the audition location, turn it on and keep it on. "It's Showtime"; you never know who is who and you want to make a great first impression.

You never know who you are first meeting; the person signing you in could be your future employer. Be professional; be pleasant and courteous to all when introducing yourself. In the end, you could be working alongside any number of the people you encounter throughout this day. Make yourself memorable. Be a dancer's dancer; be that someone whom a producer, director or choreographer would want to spend hours and hours a day with. The work we do is intimate. We can spend days or weeks on end together, first in rehearsals and then depending on the gig itself, we could spend weeks, months or years working on the same production. So, be that someone special on and off stage whom other cast members want to work with and spend time with.

When you first arrive, introduce yourself and ask if and where you should sign in. Usually, there will be a sign-in sheet and you will often be given a number and an audition form. You could be asked to fill out the form and have a photo and resume ready to be handed in at some point during the audition; perhaps after an initial type-casting or cut. Sometimes they will ask for them straight up front; while other times, they will wait until a final cut. And on that note, make sure you have a professional head-shot that looks like you, and a professionally laid out resume that is truly your resume. *You* are your resume, so *be* your resume. Remember the famous line from *A Chorus Line*, "Who am I anyway? Am I my resume?" *This is not the time to be borrowing* from someone else! Yes, you will have to spend money in this area; you absolutely must keep current, changing your photos as often as needed. This is your business and these promotional pieces are essential. You never want to give anyone a photo that does not look like you.

As for your resume, it should be no more than one page in length and should be updated constantly, making sure that all contact information is accurate. If you are first starting out and are concerned about not having any professional experience, you can list any local performances with your school, performing arts schools or dance studios, as well as any awards or accomplishments and hobbies you may have. If you have not had much experience in the area of performances, you may prefer to write a simple biography about who you are and any special interests or personal accomplishments.

Okay, let's get back to sign-in. Once you have signed in and the room is accessible, go on in, put your dance bag and resume aside, and give yourself that full complete warm-up we talked about earlier. Once again, make sure you've given yourself plenty of time to be physically warmed up and mentally prepared. Focus on why you are there; focus on your confidence, strengths and ability to give an excellent performance and audition—*visualize* a great outcome. Your mind is a powerful tool, so use it to your advantage. Rather than allowing useless non-productive chatter, (remember that fan club we talked about earlier), why not envision a fabulous ending to this day? How do you envision it? It's your story; you can write it any way you like. Bill Bartmann, a highly successful entrepreneur and motivational speaker, talks about reverse worry. Simply put, he says, "If your mind can worry, why can't it imagine? Worry is looking into the future and seeing the worst possible outcome. If you have a 50/50 shot, why not expect something good instead of bad?" Is the glass half-full or is it half-empty? Your thoughts can be supportive and constructive, or they can be negative and damaging. It's your choice.

Once the audition has begun, be present and attentive; be there completely in mind, body and spirit. You could be asked to slate your name and number, or name and agency; demonstrate confidence, maturity, and personality. You want to be captured in a good light. Videos sometimes have a way of hanging around for a long time and besides which, the person who ultimately makes the decision may not be at the audition. They could be meeting you for the first time on video. Keep in mind that they could be seeing hundreds of people this day, so you want to make yourself memorable both on and off the camera.

Encore:
It's your story; you can write it any way you like.

Practice Makes Perfect

Once again, be aware of everything and everyone around you. Get that extrasensory capacity working for you; a dancer must be able to feel another dancer's energy next to him or her. There could be hundreds of dancers in one room at the same time all trying to learn the same routine. You could start out in the tenth row. I personally would make sure I was front and center and I suggest you do the same, especially since you did arrive so nice and early. More often than not the choreographer or person teaching the routine will rotate the rows so that everyone has the opportunity to pick up the choreography as well as be seen. So if you should find yourself in the tenth row, don't fret, you will have your turn front and center. In the meantime, be courteous and patient and most important, stay present.

Dancers often express to me their concerns about not being able to pick up the routines fast enough. This is certainly a dancer's worst nightmare. Let's face it, when you only have a short time to pick up the routine and your nervous system is already working on overtime, the last thing you need is for your speed and accuracy to fail you. However, let me offer you two different thoughts on that note. Some choreographers base decisions on looks, personality, and overall dance ability, rather than speed at picking up. Others will definitely want to know right then and there that you can cut it when it comes to picking up quickly, as rehearsal time is often pressed, and there can be a great deal to learn in a short time. Here are a couple of simple recommendations that can help. First of all get yourself into a variety of classes with as many different teachers and choreographers as possible. The more exposure you have to a wide variety of choreographers and styles, the more opportunities you give yourself to pick up different combinations on a regular basis. Some teachers will offer choreography classes. These are great for practicing speed and accuracy.

We've all been told that practice makes perfect, so let me give you another suggestion: a little trick that I once learned from a great teacher. Partner up with some friends and fellow dancers. Call it a jam session of sorts. Play some of your favorite music and do some dancing. You'll want to mix things up a bit to get the most out of your session, so make sure you have plenty of music in a wide range of styles. You can start out with one person leading the dance, and everyone else following along, trying to pick up the routine as he or she free-styles, or you can break it down into partners, one leading while the other follows and then switch roles.

This is a great little exercise that you can have some fun doing while sharpening your skills on picking up quickly and accurately. Remember, variety is the key. Audition workshops can be of enormous benefit to you. The more opportunity you get to practice in life-like auditions, without standing the chance of blowing the gig, the better equipped you will be to handle the real deal. Get out those dance and music DVD's; don't stop and rewind, just follow. Every single opportunity you take to learn choreography on the spot, the quicker you become at picking up.

One of your other goals should be to develop an ability to walk into any audition and feel right at home, picking up any number of styles. As a choreographer, I can tell you that it is extremely important to me that a dancer be stylized. All choreographers have their own unique styles and believe me, if they are teaching you a routine, they expect you to get the style right. This is their creation and there is a reason for their every move. Ultimately, they want it executed just the way they do it, so your job in an audition, when learning a routine, is to ensure that you are mimicking the person teaching. You want to watch their every move. Be exact! Where is that pinky? What angle is their head at and what is the attitude of the dance? The goal is to look just like them. So as mentioned earlier, be extremely attentive to every little detail. Get that routine down; get that style down, and then perform it like it's your last. Give it everything you've got and show them what you're made of. Performance, in my opinion, is huge; I want to see you sell it, period. If you can't sell it in the audition, how can I know or trust what your performance will be like at Showtime?

Encore:
One of your goals should be to develop an ability to walk into any audition and feel right at home, picking up any number of styles.

Always Take it Professionally, Never Take it Personally

There is so much that goes into casting. Producers, directors and choreographers usually know going in what they are looking for. Sometimes, it's about a particular type or look; sometimes, it's a specific style; sometimes it's all about technique. Other times, it's all about performance, and sometimes, it's about the perfect blend of all of the aforementioned. And every now and then, we go in thinking we know exactly what we want only to be blown away by someone and so we end up re-writing the role or requirements. Unfortunately, you cannot be everything to everyone, so you go in as geared up as you can, confident of your dance ability, and give your very best performance. That is all you can do. Believe me, if you go in there and give it your very best shot, you will walk away feeling great about what you did, and so you should.

Let me backtrack for a minute; let's revisit that whole learning process. Very often during auditions you will not have a great amount of time to learn the routine; however, the process of the audition itself can be quite lengthy, so there's no need to panic. Not all auditions will have masses of dancers, but certainly some of them will, so be prepared. In this event, once the routine has been taught, the choreographer will have to break the large group down into smaller ones. Sometimes you'll be asked to leave the room while other groups have the opportunity to perform full out; this is an opportunity for you to review the choreography. Other times, they may choose to keep everyone in the room and rotate one group after another. Throughout the process, be mindful and respectful of those dancers who are performing; don't be in the sidelines practicing, as this can be distracting for the audition team and not fair to fellow dancers. This would be the time for you to review the routine in your mind, quietly visualizing the choreography. This can be an excellent exercise to calm you and help prepare you for your turn as well. You can be certain that someone is always watching and will make a note of how you handle yourself on the sidelines and how you interact with others. You will have the opportunity to strut your stuff center stage, so give your peers their moment to shine.

There will be times at large open calls when, in actuality, you may not have the opportunity to learn a routine. Some audition teams will do typecasting or a quick process of elimination by asking you to perform something as simple as pirouettes on both sides. This could be as much of the audition as you get to see. Now, if they are typecasting and you are not asked to stay past the initial lineup, you mustn't take this personally; it could be as simple as you not being the look that they are casting for. This is only one gig and it certainly doesn't mean that there will not be plenty of other parts that you could be perfect for.

Dancers often get their nose out of joint over this process, and I do understand that no one wants to be rejected before having the opportunity to dance. But what you must try to remember is that this is only one audition out of the many that you will go up for. In addition, the truth of it is there are often hundreds of dancers who turn out to audition for a gig that has very few positions available. It can be a very long and difficult process and some audition teams choose different procedures of elimination in order to maximize the time available for finding the exact talent that they are looking for. You will appreciate that additional time when you are that talent.

Some auditions will eliminate after an initial lineup or after asking for a specific technique to be executed, while others will eliminate after teaching a quick combination, all for the purpose of narrowing down to a smaller pool of talent with whom they can then spend more time. If you are chosen to stay on and learn a combination, the audition will normally continue with some sort of a cut process.

When I hold an audition, I personally like to see everyone dance, so I will often start my auditions with a lineup and ask for pirouettes on the right and left sides, and with both a jazz and a ballet preparation. However, I will usually teach the routine, or at least a section of it, to everyone. From there, I will break down into smaller groups and see everyone perform at least once. At this point, I usually do my first cut. Depending on the number of dancers, there could be several more cuts before we end up with that small chosen pool of talent. My reason for giving you this information is to reiterate how important first impressions are, and to emphasize how important your performance is from the minute you walk into the room. You may not get a second chance to perform, so you had better give 100 percent right from the get go.

Encore:
You can't be everything to everyone, so you go in as geared up as you can, confident of your dance ability, and give your very best performance. The rest will take care of itself.

Final Cut

Okay, so let's say you've spent the day auditioning and you've made it to the final cut. At this point, you could be offered a job, or you could be asked to come to a callback, and as if all that wasn't nerve racking enough, you could be dismissed and simply told that you will receive a telephone call if, in fact, you got the gig. When you've made it this far, some companies will call to let you know either way, whether or not you got the gig, but not always.

If you are asked to return for a callback, this is fantastic; you are now one step closer to where you want to be. Now I want you to consider everything, as you did for your original audition. This time, you may have more specific details, as to a particular type, style, look or character that they are looking for. They may even make a special request of you by asking you to dress or look a certain part. Pay attention and just as you did the first time out, let them see you as that person they want in their company. If no special request was made, then dress to impress and give them a performance that will seal the deal.

You may be performing the same routine as the last time, or they may choose to challenge you with yet another combination or a different style altogether. If this is a straight dance position, you could be asked to perform any special technique or tricks that you do, i.e., tumbling, jumps, leaps or turns. If you are auditioning for a chorus position and have not already been asked to do so, be prepared to sing. I will stress one more time the importance of being a triple threat. However, I am not suggesting that you cannot work strictly as a dancer; I'm just saying that you will limit your opportunities and your marketability.

Today's market is so much stronger, with the competition getting better and better every day. Dancers do everything nowadays; they just keep coming up with much superior technique and bigger tricks. Therefore, in order to remain on top of your game, it is extremely important for you to not only equip yourself with all of the various techniques and styles, but also, to add vocals and acting to your repertoire. This will make you a much more versatile performer. So, if you do not consider yourself to be the next Andrea Bocelli, Celine Dion, Michael Jackson or Beyonce, I would strongly suggest that you get yourself a vocal coach ASAP. I know I'm repeating myself, but I just want to make sure you got it. By the way, this in no way implies the caliber of vocals that is required of a dancer; however, you do want to be able to at least carry a tune.

When preparing for your vocal auditions, plan to have at least two songs available; one up tempo and one ballad. You can purchase a cheat book from any good book or music store. A cheat book or fake book is a large book full of sheet music. This will give you a long list of songs to choose from, or if you prefer, you can purchase an individual song book or sheet music for a particular piece. You will want to have your sheet music transposed in the proper key. Although some accompanists can do this on the spot, it is always best to be prepared in advance. It is also a great idea to have copies of your sheet music already taped together so that it can be easily laid out for the accompanist. It should be neat and easily accessible in a book or folder.

Here's a quick tip: a three-ring binder can be a great and easy way to organize your audition collection as it grows. Simply keep each song taped and prepared in clear sheet protectors. This will keep it in good condition and always available. This will also come in handy in the event that they would like to hear you sing more. Initially, you will probably be asked to sing only sixteen bars. Some auditioners will want to hear no more and no less, but then again, they may want to hear a different style of music than what you had originally chosen. Just as with your dance audition, do your homework—know what style of music the auditioners will most likely want to hear from you. It's best to always be prepared.

When entering the room, be confident and go directly to the piano. Have your sheet music ready and hand it to the accompanist. Show him or her the exact sixteen bars you intend to sing and give any specific requests at this time. Step away, and very important, don't forget to breathe! Greet the audition team and tell them which song you have chosen to sing for them. The idea again is to present yourself as a true professional, and by now, you should have demonstrated a strong sense of efficiency and confidence. It all comes down to first impressions. If for any reason you miss a note or a lyric, just carry on; there is no need to draw more attention to it. Maintaining your composure and the performance you give will show them how you work under pressure and it will be appreciated.

Same goes when preparing for an acting call. Are you reading for a commercial, a television show or a feature film? Are you predominantly portraying the role of a dancer, or is it mostly acting with some movement involved? You will want to know as much detail as possible in order to best be prepared. If it is a commercial, you will want to do a little research on the product; especially if this is a new or unfamiliar product, you will want to be knowledgeable. As for all readings, you will want to know what type they are looking for so that you can dress the part and prepare mentally for the character. If you are reading for a part in a television show or a movie, you could be given the script in advance or you may be asked to do a cold reading. This is when you are handed the script at the audition itself. With commercials, you are often given the script right then and there.

Last, but certainly not least, how about the audition when they ask you to improvise? This can come up in many situations, but seems to be a favorite for dancers, especially in commercials where there is only one character doing all the dancing. When looking for individuals, as opposed to a group of dancers, there isn't always a choreographer on hand, and sometimes even if there is, he or she may still prefer to see you improvise in order to see your character come through. So, as I recommended in Chapter Three: Triple Threat, you should now better understand the significance of preparing through proper training. What you don't want to do is blow several auditions in order to learn the process. I've heard a few naïve young performers say that they would prefer to learn from their own experience; however, when experience costs you a national spot or a television show or role in the next best dance movie, trust me, you would prefer to have been better prepared.

The industry is full of great expertise and you should take advantage of all that is available. You can often find workshops advertised in your local industry trade paper or posted at dance studios and acting schools. Ask around—find out from fellow dancers and your teachers who is offering what and where. Good audition, commercial, and acting workshops are absolutely invaluable in helping you to prepare for auditions. The better prepared you are, the more professional you will come off and, therefore, the more favorable your results. Remember, it's one thing to walk out of an audition, that you prepared for, and felt confident about, and it's another thing altogether to walk out of an audition disappointed because you didn't do all that you could to prepare.

In closing on the audition process, I would like to sum it up by saying that there are many factors that come into play, some of which are beyond your control. In order to really get the most out of your experience in this business you truly must learn to keep a cool head about you. Do not take things personally, and understand the difference between "being serious and getting down to business," and "not taking things too seriously." As mentioned so many times earlier in this book, making it in this business is a lot about balance. You must be flexible enough to grow, yet strong enough to stand firm for what you believe in; be secure enough to share in your colleagues' triumphs, while being centered enough to recognize your own successes, even in those moments that sometimes look like defeat.

I don't know that anything in life is ever completely perfect, but there's nothing wrong with striving for perfection, and doing all that we can along the way to keep ourselves in check and create the healthiest lifestyle we can, both in business and in play.

So, a quick recap: Do your homework, understand what you are up against, show up early, be mentally and physically prepared, be kind and courteous to everyone you meet, and be present and attentive always. Most importantly, dance, sing, act, and perform like it's your one and only chance. Have some fun with it, and don't forget *to thank* the auditioners on your way out.

Encore:
In order to really get the most out of your experience in this business you truly must learn to keep a cool head about you.

"IT'S SHOWTIME, FOLKS!"—LET THE FUN BEGIN

Play it again, Sam! "Mr. Zoot Suit," Swing Train, Celebrity Cruise Lines' Mercury

---

"You must commit to everything you do, even the smallest move or glance. It is better to make a huge mistake than a small one because at least you are committing."
—*Anne Reinking*

Congratulations! You got the gig. Now what? This is the time to put to use all that good stuff you just learned. Are you up to the challenge? Are you ready to put into practice and make a part of your daily existence your newly acquired qualities and traits, especially those covered in detail in the previous chapter, "The Audition"? Most important, are you ready to be that person, that dancer, that performer, the one your choreographer and employers want to spend days on end with? That is really a key issue here. If you focus your efforts on being the best talent and the best employee you can be, then you should have all of your bases covered. Once again, just as you did for the audition (here I go with one final review), you will want to be early and be prepared both mentally and physically, be focused and attentive, be pleasant, courteous and respectful, work hard, give them 100 percent, leave any attitude behind, and last, but certainly not least, perform like it's your last. Let them see you at your best; this is your opportunity to prove to them that they made the right decision in choosing you. Remind them of why they hired you, and let them be thrilled that they did.

At this point, I would like to touch on the rehearsal process and tell you a little bit more about what you might expect. If you don't already know, rehearsals can at times be very long and involved, they can be difficult and exhausting, and sometimes downright grueling. There is so much to learn and take in on all levels.

You will be learning new choreography and staging, while getting to know your new cast-mates and production team, as well as learning the do's and don'ts of this particular gig and any rules and regulations of the venue in which you will be performing your contract. This can all be very emotionally taxing. To cut to the chase, the rehearsal process will be by far the hardest part of the job. You need to be in your best form both physically and mentally.

We need you to be up for the task, so make sure that you are taking proper care of yourself, and that you are resting enough and eating properly. A well-balanced and nutritious diet is essential, especially now during rehearsals when you will be exerting so much energy in the long days to come. The length of your rehearsals will vary and ultimately be dictated by the production company, the demands of the show, and the type of contract.

A portion of your rehearsal time will be in the studio working in the mirrors, learning and perfecting choreography as well as learning any vocals necessary. You may also learn some of your blocking (your placement within the routines) and stage entrances and exits while learning the choreography, or you may have separate rehearsal time on stage for that process. Everyone works differently. I always like to teach as much of my staging and blocking as possible up front. This helps in making a smooth transition to the stage.

As all rehearsals are different, there is no set time you will spend in the studio and no set time you will spend on stage or on the set. When it comes to working in live stage productions, the size of the stage, the technology, any special effects, and the size of the production will determine how much time is needed to nail down the blocking and all other technical aspects of the production. The larger the production, and the more bells and whistles, the more time that will be needed on stage for the blocking and to ensure everyone's safety on deck.

Once the cast members have had this time on stage, and safety issues have been addressed, then there will be time for lighting rehearsals, sound checks, costume runs, make-up and hair requirements, dress rehearsals, and finally, full technical rehearsals. Often with various productions you will find that you can work just as hard off stage, with all of the costume changes and the need for costume presets, as you do on stage. Pre-sets are a very big part of your track in a theatrical production or revue-style show. You will have to determine where each costume will live backstage during the show in order to facilitate any quick changes with your entrances and exits and yet not interfere with other cast members. *Beware*—the number one backstage rule is, never ever touch another cast member's preset, the consequences could be catastrophic!

Encore:
*Always remember this; you get out of life what you
put in, and the same applies to your work.*

Performance Attitude

As you know "attitude" is extremely important; so much so that I dedicated an entire chapter to it (Chapter Five: Leave Your Attitude Where it Belongs: at the Door.) In that chapter, I addressed how crucial it is to have the right attitude when it comes to your career and the day-to-day life within the business. Here, I would like to address your performance attitude; this is the one time you will be given full license to give as much attitude as you want!

This is your opportunity to be a Diva (or Divo) and strut your stuff. All of those years of training are about to pay off! This is where you get to put that training and muscle memory to work for you. Throw away your thinking cap and any inhibitions and bring it on. I want to see you sell it like nobody's business. I want you to take that nervous energy and use it, turn it around to make *it* work for you, and tear up that dance floor. I want you to perform like there is no tomorrow, and I want you to do this every time you walk out on stage.

I've probably said it a few times already, but I do not want you to forget why you are here in the first place. This is so basic; but if you want to live the life and last in the game, then you better always remember where and how this journey began, and most importantly, *why* it began. That is what will drive you to give the ultimate performance at *every* performance and walk away proud, and loving what you do. We talked about what it takes to turn your childhood dreams into your reality; we talked about your love for dance and your passion for performing *and voila*! Here you now stand on opening night, just as every great performer did on their opening night. "Places" have been called and the curtain is about to rise. You're so excited, and maybe even a bit scared—maybe a lot scared and probably more than anything, just plain nervous. Finally, after all you have been through—all the hard work, the training, the sacrifices, the doubts, the fear and the rejection—you have at long last made it. So get out there and show them what you're made of!

Understand this: once you are there, you must continuously earn your place in order to keep your place. There is no shortage of dancers vying for your position; they are waiting in line and your producers have plenty of choices. You must have the same attitude as the pro athlete and know that every performance is a make or break performance. So even if you might find yourself comfortable in a long-running show, don't ever become complacent in your performance. If you don't go in with the right attitude every time, it could be your last time.

Let's go back for a moment and revisit a little of what I talked about in the first chapter, turning stumbling blocks into building blocks. I want to remind you of the importance of those building blocks; all of those otherwise frustrating moments that you must learn to chalk up as experience. All of this will help prepare you for the many opening nights and jobs to come and give you the stamina required to constantly compete with yourself, reaching new performance heights every time. Without that process, you may never even get to the stage. You may never get to see the audience from this side of the curtain; you may never get to experience the amazing sensation one gets from a standing ovation or the stir from a fully-charged audience. And that would be so unfortunate; after all, is this not a great measurement of what we as entertainers live for—the applause and the recognition? Is this not in some part a validation of our success and the long, often hard, road we've been down? Every one of those lessons along the way, which you choose to turn into a positive experience, will only make the journey so much more gratifying—the stage your home, and the business your life.

Encore:
I want to remind you of the importance of those building blocks; all of those otherwise frustrating moments that you must learn to chalk up as experience.

An Attitude of Gratitude

Ever since I was a little girl, I said that fame and fortune, "the Fred and Gingers or the John Travoltas" of this world, were few and far between, but I always believed that there was a place for me in the business. I knew that I would be happy if I could simply earn a living doing what I loved most. I thought what a special privilege this would be. I believe that I was given a wonderful gift; a talent that I could share and that I could use to bring a certain joy and happiness to others.

What greater accomplishment is there, than to do what you love most? Your talent truly is a special gift, and to have the ability to share it is an honor and a privilege not to be taken for granted; one to hold true to and always be grateful for. This passion and love that I have for what I do is what got me through years of learning, growing, falling down, and getting back up. Because of this conviction, I implore you: don't ever throw away a performance, not one single moment. The truth is you never get it back.

Further more, you never know who could be sitting in the audience. You never know how a lackluster performance by one cast member can affect the overall impact of the show and the cast; or for that matter an audience member's experience. One night while sitting in the audience of a hit Broadway show, I was absolutely disgusted by one very unprofessional young lady. She was continuously disruptive throughout the show, making gestures to her cast-mates on stage and basically having a laugh at the audience's expense. I'm sure that she thought she was being very clever and that no one would ever see; however, I was appalled that a performer in such a show would throw away her performance with this lack of professionalism. Unfortunately for her, I wasn't the only person in the audience who noticed it. After the show, I overheard a couple of other people expressing there distaste as well. Can you even imagine having the opportunity to perform on Broadway and not giving it everything you've got?

To give anything less than your very best means that you are cheating not only your audience, your fellow performers, your choreographer, and the people who hired you, but first and foremost, you are cheating *yourself*. You are utterly robbing yourself of your own true potential. This is something that I've always felt very strongly about and continuously drive home to the performers who work for me. On a few occasions, I had the opportunity to slip into the audience of one of my shows unannounced. This is always interesting because as you can imagine, everyone is on their best performance when they know that you are in the house. Bottom line: There are no shortcuts in performance and I don't care if there is one person in the house or thousands. Do yourself proud; you've aspired to and worked hard for this opportunity. Every performance should be like opening night; every performance is a first time. Tommy Tune in his book, *Footnotes*, says, "A long run becomes a launch pad that allows one to spring higher each time the curtain rises." What a great ambition to have, constantly aspiring to greater heights. If you were, in fact, only as good as your last performance, wouldn't you want each performance to top the last?

Encore:
To give anything less than your very best means that you are cheating not only your audience, your fellow performers, your choreographer, and the people who hired you, but first and foremost, you are cheating yourself.

Thinking on Your Feet

These lessons that I am teaching apply to all areas of performance, regardless of live stage, television or film. In live stage and in live television, you only have one shot at the perfect take. In film and pre-taped television, you have the added luxury of re-takes, if necessary; however, as production costs are so exorbitant, you certainly wouldn't want to be the one holding up the show. And so it's really very simple: don't waste one single moment because you'll never get it back.

Performance is a critical part of your training; both learning about performance and the actual experience of performing. There are so many varied situations that one must be prepared for at all times. Only experience teaches this stuff. Having studied and performed with a children's touring and performing arts company gave me an incredible education about the theatre and its do's and don'ts, both on and off stage. My dance director and choreographer at the time was a brilliant teacher in that respect; he, himself, had been a performer on Broadway, and was an incredible wealth of information, which he so generously passed on to all of us, his students. He taught us about being in the business and about respect for the business and respect for each other. He taught us about how to respond to unexpected situations that could happen on stage. He would say things like, "What happens if the lights go out? What happens if the music stops? What happens if the scenery falls? What do you do if you drop a prop? What if your hat or wig falls off? What if a piece of your costume comes off? What if you make a mistake or stumble? What if you fall down?" What if, what if, what if? These were ongoing lessons throughout class, throughout rehearsals, and throughout our education in his company.

The bottom line is this, everyone reacts differently in a crisis, but in a show, you can imagine that if everyone reacted differently, you would have major chaos on stage, which would not only ruin the show, but it could also be very dangerous. You may well be lucky enough to have learned much of this, either through training or through experience, and if so, you, can be very grateful. If not, I would imagine that from recital performances alone, you may have encountered a technical glitch or two, and therefore, have some idea of what I am talking about. Whenever entering new or unfamiliar territory, don't be afraid to ask for advice. Better to have a little foresight and be prepared than to be surprised and not know how to handle a situation.

Let me share with you a couple of stories that I have personally experienced. First of all, I will tell you about a situation that happened years ago when I was a young girl performing with my dance company. If I remember correctly, we were probably, on average, about thirteen to fifteen years of age. It was our annual "Showcase" and we were performing a group dance number. During this number, there was a huge prop in the shape of a crystal quartz that was suspended from the ceiling and came down from the fly space. It was motorized and therefore rotated above our heads. At the end of the number the prop was taken up into the fly space again so that it was no longer visible. However, someone forgot to shut the motor down and so this prop, unbeknownst to anyone at the time, continued to rotate high up in the rafters. By the end of the show, with twenty or so dancers on stage, the rope or cable by which it was suspended finally wore out and this tremendous prop came crashing down in the middle of all of us! First of all, let me just say how lucky we all were, as this accident could have been fatal. The reaction was unbelievable. At the outset, there was a huge gasp from the audience, but not one dancer even so much as flinched an eye. The routine continued completely uninterrupted; no one missed a beat. In the routine, there was a *grand-jete*, a traveling second to the right, and I will never forget seeing the girl who was next to the quartz leap into the air and sail over this prop to land perfectly on the other side of it. You can imagine the audience's reaction. At the end of the number, they were standing on their feet cheering in amazement. This is only one of many stories. It's simple really; we were just all so well drilled on how to expect the unexpected that we were often amazed, ourselves, at the precision in which we got through these situations.

In my early years of performing professionally, I was often quite taken aback to see how poorly some people could react in unexpected situations. Having received such well-rounded training, and gained such a vast experience, I was quite shocked to learn that not everyone had that same performance training or upbringing within the business. I assumed that everything I had learned in the company was what all children would learn if they studied dance. These lessons were absolutely invaluable throughout my career as a performer. It certainly made stepping out into the real world and the crossover between child performer and working professional a lot smoother.

Here's another story I'd like to share with you—this one many years later in a show that my husband and I produced and I had also choreographed. There I sat on opening night with my husband on one side and my assistant choreographer on the other. After a long hard rehearsal period with a great cast, we were, as always, very excited and anticipating a great show. The number was "Hello Dolly." The lead singer stepped through the center of the upstage black curtain and onto a platform that would rise up out of the floor elevating her to the top of what would become a staircase. Once at the top, with the dancers in place left and right to greet her, she would then descend the staircase through the center of the dancers. Next thing I knew, she disappeared. Rather than being elevated on this staircase, it came up backwards. Unfortunately, the stage manager had forgotten to reset the turntable after our final dress rehearsal earlier that day. This was for me the height of frustration. Instead of watching her descend this grand staircase, "Dolly" had to walk up the staircase only to stand on top of a platform with no way down or off. Thank God my dancers were thinking on their feet; the two boys downstage of the platform looked at each other, acknowledged each other, and then walked right over to Dolly. She reached her arms out to them; they gracefully lifted her off the platform to set her down on the stage and continued the choreography, "Well hello Dolly, it's so nice to have you back where you belong," as the song goes. Needless to say, I gave them my own standing ovation just for that one move! No one in the audience was ever the wiser; no one knew that this was not exactly as it was meant to be. And so there you have it; being well prepared for everything and anything that could go wrong, thinking on your feet and a little common sense can go a long way.

What about those horrifying moments when you might simply draw a blank on stage? All those long hours of perfecting and cleaning all that choreography only to space it! Oh my, is there anything worse for a dancer? Possibly only falling flat on your face right down front and center. Sad but true, it happens to the best, so whatever it is, don't let them see you sweat. You carry on like nothing ever happened and if it's a fall, make it a grand one, and if you mess up do it with conviction. Then, you will be so convincing in your performance that the audience will be certain that the rest of the cast went wrong. The truth is, even when they are aware, they appreciate your professionalism and don't give the so-called embarrassment another thought, but rather, commend you for your performance.

Life in the Real World

The transition into the real world is the beginning of yet another series of lessons. Throughout our careers, as in life, we are constantly learning. All my years in the business have been a continuous learning process. Along the way, there were definitely some lessons less pleasant than others; there were some people less pleasant than others, but over all, I somehow always trusted in the bigger picture, believing that some good would come of it; it was all just part of the test.

If ever there were times when I lost sight of this, there was always someone there to remind me that the lessons, however difficult and painful at the time, were, in fact, necessary. As I look back, I'm sure that they were well-deserved lessons. Life has a way of knocking us around a bit; sometimes when we least expect it and often, when we need it most. Sometimes it's a gentle nudge, a simple reminder when we should have known better. Other times, it's a bit of a push, maybe an eye-opening experience when we were in need of a new lesson. And then there are those times when life smacks us right in the face because we just needed to be told off or put in our place. The important thing is not to stay down, but to get right back up again. Time and experience are wonderful teachers, and although there's nothing quite like personal experience, the lessons that they teach can be passed on through others, and there is certainly nothing wrong with making the learning process a little bit easier on ourselves. We undoubtedly can learn a thing or two from the experiences of others. Besides which, you might save yourself a few of those knocks and blows. So, graciously accept all the lessons offered or handed down, take them and put them to good use in your life, in your career, and in every single performance.

Encore:
Life has a way of knocking us around a bit;
sometimes when we least expect it and often, when we need it most.

THE REWARDS—THANKS FOR THE MEMORIES

Places, please. Cast of Broadway Babies, Costa Cruise Lines' Romantica

"I do not try to dance better than anyone else. I only try to dance better than myself." —Mikhail Baryshnikov

Why choose such a difficult and tough profession? I have been asked time and time again. I'm sure you already have a good idea of my personal thoughts and feelings about this industry. But now, I want to take this opportunity to tell you a little about some of my personal highs; those once in a lifetime moments; those wonderful surprises waiting just around the corner, and those building blocks (the times that can try us) that I spoke of throughout the first section of this book.

I have already told you how fortunate I always believed I was, and I shared with you some stories about my early beginnings as a student and young professional, and the many wonderful influences in my life.

I've shared with you the lunchtime audition that relocated me from Toronto, Ontario, to Los Angeles, California. What I could never have anticipated back then was the real extent of how my life would be changed forever. Because of this one decision to go to that "lunchtime audition" for *La Cage*, my entire life and career took on a full 360-degree turn-about. I was exposed to a Hollywood that no longer exists. This was still a time when Hollywood was defined by the very legends that our parents, and maybe for some of you, grandparents, grew up idolizing. It was also a time when Madonna, Michael Jackson, Janet Jackson, George Michael, and Whitney Houston were consistently at the top of the pop charts. Paula Abdul and Michael Peters were two of the top choreographers in town; and music videos were being aired 24 hrs a day with the recent birth of MTV. It was a very exciting time, full of change, innovation and new up and coming talent. "The Brat Pack" and "The Rat Pack" coexisted in Hollywood.

How fortunate was I to have the opportunity to meet so many of the greats, true legends, and some of them the very people who made Hollywood, "*Hollywood*." Milton Berle known as "Uncle Miltie" and "Mr. Television," Lucille Ball, internationally known for the *I love Lucy* show, originally a showgirl/actress/comedienne (she was also the first woman to own her own Film Studio Desilu), Sammy Davis Jr., often referred to as the world's greatest entertainer. He was the ultimate song and dance man; Frank Sinatra, an entertainer's entertainer who bridged seven generations; Stevie Wonder, Robin Williams, Gloria Estefan, Paula Abdul, and the list truly goes on and on. For me, an extremely wonderful night at *La Cage* was the evening that Paula Abdul came in to see the show. She seemed to thoroughly enjoy herself, and on her way out, she congratulated me on the show and said that she loved the choreography. This was the most wonderful compliment of all, to be recognized by another choreographer, and one who was known for such great and popular work. It certainly made my night!

You see, here's the thing—in a whirlwind I was transported from Toronto to Los Angeles. It was as though I was dropped into the middle of a Hollywood movie scene. I was a young girl being exposed to a lifestyle that I could only have imagined, and not only was I living the dream, I was working at what I loved most, and my creative work was being performed to audiences of celebrities, night after night. Some of the most discriminating audiences of them all were raving about a show that I had choreographed; that I had a little something to do with. There is no greater honor! When people truly love what you do, there is nothing more rewarding, and when those someones are entertainers, themselves, what more could one ask for? I had the privilege of enjoying some absolutely incredible moments throughout my career, and here are a few I would like to share with you:

Let Me Entertain You

There was a show being produced for the Variety Arts Theatre in Los Angeles, and I was asked to direct and choreograph a number to "Send In The Clowns." This number was a feature presentation in the show. It was meant to introduce and pay tribute to some of Hollywood's greatest comedians, hence the reason for the song, "Send In The Clowns." Actress Terri Garr was going to star in the number, and I would stage and direct her to introduce each one of the great comedians, who would be portrayed by impersonators of the Marx Brothers, Laurel and Hardy, W.C. Fields, and last, but not least, Charlie Chaplin.

On the day of rehearsal, I got a phone call from the producer announcing to me that there was a change of plans, and that unfortunately, Ms. Garr would not be able to make the show. Could I perform the number, in her place? Of course, I can. Was there any other answer? I don't think so! Once again, I was excited and nervous all at the same time. I knew who was going to be in that audience, some of the people I most admired, and now this flawless presentation that I had envisioned was going to rely not solely on my creative abilities as a choreographer, but on my performance as well.

Okay, fast forward to the night of the show. Rehearsals had gone very well, and I would be dancing and introducing one by one, some of the best look-a-likes of those famous comedians I mentioned earlier. Honestly, it was like being on stage with the celebrities, themselves. They were so dead on; every gesture, every innuendo took you back in time. I was mesmerized watching their performances. "Places please," and I climbed the back side of the staircase to reach the top, my opening position. Next, I heard the intro and I could feel my whole body shaking; I was so nervous. The spotlight hit me at the top of the staircase and I began my descent, I immediately sensed the audience and it was such a lovely feeling being on this incredible stage in this wonderful old Hollywood theatre. I was dancing and I was loving it. As the choreography went, I worked my way downstage, left. I paused to introduce the first legend, the spotlight faded on me, and slowly came up on our first set of clowns. The audience gasped as they came to life. As I told you earlier, the look-a-likes were phenomenal, and this was a Hollywood audience. Who better to appreciate such a tribute? The spotlight faded on our clowns and restored on me. I carried on the dance only to introduce my next guest and so on and so on, until each of these famous personalities was brought to life. The number culminated with all of us performing together, and the dancer bringing the lights down on all of them to be left standing, center stage alone, as though it was all a dream. By the end of the number, I was told, there wasn't a dry eye in the house. The audience were on their feet and I was blown away by the reception. Apparently, "Uncle Miltie" wanted to know emphatically who the audience was cheering for so loudly, I was told that when they told him it was my number, he gave a smile and approved. Talk about a natural high!

Mr. Bojangles

Sammy Davis Jr. was no stranger to *La Cage*. He was a big fan, he loved the show and had seen it several times. We recently had added a wonderful tribute in the show to Sammy Davis Jr. Our impersonator was just spectacular. Several of Sammy's friends and family had been in to see the addition and told him all about it. One night, he sent his dresser in with a message for the show and a personal gift specifically for our Sammy impersonator. At the end of the show, his dresser came onto the stage with our brilliant Master of Ceremonies, Gypsy. Gypsy handed him the microphone. He proceeded to make the most wonderful speech on behalf of Sammy Davis Jr. Unfortunately, Sammy was not feeling well and couldn't be there himself. His dresser told the audience that Sammy loved our show and wanted to give us his blessings, and with that, he called our Sammy impersonator forward and presented him with Sammy Davis Jr.'s personal bowler hat, the very hat worn when he performed "Bojangles." Wow, moments like that just don't happen everyday, and lucky me, I got to be a part of it all.

This Show's Too Hot to Put Out

It was about 5:00 p.m., only one hour away from the doors opening. This was opening night in San Francisco at The On Broadway Theatre, and if you could have seen the interior of the main showroom, you would have been certain that we were a month away from opening. I was busy on stage still fitting in every last minute show note, while the showroom floor, which should have been set for dinner and a show, was covered with sets still getting final touches. There were props and tools strewn everywhere and sawdust to boot. We had, as we always did, a tremendous line-up of guests for our "Grand Opening," just an hour away and the room was in shambles. And to add insult to injury, the fire department was threatening to close us down, or rather, not let us open. Can you imagine a worse possible situation for an opening night? I carried on until the last moment when I finally had to let the dancers get into costume and warm up, or we wouldn't have had a cast to perform.

One of the reasons we were down to the wire was because of major last minute changes that I had to make to the staging, due to complete sets not being ready on time. The two or three days leading up to opening were crazy. Every day I was told by my stage designer of yet another set or prop that I wouldn't have, down to the last day, when I was told that I wouldn't have the famous bar for my "Big Spender" number. Ready to scream, I turned upstage, and as I looked up to my left, there was a magnificent little balcony. So instead of losing it, I ushered the dancers upstairs to our newly-discovered set and restaged the number accordingly. It turned out to be an even better number with more impact! Ever heard the expression "there is no such thing as an accident"?

Back to the opening, somehow as though magically, within that final half hour or maybe a little longer (holding the door just that bit more), we managed to transform this theatre from a construction site to a flawless showroom. All that, and the fire department allowed us to open as long as we had three firemen, including the chief, himself, on the premises. The doors opened to an awaiting guest list and the show went on without a glitch. The evening was a huge success, the show was a smash hit, and the reviews reflected exactly that. Even the chief of the Fire Department gave us a quote we still talk about, and that was: "This show is too hot to put out!"

Take A Bow

Milton Berle was a huge fan of *La Cage* and a tremendous support; he loved the show so much that he came to almost every one of our opening nights. I had been privileged enough to be in his company on several occasions, and this time was an evening to write home about. It was the San Francisco opening, which I just told you about, the show was over, and Uncle Miltie took the microphone. He always did a little special shtick and then proceeded to congratulate the cast and introduce the producer. This night, as he did on several other occasions, he began a lovely introduction; he went on to say "I want you to meet the very talented person responsible for this fabulous show that you have just seen." As the producer was getting ready to stand and take a bow, "Uncle Miltie" went on, "There is a young lady in this audience who is talented beyond her years. She is the director and choreographer of this show, and her name is Mande Dagenais. Mande would you please come up here and take a bow?" Oh my God! This was truly a spectacular moment. I immediately called my best girlfriend back home in Toronto, and when I told her, the first thing she said was "Wow! I hope you got that on tape." And to this day, the producer, Lou, and I still laugh about that story.

The point to these stories is simply to share with you some of the wonderful moments that I experienced as a choreographer or as a performer. Not to sound boastful, but rather, grateful, these are those moments that I've talked about: the once-in-a-lifetime moments. The very moments that make this business like no other, they carry with them a huge amount of wonderment, a sense of humility and a gratitude for some of the best memories a person could ever ask for.

MILTON BERLE

January 1991

La Cage Aux Folles
643 North La Cienega
West Hollywood, California 90069

Dear Mande:

I don't write many fan letters (only to myself).
But I just had to write YOU this letter...

Your expertise and the shows at La Cage are
tremendous! Words can't express completely
what I think about you as a choreographer,
producer and director...and as a person.

For the nnth time I was at La Cage and the
production numbers were superb, thanks to you.
The timing absolutely terrific, the staging
perfect. This note is just to tell you that
I'm proud of you and I think you're so very,
very talented.

When you get your first Broadway show or motion
picture assignment, I guarantee that you'll
knock 'em dead.

Mande, you'll always be my first choice. And
if this sounds like a big fat fan letter...it is,
from the bottom of my heart.

You're wonderful,

The Tonight Show Starring Johnny Carson

We were engaged to perform at the 28th anniversary party for Johnny Carson and *The Tonight Show*. Both Johnny and the producer wanted it to be a special surprise for their staff; no one knew what entertainment was being brought in for their special event. We did the show, it was a huge hit, and afterwards, Johnny invited us to perform a special segment on *The Tonight Show* on NBC. What a thrill—of course, it goes without saying that we were ecstatic at the invitation. We decided to feature our Madonna number. Johnny gave us the most wonderful introduction, telling the viewing audience at home that this was their best anniversary party in twenty-eight years. The performers did a fabulous job and I couldn't have been prouder in that moment!

JOHNNY CARSON

January 30, 1991

Ms. Mande Dagenais
1155 N. LaCienega # 312
Los Angeles, CA   90069

Dear Ms. Dagenais:

I'd like to take this opportunity to thank you for
the wonderful choreography you did for the Tonight
Show's 28th anniversary party this past September.

The La Cage aux Folles dancers were great and the
entire staff thoroughly enjoyed the act.

Thanks again for your contribution to our anniversary
party.

Best wishes,

JOHNNY CARSON

JC/pas

Happy 80th Birthday Uncle Miltie

July 12th, 1988, Milton Berle's 80th birthday at *La Cage*, this was certainly a star studded night to be remembered. The guest list was incredible and just a little intimidating—from Frank Sinatra, Nancy Sinatra, Sammy Davis Jr., Lucille Ball, Warren Beatty, Johnny Carson, Jill St-John and Robert Wagner, to Steve Lawrence and Eydie Gorme, Arnold Schwarzenegger and Maria Schriver, George Burns, Red Buttons, Sid Caesar, Jack Lemon, Walter Matthau, Bob Newhart, and so many more. I was in my early twenties, and many of these people had been in the business longer than I had been alive. Some of them played a huge role in helping to define show business as we know it today. What an honor to perform for them.

We created a show line-up catering specifically to this entertainment audience; we wanted to make sure that we pulled out all the stops! I restaged several numbers to include more cast members, and choreographed and added a few new ones especially for Uncle Miltie and his guests. It was a very exciting night; there was a buzz about the showroom like none I had ever experienced. The show went off with a bang and the audience was like no other. We were no strangers to celebrity audiences at *La Cage* and it was always such fun to see who might be in the house on any given night of the week. However, this was no regular night by any means, for this night they were *all* there. It was the ultimate fantasy for anyone who might be a bit star-struck; legends, film stars, recording artists, and the heads of networks (young and old alike).

The evening ended with an even bigger bang, this list of "who's who" were standing on their feet cheering and applauding our show.

"I have been in show business twenty-nine years"; (his wife muttered, *thirty-four years…*) he gave her a smile and continued, "I've been in film, radio, television, and stage, and I have never been more entertained in my whole life."—*Jack Lemon at La Cage*

If at First You Don't Succeed

I had heard through a friend that the Entertainment Director at Costa Cruise lines was looking for a choreographer. This friend had worked with me as my lighting designer on a few of my openings here in Miami, as well as New York City, and St-Maarten. He called to tell me that he had mentioned my name to this acquaintance of his and suggested that I give him a call. No sooner had I heard, that I made the call and was on my way to meet with the entertainment director of whom my friend had spoken. We had what I thought to be a very nice meeting and mutual interest in working together. I left my promotional reel and biographical information with him, and he said that he would give me a call very soon as he would be making a decision straight away. He also let me know at the time that the other choreographer he was considering was a gentleman whom he had worked with previously. I left the meeting feeling very good about it, and thought to myself that if I didn't get the gig I wouldn't feel so bad as the other candidate was someone that had previously worked with him. Not long after our meeting, I did get the promised phone call, in which he explained to me that he had decided to go with the other choreographer as he had a previous relationship with him. *No problem, perfectly understandable,* I thought and left him with the idea that should it not work out for any reason, or if he needed me in the future to please feel free to contact me any time. I kept in contact with him over the months that followed, first with a thank you note, and then with a phone call every month or so to check in. I think it was in December, approximately six months or so after our initial meeting, when I received a phone call from him saying it was time for us to talk. For whatever reason, the position was now available and he wanted to know if I would still be interested. That first meeting, which some would have written off and chalked up as rejection, turned out to produce a long-standing work relationship, almost ten years, nine different productions, two different cruise lines, and a few recommendations along the way.

Another Opening, Another Show

It was this same Entertainment Director who introduced me to Opryland Productions and Gaylord Entertainment. I was brought in to re-direct and re-choreograph two existing shows that the client, Celebrity Cruises, was not happy with. This was somewhat of an interesting situation as I would be working with both the client who was recommending me and the production company. Actually that part was quite easy for me as I had a good standing relationship with the client, I developed a wonderful work relationship with Opryland, and a long-standing friendship with many of the people whom I got to know. The real challenge was that I was being brought into a situation where the cast, who were already on board, and halfway through their contract, were quite happily performing the existing shows. Suddenly, with little to no warning, they were about to be thrown back into rehearsals. Basically, they would be working day and night. This was somewhat of a delicate situation for several reasons. Many of the cast and crew members had worked with Opryland for some time and had a good relationship with the director and choreographers before me. And as I said, they were already under contract so the thought of having to rehearse daily and perform nightly was a bit of a nightmare for them. I could have walked into a minefield. This situation would require a great deal of sensitivity, diplomacy, organization, hard work, and most of all, cooperation from the cast. My assistant, Jemma, and I were there and ready to work, regardless of what it took. I had exactly one cruise itinerary to recreate this first show and give them nothing short of fabulous. I certainly had my work cut out; first I would re-choreograph and re-stage the show; then I would have to re-write the technical stage direction for the crew. I always love a challenge, and what better challenge than this! If we did the great job that I knew we were capable of, we would save the day. And there was only one way I saw this going.

I would be working with an entirely new automation system (that's the system that controls intelligent lighting, some of the scenery, and hydraulic stage movement etc.) and, we would work through the wee hours of the night preparing. I always liked to have my choreography ready in advance of rehearsals with the cast so as not to lose any precious time. As planned, we rehearsed days and any other opportunity I was able to grab, late night, sometimes even through the night. The cast and production team were gems, they truly were, and they were talented at that. The caliber of dancers and singers was exceptional. It was an absolute pleasure to work with them and they worked hard for me in spite of the difficult schedule they were up against. They were true pros and it showed on opening night. They'd had approximately ten days of rehearsals to learn an entire show of choreography and staging, not to mention re-lighting and full on technical and dress rehearsals. Everyone was so pleased with the response they got after all that hard work, they received a standing ovation and the ship's ratings were through the roof. Two weeks later, I was back to put them through the paces one more time for the second show. I won't pretend that it was anything less than grueling, but in the end, our hard work sure paid off. The cast did another outstanding opening and the show ratings shot up to Number One. As a matter of fact, the ship was rated Number One in the fleet consistently that season. Opryland and their client couldn't have been happier with our results, and from that came several other great opportunities to work with Opryland. I went on to direct and choreograph the *General Jackson River Boat* in Nashville for several seasons, as well as the *Alabama Theatre* in Myrtle Beach. Some of my favorite talent, favorite people, and many wonderful memories came from this period in my career.

Two Sides to Every Coin

In previous chapters, I referred to the tumultuous turns and the ups and downs of our business. Here is a short story that depicts just that. As I mentioned above, the Entertainment Director whom I worked with at Costa and Celebrity also introduced me to Opryland Productions.

I was on my way home, having just opened *Swinging on the River* for Opryland Productions in Nashville, when I received a phone call from one of their producers, the one I had worked with on the ship projects. He announced to me that they had just lost their contract with the cruise line and would not be doing the next season. I felt very sad as I genuinely liked them as a production company. I really loved what they did and how they worked, and had grown to care very much for the people who had brought me in to work with them in the first place. They, as a company, had since undergone huge changes, and most of the people whom I had originally worked with were no longer there, and now, for whatever reason, they had lost this contract.

You may remember from my earlier story that I had been recommended to them by the very client they were now losing. This was a horrible, gut-wrenching reality for me. I was torn and wanted to pick up the phone to call my friend at the cruise line to find out why, but a part of me just couldn't make that call. Certainly, had I made the call, I could have saved my own gig, but I could never take advantage of their misfortune. Call me foolish. A short while later, I received a phone call from *yet another* production company who had been assigned the new contract for that same ship. I was referred to them once again by the Entertainment Director as these were my shows, having previously directed and choreographed them for Opryland. I immediately called my friend, whose first words to me were "Why didn't you call me? This should have been your contract," and to that I answered that I just didn't feel right, and I didn't want to gain from someone else's loss. So now, here I was in an entirely new situation, being offered once again to work as director and choreographer of the very shows that were already creatively mine. Talk about a strange twist of fate.

I believe the lesson here is two-fold. Throughout the book, I speak a great deal about integrity and loyalty, and this story brings up both. There I was trying to handle the situation correctly and diplomatically. Of course I would have loved the opportunity to carry on doing my shows with the cruise line, but I felt a sense of loyalty to both companies, and, therefore, chose not to take action by remaining somewhat neutral. If I had made the call, the production company might have felt slighted, but surely they should have understood. After all, it was the cruise line that recommended me to them. However, I didn't make the call, and by not calling, I compromised my own opportunity to take over the contract, and who knows, I might have (unintentionally) slighted my friend by not calling him in the first place. So I reiterate, first and foremost, always come from a good place, use integrity and loyalty, add to that the facts, and weigh your decisions carefully while taking care of Number One. Anyone who is a true professional should, in fact, appreciate that, and understand where you are coming from. If not, it will be their loss not yours.

Berne Baby Berne

The Berne Convention for the Protection of Literary and Artistic Works, is the law that governs Copyright protection for the author, or creator of an artistic work. And yes this does include choreographers. In Chapter Thirteen: No More Starving Artist I reference copyright when I discuss you putting together any promotional material, specifically when creating a demo reel and using video footage of your performances. I recommend that you obtain permission to use any footage of choreography that you may have performed, but did not create, for the mere fact that the choreographer of that work is the owner of the copyright to that work, unless he or she gave the rights to another.

I'd like to share a few incidents with you, which, unfortunately, are not on my list of favorite memories, yet are very important lessons that may help protect you or another person in the future. These can be hard lessons if you were to find yourself in a similar situation. So heads up!

I was in my fourth or fifth season of working with this company (whose name will remain anonymous) when there was a sudden change of upper management. I had been working as director/choreographer in charge of several productions for them and I had a small production team that worked with me and relied on these contracts from season to season.

As can often happen when there is a new sheriff in town, the new head honcho decided that he wanted to change how the old team did things. He decided that he was no longer going to use my services or the services of my company and, unfortunately for us, gave us little notice, leaving us without much time to recoup the damage of a lost season. Regardless, he did however decide that he still wanted to use my choreography; he just didn't want to pay for it. And so he hired a couple of dancers to come in and learn all of my work so that they could then teach the new cast members from season to season. This way, he could have the benefit of all my work, which they obviously liked enough to want to continue using in their various shows, and he wouldn't have to pay the fees of a choreographer. Instead, he would pay some lesser amount: a salary, to a dancer who would basically go along with the idea of plagiarizing my creative work and using it as theirs. When I questioned the company's intention and sent a letter informing them of my copyright ownership and requesting that they cease and desist using my work, this new entertainment director further showed his ignorance and arrogance by claiming to be in the business for twenty-five years and had never heard of such a thing as a choreographer owning the rights to his or her work. This man claimed to be so knowledgeable and experienced in the entertainment industry, and even had the audacity to mention having worked at the Lido in Paris as a lead, yet he didn't know about simple copyright laws, which protected my rights as a choreographer. In return, my copyright lawyer followed up with a letter giving him and the company the facts about copyright and copyright usage. We never heard back from them, and in the end, I chose not to pursue it further, as it would have been a very costly endeavor and a lot of wasted time and negative energy. What I did instead, was simply insure my copyright protection in all future contracts by clearly adding a copyright clause. Several years later, an assistant choreographer of mine happened to see shows produced by this same company in a new venue and called to tell me that my choreography (or some semblance of), however mutilated, was still being used. Although infuriating, someone told me I should be flattered that they liked my work so much!

The bottom line is that it is not uncommon in our industry for people to either not know or understand the laws governing copyright, or to plead ignorance about the matter when convenient. Furthermore, when hiring choreographers, producers and/or production companies will often want to own the copyright to the work being created for them. This is perfectly fine, if, in fact, it is addressed and discussed up front, and mutually agreed upon by both the company doing the hiring, and the choreographer. In this event, an agreement will be drawn up to reflect what is known as a "work-for-hire," or a copyright clause with a clear definition of their agreement will be added to the contract being signed. Should you decide to become a choreographer, you will want to be fully aware of your rights so that you can protect yourself and understand the laws when giving others the rights to your work, or when working with a work-for-hire contract.

And that brings me to yet another similar story. This one has a slightly different ending. Once again, I will not disclose the names of the parties involved. In this particular situation, I had also worked with this company for several years and had now moved on. I received a phone call from a performer warning me of a situation, where once again my choreography was being utilized in this show long after I was no longer working with them. A video tape of the show was then sent on to me. So I immediately called the company and addressed the situation with the producer. I explained that the material was copyrighted material and they did not have the authorization to use it. That very afternoon, I received a phone call from the choreographer who was now working with them. We knew of each other, had met briefly in the past, and displayed a mutual respect. She expressed to me how sorry she was for any injustice or damage that might have been done to me. She also explained that she had no knowledge of copyright laws. She had worked with this same company for many, many years, and as far as she was concerned, they owned all the rights to the work she had done for them, and assumed the same of mine. She had always worked under a "work-for-hire" contract. We had a very pleasant conversation and ended it on a nice note. I was assured that they would cease and desist from using my choreography in the future and I was very grateful to her professionalism in addressing the situation with me. I believe that when people have mutual respect for each other and their work, and they handle matters between them rather than allowing them to become greater than necessary, things can be resolved in a professional manner.

On several occasions, I have been that choreographer who was called upon to re-choreograph an existing show. Whenever there was material from other choreographers left over in a show or venue, I always did my best to ensure that they received proper credit in a show program for whichever part of the work was theirs. I would only hope that someone would do the same for me.

If you are interested in reading more about the Berne Convention, you can visit the World Intellectual Property Organization's website at www.wipo.int. You can also learn more about Copyright in general by visiting the United States Copyright Office website at www.copyright.gov.

There's No Business Like Show Business!

As Ethel Merman said, "There's no business like show business, like no business I know."

I hope that these stories I've shared with you in this chapter and throughout the book have entertained you, have inspired you, and will help to guide you. Some of them will reinforce the lessons I am teaching. Lessons like, when opportunity strikes, never give up, don't let anyone take your dreams from you, and look out for Number One. You never know where things come from or what is waiting just around the corner, and last, but not least, there are plenty of highs and lows. I believe that there is good to be found in all situations, which I have shared several times over. However, in an effort to always find the good, we mustn't be foolish or ignore what is real. This business also comes with a certain amount of jealousy and a whole lot of ego. Someone often wants what you have, or the very thing you are going after, so here's one last bit of advice. I want you to stay positive and keep your focus, keep your eyes wide open and squarely on the prize, but don't forget to also watch your back. I could go on and on…I've been working in this business in one capacity or another since I was a young girl, either as a performer or later on, as a director/choreographer and producer, and that can make for a whole lot of story telling. However I will leave you with this.

There may very well be as many difficult moments as there are great ones, if not more, but the bottom line is, if you always maintain the utmost integrity in all that you do, keep your chin up, and never give up, you can survive the trials and tribulations and revel in the highs along the way. If you see that a door is slightly ajar, go ahead and open it. You just never know what is waiting on the other side.

Encore:
If you see that a door is slightly ajar, go ahead and open it.
You just never know what is waiting on the other side.

CHAPTER TEN

FIT TO DANCE— YOU ARE WHAT YOU EAT

Strike a pose. "Vogue," La Cage, the Blue Angel, New York City

"The wise man should consider that health is the greatest of human blessings. Let food be your medicine." —Hippocrates

In this next section, I would like to discuss the significance of keeping fit and healthy, thereby giving you, the dancer, the best possible shot at preventing injury and creating longevity for your career. We will also address what to do should you become injured, and the importance of proper care and recovery.

Through my own experiences and research, I have learned the importance of keeping healthy and fit, and believe me, I'm still learning. It is truly a never-ending process. There are always new studies being made and, therefore, new discoveries. In order for you to stay on top of your game as a dancer and performer, it is crucial for you to be informed. Read everything you can about your business. Taking care of yourself is a huge part of your business; after all, your body is your business and if you don't take care of it, you won't be in business for very long.

Please understand that the information in this section is merely meant as suggestions with the intent of helping you find the correct path in your own quest for optimum health and fitness. There are many wonderful books and websites that will help substantiate and elaborate on what we discuss here, as well as offer you other great ideas that may be suited to your own ideals. It is so very important to remember that when we talk about "diet," we are talking about nutrition as a way of life and not some fad diet that you go on for a week or two at a time.

In an effort to further educate myself and to be able to offer the best possible advice in the area of health and fitness I sought the help of a very dear friend of mine, Dr. Spencer H. Baron. He is a highly revered Chiropractor and sports injury specialist, not only in his field of Chiropractic, but also in the world of athletics and dance.

He has held many prominent titles and has been the treating physician for many Broadway shows, *CATS, Crazy for You, and Les Misérables* to name a few, not to mention every show I ever had come through town, here in Miami. Dr. Baron has been appointed the Team Chiropractic Physician for The Miami Dolphins and the Florida Marlins. Additionally he's treated the New York Mets, The San Francisco Giants, the Colorado Rockies and the Florida Panthers. Dr. Baron is the author of *Secrets of the Game: What Superstar Athletes Can Teach You About Health, Peak Performance and Getting Results*. You can visit Dr. Baron's website at: www.drspencerbaron.com.

Your Health Pyramid

Much of this section on health and fitness will revolve around what we will refer to as the *health pyramid*. Simply put, Dr. Baron asks us to view our health as having three sides—nutritional, physical, and mental; thus the comparison to a pyramid. He points out that the pyramid is one of the most stable and balanced geometric structures in the world; and in order for us to have the same stability and balance in our health, we need all three areas—nutritional, physical, and mental—to be in balance. In terms of health, this is what we call homeostasis, and it is paramount to any athlete, including dancers.

It is essential for you to realize that all three of these areas are integrated and extremely intimate with each other. Any faltering of one of these three categories and you could end up with an injury, if not this time, almost certainly in the future. It's almost like a trickle down effect: if you weaken one side, the others will eventually follow. When you understand the importance of homeostasis, you can go a long way towards avoiding this and preventing both injury and illness.

Good Nutrition—a Way of Life

Good nutrition is the foundation of good health. It is so very important to remember that when we talk about diet, we are talking about nutrition as a way of life and not some fad diet that you go on for a week or two at a time. When it comes to creating an actual diet plan for yourself, you will want to have a good understanding of what a healthy diet should consist of. First of all, the food and the quality of the food you are putting into your body, and whether or not you are getting the proper balance of water, carbohydrates, proteins and fats. All of this should be within the correct amount of calories necessary to counter and/or support your activity level.

You will also want to consider whether you are getting the correct amount of vitamins and minerals and whether or not you should be taking supplements. Yes, it can all seem a bit daunting; however, the more you learn, the easier it becomes to make intelligent choices for yourself.

Encore:
Good nutrition is the foundation of good health.

You Are What You Eat?

I'm sure you've all heard the familiar saying "You are what you eat." When I was a young dancer, I certainly heard it many times. I was constantly told what not to eat and which body part it would end up on if I did. However, the one area that I would have liked to learn more about was *proper* nutrition. I'm certain there are teachers and company directors out there teaching about the importance of proper nutrition and good eating habits. Unfortunately, a great number of dancers don't receive this education and, therefore, adopt many unhealthy habits which can then lead to illnesses or eating disorders.

At twenty years old, 5'3" and 110 lbs., I was told by my producer that I needed to lose weight or it would cost me my job. I was told I had to lose it straight away as I was already in a performance contract, so I did; I lost twelve pounds my new weight was 98 lbs. Then I was told that I was too thin and needed to put some weight back on... And people wonder why dancers are so obsessed with food and the way they look. I mention this to make a point; this is a minor story, but one of thousands of incidents in which dancers' jobs were on the line for a few pounds. Whether you think that this attitude towards weight and over all picture-perfect body image is right, wrong, or indifferent, you have to admit that in choosing this profession and going into it, you must understand that this attitude is prevalent and goes with the territory. Unfortunately, the people making these calls don't always have a good enough understanding of nutrition to really be of any help to you. They may suggest loosing ten pounds, when, in fact, all you need is to drop a few pounds and tone up.

This is why it is so important for you to have a good understanding and grasp of health and nutrition. You should know your ideal performance weight, and what for you is the most nutritionally sound way to achieve a realistic goal. As you well know, it's not always about the numbers you see on the scale, but what you see in the mirror. What I want to stress here is that there is a right way—more importantly, a healthy way—to approach weight control.

I say that today with a strong conviction, due to many years of trial, error, and self-education. I know now that back when I was twenty and told to lose weight, I went about it the wrong way: I basically didn't eat, or ate very little. It was so easy for me to get caught up in the need to lose weight and ignore the importance of health; something we can all do when we are younger and convinced that we are invincible. Over the years, on several occasions I have had to speak to my own dancers or cast members about weight issues. This is never an easy subject, but I always take a very strong attitude toward them handling it in the right way. For any dance teachers reading this book, I ask you to handle this topic with the utmost sensitivity and to be prepared to help educate your dancers so that they can accomplish their goals in a healthy manner with proper nutrition as the number one focus. We all know that a dancer's work is not only extremely physically demanding, but it can also be emotionally taxing; a balanced diet for optimum physical and emotional health is imperative.

A big concern in this area especially relating to young female dancers, is the nutritional deficiencies that often result from eating disorders or even simply from bad eating habits. The combination of such nutritional deficiencies and low body fat can very often cause menstrual irregularities known as *Amenorrhea*. When you interrupt the fine hormonal balance of a teen or a young woman in her twenties', you can provoke skeletal abnormalities or conditions which can then cause stress fractures. Needless to say, this is not a good thing for a dancer. Again I want to remind you of the trickle-down effect I mentioned earlier. In this classic example, we have an eating issue, which may have started out as an emotional problem, which turns into a nutritional problem, which turns into a physical problem. Get the picture? It is important to realize that an eating disorder doesn't just mean bulimia or anorexia; these are the full-blown medically diagnosed versions we are all too familiar with. However, in their infancy stages, eating disorders begin when someone is simply missing a few vital nutrients from their diet. Nutritional deficiencies, and specifically eating disorders, can cause a wide range of health complications. In this book, I will not go into all of the possible complications; however, if you or anyone you know has any concerns in this area, please learn all that you can about these illnesses and the possible complications, and seek professional help immediately. There are organizations that deal specifically with these issues; there is much information and help available today. The complications are far too great and too dangerous not to be addressed seriously.

Encore:
We all know that a dancer's work is not only extremely physically demanding, but it can also be emotionally taxing; a balanced diet for optimum physical and emotional health is imperative.

Mother Knows Best

Mom knows best! For me, my mother was a huge influence on the healthy habits I later took on in life, from my food choices to alternative therapies. First of all, just about everything we ate growing up was made from scratch—from fresh-baked bread to desserts of every kind. Also, it seemed that Mom always had a natural remedy for just about any ailment; she grew up on a farm during a time when people relied on what was naturally grown—often herbs from their own gardens or from the fields. Although she probably thought I wasn't paying much attention as a teen, something obviously sank in, for when I was old enough to know better, I found myself doing the exact things she had recommended to me all those years ago, following a natural, healthy diet and always looking for natural remedies.

Encore:
For me, my mother was a huge influence on the healthy habits I later took on in life, from my food choices to alternative therapies.

Making Healthy Choices

On that note, I will discuss some guidelines for both healthy and not-so-healthy habits. When it comes to proper nutrition, a pretty safe bet would be to start by making healthy *whole food choices*. You know, the foods your parents or maybe your grandparents and great grandparents ate before the birth of so many preservatives and additives. Making healthy choices is one of the most important things you can do for your over all health and diet. So, what are healthy choices? I am often amazed at the false or misconstrued beliefs many people have when it comes to what is healthy and what is not. The truth is, it often comes down to what we've learned as children, as well as which marketing and advertising ploys the food manufacturers have led us to believe in. I will outline below certain guidelines for you to consider when making food choices. The bottom line is to try to eat whole foods. Think "Mother Nature" foods in their natural state, or as close to their natural state as possible: foods that have not been or have been minimally processed or modified. Granted, this is not always easy to do when a tight schedule has us eating on the run, but this is where a little creativity with food and meal planning is extremely important. It is definitely doable; it simply requires some thought, commitment and preparation. Always remember that you have everything to gain from your efforts!

I can attest to my own experiences over the years and I can honestly tell you that I am at my best when my diet is clean and loaded with an *assortment* of fresh and whole foods: fresh fruits, vegetables, legumes, whole grains, nuts and seeds. I love fish and try to have it a couple of times a week. I prefer to eat chicken and ground turkey to red meat, but do love a good steak once in a while. I have always been a protein junky and I have learned the importance of moderating my intake of animal proteins. I do so by having a couple of vegetarian meals every week. I also avoid refined flour and white sugar (except for a chocolate fix, which I allow myself every now and then). Although studies have proven that dark good-quality chocolate is healthier, I still prefer the taste of good-quality milk chocolate. Again, I am simply sharing with you what I like and what works for me. The variety I'm talking about will give me a good balance of nutrients. One of my very favorite foods is sushi, and an excellent way to create a balanced meal. You have your vegetables, such as asparagus, carrots or cucumber; then you have seaweed, which has several vitamins and minerals, lean fish for your protein, and rice for a complex carbohydrate. (I prefer brown rice over white whenever possible.) Plus, you have wasabi and ginger, which are huge in anti-oxidants. So as you can see sushi can be loaded with goodness!

Encore:
Think "Mother Nature" foods in their natural state, or as close to their natural state as possible: foods that have not been or have been minimally processed or modified.

Colors of the Rainbow

When shopping for foods, think colors of the rainbow and try to select a wide variety since many nutrients are associated with various colors. Your richly-colored fruits and vegetables are of premiere importance to you because they have the most vitamins, antioxidants and carotenes.

When it comes to salads, you want dark leafy greens, these could be the most important greens of all because they have the most vital nutrients, dark greens such as spinach, kale, romaine, and collards.

Other great greens include: green apples, green grapes, kiwi, broccoli, cabbage, brussel sprouts, watercress, asparagus, green peppers, celery, cucumbers, and the green portions of scallions, chives and leeks. Although we have given specific mention to those all-important greens, don't forget the rainbow, and make sure to select a wide spectrum of color from deep yellow and orange, deep red, blue and purple, and last but not least white. Try to eat as much color daily as possible and preferably raw or lightly steamed when it comes to your produce. I love fresh juices, which I prepare at home. I am a big fan of juicing for two reasons. One, this is a great way to ensure that you get your daily recommendations of two to three servings of fruit and three to five servings of vegetables per day, and two, this is a superb way to get some raw food into your diet, thereby ensuring the maximum nutritional value.

- **Deep yellow and orange:** pineapple, nectarines, peaches, yellow apples, yellow peppers, yellow winter squash, spaghetti squash, and corn, oranges, melons, tangerines, apricots, papayas, orange peppers, carrots, pumpkin, sweet potato, and yams.
- **Deep red:** red apples, cherries, red grapes, pomegranate, cranberries, watermelon, strawberries, tomatoes, beets, red cabbage, red peppers, radishes, and red onion.
- **Blue and purple:** blackberries, blueberries, purple grapes, raisins, eggplant, and plums.
- **White:** bananas, pears, garlic, onions, white potatoes, mushrooms, turnips, and parsnips.

Encore:
When shopping for foods, think colors of the rainbow and try to select a wide variety since many nutrients are associated with various colors.

Keep It Lean

When it comes to protein, stick to lean meats, chicken or fish; and for vegetarian choices, you have beans, tofu and low-fat cheese, such as cottage cheese (most varieties make lower fat or fat-free versions; once again, just read your labels). Your lean protein sources provide you with the essentials that your body needs for the building and repairing of soft tissues: muscle, tendons, and ligaments. When you eat protein, the first thing your body does is break it down into amino acids. Calcium and iron are often derived from a good source of protein, which can help reduce the soreness that you usually experience the day after a work-out, and will help improve recovery time. Not just recovery time from an injury; but recovery time from a great performance, a class or rehearsal without injury. Protein prevents one from becoming easily fatigued by allowing the body to express stamina and energy.

Nuts and seeds, which are also a great source of protein and good fats (the heart-healthy kind), are an excellent and easy to take-with-you snack. They are also simple to add to other foods such as salads and cereals, and can be used as a topping for fruit and yogurt. Whole grains are composed of minerals, protein, and carbohydrates and have been the staple food for a wide variety of cultures for thousands of years. When it comes to adding them to your meal planning, consider a good vegetarian or specialty recipe book for a little variety in preparation. Otherwise, the truth is that grains are easy to cook and need little or no preparation. For the most part, all you need to do is to rinse them, add water and place on low heat. There is much natural goodness to be gained from adding whole grains, such as barley, bran, whole wheat, oats, brown rice and wild rice, corn, millet, buckwheat, and quinoa to your diet.

Let color, whole foods, whole ingredients, organics, (when you can), simple natural goodness, unrefined, and unprocessed be your mantra when shopping.

Stay away from junk food, fast food and processed food.

The truth is they're *all* the same; *bad for you*! Do your best to exclude them from your diet. They are, for the most part, loaded with artificial or processed ingredients and offer little to no nutritional value whatsoever. Firstly, it's important to understand that the term "fast food" does not just mean the numerous chain restaurants, it also includes things like frozen dinners and the countless prepared meals in a box or can, as well as a candy bar or bag of chips. Fast, yes, but not good for you. I suggest that if it comes in a box or bag with some great big fabulous claim printed across the front, you should immediately read the ingredients on the back. It can be quite shocking. First things first: start paying attention; *read those labels*!

Being somewhat of a reformed chocoholic myself, I understand every whim when it comes to having a sweet tooth, and sure, a little cheat once in a while never hurt anyone; just try not to make it a daily habit. On those rare occasions when indulging, you have a choice to make, and that is whether or not to go with a natural and healthier version found in your local health food store—the kind that may be sweetened with organic cane sugar, molasses, apple juice or honey, instead of the refined white sugar, or to just simply go for that Snickers or Cadbury bar you've been craving. When it comes to choosing healthier versions, again read your labels. Just because it is sold in a health food store doesn't mean that it's automatically healthy. Although you will find healthier choices, the same rules still apply. And that, I will leave to your discretion, and simply remind you that moderation is everything.

If you haven't seen the movie *Supersize me*, be sure to do so. If eating on the road or on the run, and Burger King or McDonald's are truly your only choices, then go with a salad—one of their attempts at convincing us that they, too, can offer healthy choices. At the end of the day, one big, fat juicy burger once in a while is probably not the end of the world; this is more about your everyday habits. And that is all I will say about fast food specifically.

Processed food, which basically includes everything that is not a whole food in its natural state, can easily be found in abundance. (Processed meaning altered, or added to in some form, and whole food meaning as close to the state in which Mother Nature delivered it to us.) Processed foods have been, and continue to be defined by many, in *many* different ways, and one can certainly get carried away with the topic. So, in an effort to help you understand, I say keep it simple. If a food is not in its natural state, then it has been modified to some extent, and, can therefore, be considered processed. However, some processing is necessary, and some advantageous. You want to stay away from those foods which are over-processed, often with chemicals and mostly loaded with artificial ingredients. These make for very poor choices; some are potentially harmful, and most are nutritionally deficient. Here's a good rule of thumb: if you were to shop the perimeter of the grocery store, you would avoid many of the over-processed foods as this is where you will find your produce, meats, dairy products etc. Think about what food items you find in the aisles, in the interior of the grocery store. Not to say that all foods in the aisles are processed, but this is where you will find most of it; like your junk foods and so on. So keep these items to a very minimum, and keep your minimum to the minimally processed when shopping.

One area in particular to try to avoid, and to certainly beware of, is salad dressings and marinades. Dressings can be one the most deceptive areas in a person's diet. How often do you go to a restaurant, and in an effort to do the right thing you order a salad, only to then pour an undisclosed dressing all over it? Before you know it, you've added hundreds of calories full of bad fats and sugars to your wonderful healthy choice. How about all of those choices in the grocery stores? So many to choose from, so I will say it again: first and foremost, *read your labels.* Just because something says fat-free, no sugar added, low-calorie, light, or no carbs, doesn't automatically make it the healthiest of choices. When eating in, you can make yourself a lovely healthy salad dressing with a few basic ingredients: a little olive oil and balsamic or fresh lemon juice, a touch of mustard and some fresh crushed garlic makes for a great-tasting and healthy choice. Personally, I say the least amount of packaged goods you can buy and consume, the better off you will be.

Encore:
*Let color, whole foods, whole ingredients, organics
(when you can), simple natural goodness, unrefined,
and unprocessed be your mantra when shopping.*

Low-fat Options and Good Fat Versus Bad Fat

It is important to understand that although fat was the first to receive bad press as being the main culprit of obesity and cardio vascular disease issues in the United States, fat is indeed necessary, and when eaten in moderation, it is important for our body's development and growth and our overall health. However, what you *must know* is the difference between *good fat* and *bad fat*. There are four major categories—monounsaturated fat, polyunsaturated fat, saturated fat, and trans fat.

Trans fats are getting the majority of the media's attention and bad press today. And rightfully so, thanks to the efforts of *BanTransFats.com, Inc.* a California non-profit corporation which began an international trans fat campaign by suing Kraft in 2003 to eliminate trans fat in Oreo cookies. Trans fat is made when manufacturers add hydrogen to vegetable oil, a process called hydrogenation. It is the worst kind of fat, far worse than saturated fat and should be avoided entirely. These trans fats are often found in products such as margarine and many other packaged foods. Many of these packaged foods are also used in restaurants to prepare, or cook other food. These oils are often blamed for contributing to the ever-increasing number of heart disease problems in the world. In December 2006, New York City passed a regulation banning the use of all *trans* fats in all New York City restaurants; in February 2007, Philadelphia followed suit, and today the initiatives by other cities and states have been overwhelming and too numerous to list. If entire cities are banning the use of trans fats, don't you think *you* should?

Generally speaking, you should also try to limit your intake of saturated fats, the kind that are solid at room temperature. Saturated fats occur naturally in many of the foods we consume. They are predominantly found in animal sources, including dairy items, especially whole-fat versions, and in fatty meats, such as beef, veal, lamb, pork and chicken with the skin on. Many baked goods and fried foods may also contain high levels of saturated fats. Saturated fats are certainly amongst the most harmful fats in the every day diet and when consumed in excessive amounts, they can be a major source of bad cholesterol and blood fats that can lead to cardiovascular problems. When it comes to dairy products, consider fat-free and low-fat options.

Monounsaturated fats and polyunsaturated fats don't seem to raise bad cholesterol levels and are beneficial when consumed in moderation. Monounsaturated fats, which are some of the best fats, are extremely important to your diet and can be found mostly in vegetable and nut oils, such as olive oil, canola oil and peanut oil, as well as avocadoes and many nuts and seeds. You should consider replacing the lesser quality vegetable oils in your diet with olive oil. Olive oil is a staple of the Mediterranean diet, which has been proven time and time again to be one of the healthiest diets.

Polyunsaturated fats are found in a number of vegetable oils, including soybean oil, corn oil, safflower oil and sunflower oil. Omega 3's, which are a very important group of polyunsaturated fats, are absolutely essential to optimum health and not as abundant in the average every day diet. Omega 3's can be found in certain fish, especially fatty fish like mackerel, lake trout, herring, sardines, albacore tuna and salmon, as well as walnuts, hemp seeds, and flax seeds. When purchasing salmon, try to choose wild salmon, not farm-raised and color enhanced. Aside from the questionable diet which farm-raised fish are fed, once you taste the difference, you'll understand why.

Encore:
Monounsaturated fats and polyunsaturated fats don't seem to raise bad cholesterol levels and are beneficial when consumed in moderation.

Five to Six Meals per Day

Brace yourself! Here it comes that terrifying five to six meals a day topic. I remember the first time I went to a nutritionist in Los Angeles many years ago. The first thing he said to me was that he wanted me to eat five to six meals per day. I immediately thought to myself, "How can I possibly eat five to six meals a day?" I'll be as big as this building! Like most people I was appalled at the thought. Well let me tell you that in three short months on this program I went from 17 percent body fat down to 10 percent body fat and learned the importance of food and "fueling the furnace" as he called it. Let's use this analogy of your body being the furnace and your food being the fuel. You have to put fuel into your furnace in order for it to run, same goes for your body, if you don't put any fuel in it, how can you expect it to operate at optimum level. If you don't feed your body regularly it doesn't know when you are going to feed it again, so instead of burning calories it learns to hoard them as a means of preserving itself. This is the worst thing you can do for your metabolism.

First of all, a meal doesn't have to mean one meat and two vegetables. Small meals, more often, are much better for your digestion and overall weight control. You will be most successful if you plan and prepare meals in advance and get creative with your food choices. Five to six meals a day should consist of a good breakfast, lunch and dinner, a midmorning snack, an afternoon snack and a light evening snack (if you like), but no later than one hour before you go to bed.

In the morning, before you go to class or rehearsals, make sure that you have a good source of carbohydrates to give you the energy you need. Fruit, a dark or multi grain bagel, oatmeal and other whole grain cereals, or whole grain bread are all great sources of complex carbohydrates. When it comes to snacks, nuts and a bottle of water, can be a great choice. If you're worried about salted versus unsalted nuts, Dr. Baron actually prefers salted for athletes as they perspire so heavily while in training or performance. Not only is your salt being replaced, but you are also increasing your thirst, so you're more likely to drink more fluids, and this, of course, is a good thing. He doesn't advise this for someone who is sitting at a desk all day, but you, the dancer, are moving; you are active. As a side note, nuts are loaded with good fats, primarily the "heart-healthy" monounsaturated and polyunsaturated fats, which are very good for you, so don't let anyone tell you that nuts are not a good diet food. You probably won't want to eat two pounds in one sitting as they are high in calories. That's just common sense, but we all need those little reminders: *portion control is everything.* As for other snacks, try to keep them light and clean; consider your overall daily calorie intake. Here are a few ideas: individual servings of apple sauce (the all-natural-no sugar-added kind is best) and a couple of graham crackers, a natural brand yogurt, a fruit smoothie made from all fresh ingredients, or a protein shake. Last, but certainly not least, any fresh fruit or vegetable, and for something a little different and refreshing, try freezing some blueberries, grapes, or cherries.

As for lunch and dinner, try to eat a good balance of protein, carbohydrates, and heart healthy fats. Protein should be lean and no larger than the size of your fist. As for carbohydrates stick to your healthier and cleaner carbohydrates such as your vegetables and whole grains, as opposed to those over processed versions we spoke of earlier. Once again, remember your portion control. Lunchtime can be a great time to load up on your veggies, especially those dark leafy greens; they make a wonderful base to your salad. Also if you like your pastas, which happen to be a good energy source, it's not a bad idea to eat them earlier in the day, and just remember to keep your portions smaller, unlike the often heaping servings you might get when ordering in restaurants. Dinner is a good time to load up on your protein and choose carbohydrates that are easily digestible, such as steamed vegetables. This will prove especially important if you are having a late night dinner after a show. Easy reminder, keep your *protein lean* and your *carbs clean*! Whenever possible, try to keep your last full meal to at least three hours before bedtime.

Encore:
You will be most successful if you plan and prepare meals in advance and get creative with your food choices.

Read the Labels

I'm sure by now you've gathered that I have never been a fan of processed foods and anyone who has spent any time around me would likely say that I could make them a bit crazy with reading labels and conversations about ingredients! It's very simple—if you don't know what you're reading, you don't know what you're eating. Luckily for us, the law dictates that food manufacturers list ingredients, and outline the nutritional breakdown on the packages of most foods. This is known as the Nutrition Facts Panel and is regulated by the FDA (Food and Drug Administration), so take advantage of this feature. Have I said it yet? Read your labels and not just the calories and fat count.

Overall calories and the breakdown of fats, proteins, and carbohydrates are all important; however, you will also want to read the ingredients list. What are you eating? Ingredients are listed from the largest quantity to the smallest, so if sugar is first on the list, then that is the Number One ingredient in the food item. If it is last on the list, there is a smaller quantity in the product.

So pay attention! Maybe the front label boasts some natural ingredient that is good for your health; however, in the ingredients list, it might be last on the list, and the product could have very little of the one ingredient you thought you were buying, not to mention the fact that it has been processed beyond recognition.

The other area which can prove to be very deceiving is the advertisement and promotion by companies of items for the diet-conscious consumers.

"Fat-free" often means loaded with sugar, and "sugar-free" often means chemically processed sweeteners, while "low-carb" could mean loaded with fat, and not necessarily the "good" fat. The truth is that some people can, and will, eliminate all processed foods from their diets, while others will find it difficult. At the very least, do your best to keep these purchases to a minimum. By reading your labels, you can begin to eliminate the worst ingredients first. Refined white sugar and white flour are right up there with hydrogenated oils as ingredients to avoid. Keep in mind that if something is listed near the top of the ingredients list, it means that it is one of the main ingredients.

Over the last century, we have seen food manufacturers use everything possible to get their products out quicker, cheaper and bigger. Along the way, they have ended up using more and more chemicals for processing, and have supplemented diets with growth hormones in order to cut corners.

Research is slowly determining that not only do these procedures reduce the nutritional value of our foods, but they can actually be detrimental to our health. Let's face it, in this day and age, when we witness ever-increasing health issues, one sure fix is to simply go back to basics. Try to obtain foods in as natural a state as possible; you may want to consider shopping at your local health food store, whole-food markets, and/or local farmers markets if available.

Encore:
It's very simple—if you don't know what you're reading, you don't know what you're eating.

Meal Preparation and Planning

If you truly want to control what you put into your body, one certain way to accomplish this is to plan and prepare your own meals. Yes, this means you will want to brush up on your gourmet flair and a few great cookbooks could help you with exactly that. Truth is, you can make it as simple or extravagant as you like; most important is simply that you take the time to prepare, make sure you have all those healthy choices on hand, and get a little creative.

Vitamins and Supplements

I'm going to touch lightly on this topic merely for the purpose of introduction, when speaking with Dr. Baron I asked him which vitamins and supplements he recommends, and which, in particular, he most recommends for strength and endurance, or for healthy muscles and bones? His response was, "A multi vitamin is always important, and having said that, I want to make it clear that what you cannot do is eat a terrible diet and then pop a multi-vitamin expecting it to be a cure-all. When you are eating properly, you get a lot of nutrients naturally. Unfortunately, unless you eat an absolutely impeccable diet, it will be difficult to get all of your nutrients from food alone—not impossible, but certainly difficult. Therefore, your multi-vitamin will be important to help supplement your diet." If you are interested in taking vitamins, it is a good idea to spend some time reading about the benefits of vitamins made from whole foods versus synthetics. Just as it is recommended that you eat whole foods in as natural a state as possible, you should also try to take good quality vitamins from a trusted brand, that are at best made from certified organic whole food ingredients. If your budget won't allow for certified organic, try to at the very least purchase vitamins made from whole food ingredients.

"Antioxidants naturally occur in all of your fresh fruits and vegetables and are very important to us. They are exactly as they sound, anti-oxidation; they block or inhibit destructive oxidation reactions. Oxidation is what happens during the aging process. Antioxidants give you the ability to fight off some of that damage. Does it not stand to reason, that if antioxidants help to retain the elasticity in the skin, they can also do the same for what lies beneath the skin, our ligaments, tendons and muscles?" And that elasticity is so important to a dancer. If you are interested in taking antioxidants in supplement form, I suggest that you do some research, as the list can be overwhelming. You will want to learn more in order to determine what is right for you, based on your personal nutritional habits and needs. Most multi-vitamins should include some antioxidants. ACE is a quick simple acronym to help you remember a few important antioxidants, vitamins A, C and E, but the list does not end there.

In reference to our joints, ligaments and bones, "Vitamins like E, A and D, which are oil-based are very good; E specifically is going to be extremely important because it helps to lubricate the joints. Other supplements that are super and are proven to show merit for arthritic joints are Glucosamine,

Chondroitin and MSM. Glucosamine and Chondroitin are probably the most important arsenal for a dancer, due to the fact that they help repair and support cartilage. After all, the cartilage is what often takes the abuse, constantly absorbing the shock from your landings of all those jumps and leaps, and, therefore, suffers repetitive micro traumas." Some joint formulas or complexes can also be found with ginger and turmeric in them; these additional ingredients are known for their antioxidant properties, anti-inflammatory agents, and pain relief. I have found the combination to work very well for me.

"Papain and bromelain, which are enzymes found naturally in papaya and pineapple, are both fantastic for muscle repair. After an injury, it would be a good idea to add some extra papaya and pineapple to your diet. Again, these can also be taken in supplement form."

Encore:
*Antioxidants naturally occur in all of your fresh fruits
and vegetables and are very important to us.*

Drink your Water

"Water constitutes about two-thirds of your body weight. So, what's the best thing for it? Water, *not diet soda*, and *not fruit drinks*, as they are loaded with sugar and can defeat the purpose. Your body needs water. It is extremely important to constantly keep hydrated." Every system in your body depends on water. For example, water flushes toxins out of vital organs, carries nutrients to your cells and provides a moist environment for ear, nose and throat tissues. I'm sure you have often heard that you should drink at least eight 8–12 oz. glasses of water per day. The average adult loses more than ten cups of water every day simply by sweating, breathing, and eliminating waste. You also loose electrolytes—minerals such as sodium, potassium, and calcium which maintain the balance of fluid in your body. Normally you can replenish sufficiently through the foods and liquids you consume. However if you eliminate more than you replace, this can lead to dehydration.

> **Encore:**
> *Your body needs water. It is extremely important
> to constantly keep hydrated.*

Eight Quick Reference Tips

1. Make healthy choices:
    Eat whole foods as close to their natural state as possible.
    Shop for the colors of the rainbow.
    When it comes to animal protein, keep it lean.
    When it comes to carbohydrates, keep them clean.
    Good fat versus bad.
    Grains are easy to prepare.
    Nuts and seeds are easy to pack.
2. Stay away from junk food, fast food, and processed food.
    Bottom line is, it's all the same: "bad for you!"
3. Five to six meals per day:
    Not every meal has to be a meat and two vegetables.
    Don't skip meals.
    Nuts and a bottle of water are a great snack.
    Make sure that your last meal of the day is at least three hours
    before bedtime.
    A light evening snack should be no later than one hour before
    bedtime.
4. Portion control:
    Small meals more often, hence the five to six meals.
    Protein portions should be the size of your fist.
    Stop when you are no longer hungry; don't wait until you are stuffed.
5. Read the labels. (Can't stress this one enough):
    If you don't know what you're reading, you don't know what
    you're eating.
    Ingredients list is important—not just the fat, calories, and
    carb count.
6. Meal preparation and planning:
    The healthiest meals start in your own kitchen.
    Load up on good-quality ingredients.

Buy yourself a good "healthy" cookbook.

Get creative and try new cuisines.

Take a leaf from the Mediterranean, Indian and Japanese diets.

7. Supplements and vitamins:

Try adding a daily multi vitamin.

Supplements made from whole foods versus synthetics.

Read and learn more about antioxidant-rich foods.

8. Water:

Keep hydrated with a minimum of eight glasses (each 8–12oz) of water per day.

Encore:

Mom's Know Best—Isn't that why we refer to Nature as Mother Nature?

CHAPTER ELEVEN

LET'S GET PHYSICAL—INJURY RECOGNITION AND PREVENTION

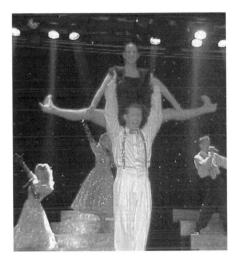

A natural high. "Jump Jive and Wail," Las Vegas Then and Now, Celebrity Cruise Lines' Century

"The doctor of the future will give no medicine, but will interest his patients in the care of human frame, and in the cause and prevention of disease." —*Thomas Alva Edison*

The information transcribed by me and extensive quotes you are about to read in this chapter are the results of an in-depth interview with Dr. Baron, as previously mentioned.

Dr. Baron has always had a special interest in dancers, he refers to dancers as, "One of the ultimate athletes, they are the only athletes that have to present their art using their bodies while making it look beautiful and effortless. If they are in pain, you will never know." He also reminded me of how often I have said to him, "The show must go on," and that, concisely, is why he finds dancers so fascinating. To me the *ultimate dancer* is exactly that, fascinating. When a dancer is driven by passion it's no wonder they can endure just about anything and achieve such great feats. One of my favorite quotes by Albert Einstein sums it up: "Dancers are the athletes of God."

"Recognition and prevention are keys to your longevity as a dancer or an athlete" Dr. Baron says. "And a fail-safe way to really accomplish this is to have an imaginary checklist in each area of your health pyramid—nutritional, physical, and mental. Think about everyday life; emotional upsets tend to create stress. With a dancer, there is always a tremendous amount of pressure, from the need to constantly perform at the same level or better, to vying for a job or specific role at an upcoming audition. Either of these could cause a great deal of stress, and if you are so preoccupied with stress, then your performance will undoubtedly be affected. Here's why. First it creates tension, next you're not sleeping, and before you know it, you're not eating well, or you may not be eating at all. I understand that sometimes you can't help getting stressed. If that's the case, then you have to make up for it, and compensate in other areas by taking extra care, and ensuring that you eat properly, and stay away from unhealthy choices. For instance, if you had a bad night's sleep because you were stressed out, and to add insult to injury, all you have for breakfast the next morning is a cup of coffee, where are you going to pull your energy from? If anything, this will provoke more anxiety and more anguish as your system is being driven by poor fuel; hence, you are mentally and physically unstable. One small mistake during a jump, and before you know it, you've landed inaccurately and injured yourself. You can see from this example how integrated and intimate everything is."

Encore:
*Recognition and prevention are keys to your
longevity as a dancer or an athlete.*

In Your Control and Out of Your Control

The previous paragraph relates to recognition and prevention in areas that are within our control. Next, we want to stress the importance of recognition in areas that are outside our control. Environmental factors, such as a dance floor, a cold-drafty atmosphere, or humidity and high temperatures, can often be the cause of injuries. You don't always know the kind of environment you will be working or auditioning in, so at all times, you should be prepared for the worst. Never slack on your footwear; it is your most important piece of equipment. There are many types of flooring that you might encounter at auditions or during rehearsals. Some may not have been originally intended for dancers, so don't cut corners on your footwear. When it comes to a drafty environment, you have to be very careful, especially in hot climates where you have air conditioning.

The air from such systems is cold and dry, so you want to make sure that you are appropriately dressed and properly warmed up, a few extra layers can go a long way towards injury prevention. Something to be aware of in the summer months, and something we see here in Florida year-round, is humidity and high temperatures. This can provoke dehydration, cramps, and exhaustion, so the components of nutrition and re-hydration become absolutely imperative. Be sure to eat balanced meals and drink plenty of fresh water.

I want to emphasize that preparation is always the best form of defense even when confronted with unfamiliar circumstances. Dr. Baron remembered a story that reiterates this point succinctly. "It was the cast of *Les Misérables* and they were performing on an incredibly raked stage, certainly the worst one the dancers had ever worked on. This was the only time that I ever had to send a dancer to an orthopedic surgeon. Due to the extreme rake in the stage, he lost his footing, and unfortunately injured himself on the spot. Sadly, he ended up having knee surgery."

Of course accidents do happen, but awareness and preparation are key under these circumstances. Sometimes spending just a little extra time familiarizing yourself with your environment can help you prevent such accidents. In fact think about the dancers working on cruise ships. Very often, they are performing on a stage that is moving up and down, and side-to-side. The way to handle this is to first of all be open to the situation at hand, and be completely focused so that you are fully aware of exactly what is happening. This will allow your body to compensate and adjust as necessary; your muscles will naturally adjust their tension, motion and memory, but it does take some time. So you must approach it intelligently, taking the necessary time to become familiar with your new territory.

Encore:
Sometimes spending just a little extra time familiarizing yourself with your environment can help you prevent accidents.

Chiropractic and the Dancer

Year in year and year out Chiropractic has become one of the chosen treatments for athletes and dancers alike. Dr. Baron explains: "Chiropractic offers an understanding of physiology and of biomechanics, so we, as Chiropractors, observe the athlete and identify what actually went wrong and why, and then we can treat the injury from that perspective. As Chiropractors, we help to create balance and strengthen weak muscles. We work with the way the body naturally heals, so you are not misguided by an impression that you are better when, in fact, you are not.

"Part of the beauty of being a Chiropractor with a specialty in sports injury is that we look to identify things that are actually compensations to the original injury. So, for example, let's consider a torn hamstring. In traditional medicine, it would be all about your hamstring, and yes, of course, Chiropractors pay attention to the hamstring, as well, but we will delve further. What you may not have known is that your injury was due to the fact that your pelvis was out of alignment, or that you had pressure coming off the nerve at L5, 4, or 3 (L stands for lumbar region of the back, while the number relates to the exact vertebrae). This pressure was slowing down or hindering the full potential of that hamstring muscle, both in strength and coordination. Because it was weak and not operating at optimum level, it became injured. A different scenario could be if the ankle on the opposite leg to the injured hamstring became a problem. Maybe your dance shoe didn't fit properly, and you were compensating for it. Whenever there is an ankle or a foot injury, we always look to the joint above on the opposite side, so a bad ankle on the left can produce a bad right knee, and what is hooked up to the knee but the hamstring? So before you know it, you have a hamstring strain. The problem is this: if you never fix the ankle, you'll constantly have hamstring strains. Now that's putting it so simplistically for the purpose of clarity; however, there is a whole web of other biomechanical compensations. It's like peeling back the skin of an onion to get to the core of the injury."

Traditional Medicine and Your Injury

"Unfortunately, the primary health care choice that most people know and use is traditional medicine. This is all well and good, but the form of treatment they generally use is medication. Medication is the very short-term approach to getting better, and it's not necessarily getting-better it is simply shutting off the fire alarm, and never really addressing the fire. So, when a dancer rehearses or performs with the fire alarm shut off, he/she is magnifying the potential for re-injury. They are actually shortening their life span as dancers. Dancers have very strong wills, and are already accustomed to and capable of shutting off pain in their mind. Unfortunately, with medication, you have a double whammy: first the dancer shuts it off in their mind, and then the medication shuts off the actual sensation. It's one thing to control the sensation and modulate it; however, to eliminate it artificially is a completely different situation. Together, the two are an extremely dangerous combination for a dancer. Depending on the injury, the other option recommended by traditional medicine is surgery, and when you are a dancer, surgery is not a good thing. It can impose great delays and often, it can even be the end of your career. You want to avoid surgery at all cost."

Encore:
Medication is the very short-term approach to getting better, and it's not necessarily getting-better it is simply shutting off the fire alarm, and never really addressing the fire.

Other Alternative Approaches

"In addition to Chiropractic, here is a list of other healing arts which can also be very beneficial. Massage therapy should be a part of your standard practice whenever possible. Pilates is one of the most superior practices for a dancer because it is both a rehab and preventative program. It is perfectly made for the dancer. A physical therapist can be helpful; try to find one that has a specialty in sports injury. Some are meritorious of having the ability to treat conservatively without drugs or surgery. An athletic trainer who is certified in treating pro-athletes, a good nutritionist, a dance or sports psychologist, and an acupuncturist might all be helpful. These are all good people to know and to have on hand.

"One other area is Osteopathic Medicine. The beauty of it is that it's meant to be the combination of the traditional medical doctor who prescribes medicine with the philosophies of manipulation of the spine and extremities, which is what the osteopath does. The only unfortunate thing is that many osteopaths here in the United States have found it easier to put a greater emphasis on prescribing medication than on performing the art of manipulation."

Different practices work for different people, so sometimes you have to try things on for size and see what works best for you and your body's needs. The above list is merely intended to serve as a guideline and provide information to help you in determining what natural approach will be best for you in both injury prevention and rehabilitation. The bottom line is, as I've said previously, your body is your business and it is your responsibility. You have to ensure its proper care by putting yourself in the right hands in order to sustain the maximum longevity possible.

Minor Inconvenience, Warning Signal or Injury

Because of the strong will that dancers have and that innate ability to dance through much pain, I want to pay special attention to the differences between a minor inconvenience, a warning signal, and an actual full-on injury. From the time I was very young, I was taught that what the average person considered pain was simply a minor inconvenience to a dancer. Although I hope that dancers today are more informed and better educated in the area of health and fitness, it is still in their blood as a breed to endure and live by the wonderful old adage, "The show must go on." So how does this same dancer—the one who is capable of shutting off the sensation of pain—understand the difference between a warning signal, an injury, and just a minor inconvenience?

Dr. Baron reiterates the importance of prevention and recognition: "A good warning sign is a weakness in the muscles. For example, if a dancer is on point, and she is losing control of her stability, that could be a sign of fatigue. This is usually a sign that there is a potentiating injury ensuing, so you must be aware. There is nobody more body-conscious than a dancer; therefore, I suggest that you learn to use this to your advantage. It is possible to be aware of the pain and still maintain that same mentality so that it will not get you down—"the show must go on" attitude. But you must heed the warning and take care. An even stronger warning would be, if you suddenly found that you could not hold a position like you used to. This could also be due to a weakness and it might be an early warning sign that something is building.

"There is a first sign that people do not heed, and that is called a loss of *proprioceptive skills*. Proprioception is one of the components of nerve conduction; nerve fibers conduct four senses—the sense of pain, the sense of temperature, the sense of pressure, and the sense of proprioception. Proprioceptive fibers allow you to understand where your body is in space without looking, for example, when you land from a jump or leap without looking at the floor. If you begin noticing that you are no longer able to land pinpoint, then you should start questioning your proprioceptive skill, as this is one of your first signs of a potentiating injury. Proprioception is critical to a dancer; it is a sensory perception that everyone has, but is definitely enhanced in dancers; so if you start to see this falter, you should beware.

"This is why in the athletic training camps, you hear more and more about football players learning ballet. It helps them to develop that ability of balance, which is proprioception. When it comes to recovering from an injury, there is much rehabilitation being done today with balance boards for this exact reason. If we can rehabilitate an athlete's balance and proprioceptive skills, we have a much stronger and more stable foundation, and, therefore, can secure far less chance of re-injury. The old way was to simply get them back into the game, or on stage, as quickly as possible with not much foresight as to their overall career longevity. Back then, the reason people were not rehabilitating correctly from ankle strains and similar injuries, was because they were not developing their proprioceptive sense. Without developing and re-strengthening that sense, you cannot ensure that you will dance or perform and not do the exact same thing again, hence the constant re-injury. If you cannot feel where the floor is, how are you going to land? Today there is so much more beyond just pain control that can be done for injury rehabilitation." In the event that you might notice this sort of early warning sign, you should immediately go back, default to your nutritional, physical, or mental checklist, and find out what is going on. You may realize that you are over-training, or are becoming overtired. You may not be giving your body adequate nutrition. *Something is out of whack*, and this could mean an impending injury. Your checklists are your ways of identifying some of what may be lacking.

Encore:
Without developing and re-strengthening your proprioceptive sense, you cannot ensure that when you dance or perform, you will not re-injure yourself.

R.I.C.E.

In the event of injury, you cannot go wrong with the acronym *R.I.C.E:* rest, ice, compression, and elevation. This should be done for the first three days of an acute injury. Current research suggests that one should ice intermittently immediately following an acute strain. For best results, recommended protocols are ten minutes with ice, ten minutes without ice, and ten minutes with ice again, repeating every two hours or as often as you can for those first three days.

After the first three days or so, when all swelling has stopped and has definitely been reduced, then you can start to do a contrast of ice and heat, alternating ice for ten minutes, then heat for ten minutes, and ending with ice. This will serve as a vascular exercise to pump all of the injured or dead blood cells and tissue out of the area. Heat expands and ice contracts; when you alternate heat and ice a couple of times back-to-back, then you create a vascular exercise. Heat re-accommodates the blood vessels to open and forces fluid and nutrients in; ice closes them so you don't cause additional swelling. Swelling is where further injury can happen, because it distorts the tissue from the onset of the injury. You can control tissue distortion by suppressing any swelling that is going on. Even though some of it is natural and is supposed to happen, you still need to control it.

There is a time to use heat only, however, Dr. Baron stresses that you must be very clear on this point. "Heat is good as long as you don't continue to aggravate the situation. So, for example, let's say that you are into day number seven and you are back to doing some moderate performing, moderate level of activity, or full performance. Let's take it a step further. Let's say that the original injury was to a shoulder, although this is not a weight-bearing joint. Imagine that every time you do a certain move, you re-aggravate the injury; this is when you must not use heat or you should stop using heat if you have been. When you re-aggravate an injury, you have to use ice again, and restart the cycle. Heat, you only use if you're not re-aggravating the situation. If you're into day six, seven or eight, then you should be using heat only to warm up the muscle, without allowing it to swell. Whatever you do, you do not want to re-potentiate the swelling. Here's a good rule of thumb to help you better understand. Because the injury is under the skin, you can't see it, so think of it as a cut on your knee. Every time you feel pain or pulling, you're opening up the wound again. You wouldn't put heat on your wounded knee because it would actually deteriorate the scar tissue (the scab), and it would start to bleed again. So consider that the same is happening below the skin, and the last thing you want to do to a fresh injury or re-injury is to make it bleed. This is why we always use ice first."

Encore:
R.I.C.E: rest, ice, compression, and elevation.
This should be done for the first three days of an acute injury.

Pull, Tear, Sprain or Strain?

Dr. Baron explains in layman's terms the difference between a pull or a tear, and a sprain or strain to a muscle, a ligament, and a tendon. "A pull is a word used so freely," he says. "When people say a pull, it is usually a tear. This sounds very aggressive, but all strains and sprains are, in fact, tears to the soft tissue; they are micro tears. Because the word tear sounds so overwhelming,

I don't often use it. A sprain is what happens when the ligament tears, whereas a strain is what happens when the muscle or tendon is injured or tears for the sake of explanation. If you were to take a piece of toilet tissue and not tear it apart, but just start pulling on it to the point where the fibers start to separate, then you would have an idea of what happens to muscles, and ligaments, and tendons. To further clarify, ligaments are found much deeper than the muscles and tendons; ligaments attach bone-to-bone and tendons attach muscle-to-bone. So to connect the tibia to the femur, you have a lot of ligaments. Ligaments provide stability. They do not provide any power, whereas muscle, which turns into tendon and attaches to the bone, provides you with power and propulsion. Many years ago, when soccer players would suffer ligament sprains, surgeons often recommended cutting certain ligaments out. Since the technology for healing ligaments was so inadequate back then, the players just continued to re-injure them, and so the simple solution was 'Let's get rid of them.' It was believed that they didn't really need the ligaments, because one could manage without them. Because soccer players have such incredibly strong leg muscles, and since that is where their propulsion comes from, this very strength is what they relied on to carry them through. But you see the problem is this, when they get older and their muscles get weak, without those ligaments, they are left with a sensational amount of instability." Thankfully this is no longer common practice.

Encore:
Ligaments are found much deeper than the muscles and tendons; ligaments attach bone-to-bone and tendons attach muscle-to-bone.

Healing Time

"Why does it always seem to take so much longer to heal a strained muscle or sprained ligaments than to heal a bone fracture?" He answered, "It has often been said, 'I would rather you fracture a body part than strain it'. Why? When something is fractured, we pay a lot of attention to it; we cast it immediately, and it's a big deal. When it comes to a strain or sprain, no matter to what degree, you think that it's only a minor injury and so you don't take care of it as well; hence the elongated healing time. You simply never really take care of these minor problems with the same concern as a major problem. The truth is, when properly addressed, a muscle or tendon can take four to six weeks to heal; a ligament can take six to eight weeks; whereas a bone can take eight weeks or more.

"With dancers, the most common injuries are stress fractures in the feet. Unfortunately, what usually happens is that we wait until a strain leads to a fracture before we take care of it. The lower extremities are nearly always beaten up from various injuries, but when you let them go on and on, and do not take care of them, then they become stress fractures. Bones are strong, and it takes weakened ligaments or tendons to create a lack of support; without that support, the bone takes the brunt of the problem. Usually, the first to go is a muscle, then tendon, then ligament and finally bone." So you can see the importance of paying attention to those early warning signals and properly addressing them before they become debilitating injuries.

Encore:
The truth is, when properly addressed, a muscle or tendon can take four to six weeks to heal; a ligament can take six to eight weeks; whereas a bone can take eight weeks or more.

Injuries and Sleeping Patterns

I've had a few dancers over the years with injuries that we discovered were being aggravated in their sleep, although it's difficult to tell which came first, the potential injury and the improper sleeping patterns, or the improper sleeping patterns which provoked the injuries. "Allow me to explain: Most important to the aesthetics and performance of a dancer is balance and symmetry. Therefore it only stands to reason that if you were to sleep in awkward or funny positions 365 days or nights out of the year, you would be damaging your balance and symmetry? The worst way you can sleep is belly-down; your head might be turned to one side, with one arm over your head, and one leg in a passé position. Imagine if you are absolutely exhausted, and you just don't move from that position all night, when, in fact, our bodies are meant to move countless times throughout the night. Do that all night for six or eight hours and see how you feel! The best way to sleep is on your back with a pillow that provides curve to the neck. Your head should be slightly back with your ears in balance with your shoulders, and maybe a couple of pillows under your legs. The second best way to sleep is on your side in the fetal position with a pillow between your legs and one placed underneath your head. Your shoulder should be slightly forward; you should not be lying on it.

"Bad sleeping habits are hard to break, but because they can be the culprit of chronic aches and pains, they are definitely worth your consideration." How many of you sleep in turn out, passé positions or legs and arms extended in all angles? Some of you may be doing full-on choreography in your sleep! Give it some thought and try to retrain yourself to sleep in one of the more favorable positions recommended. I have seen a few dancers, including myself, eliminate a fair bit of pain through a good night's sleep.

Encore:
*Most important to the aesthetics and performance
of a dancer is balance and symmetry.*

Home Rehabilitation

When it comes to at-home rehabilitation and exercises that are best for preventative measures, Dr. Baron strongly recommends Pilates, a method, which has been widely embraced by dancers for years. I trust that most of you are familiar with it. Created by Joseph Pilates in the early 1900s, he was a performer and boxer who developed his concepts and exercises from over twenty years of self-study and apprenticeship in Yoga, Zen, and ancient Greek and Roman physical regimens. "Pilates is the ideal thing for dancers; it's as though it was made just for them.

"When it comes to rehabilitation, you want to use a non-trauma approach. I wouldn't recommend jogging, I would, however, recommend a therapy ball or if you're looking for more conditioning, I would suggest doing all non-traumatic activities, like a recumbent bike, the elliptical machine, and stairmasters, rather than jogging or using a tread mill. You want to avoid trauma—you've already done so much of that in your dance."

Encore:

When it comes to at-home rehabilitation and exercises that are best for preventative measures, Dr. Baron strongly recommends Pilates.

Off-season Training

In chapter Three: Triple Threat, I talked about the importance of constant training for a dancer. The reason I put so much emphasis on this is because over the years, I've seen many dancers develop bad habits. Often, when they are traveling for work and not able to get to class, many are not disciplined enough to give themselves a class or get to the gym. Even worse, when doing a long-running engagement, many think, because they are performing every night, they don't have to be in class every day, but there is no greater misconception. Although I have stressed the importance of training even when you are in contract, Dr. Baron made special mention of what he refers to as off-season conditioning, or for clarity, out of performance season or out of contract training. "Off-season conditioning is so important because you want to be as close to performance ready as possible, without enduring the trauma of what it is like to be in training during performance season. So, you really want to gradually ramp up your activities throughout your off-season in order to prepare for performance season, or an upcoming contract rather than waiting until the last minute. This could be really simple stuff, because what you don't want to do is suddenly shock the system as that will take its toll on you, and defeat the very gradual approach necessary for building your stamina."

I can certainly relate as a choreographer in and out of rehearsals on a regular basis. My dance schedule changes with my rehearsal schedules, and so it is even more important for me today and has been since I stopped performing, to maintain a strong training and workout schedule, outside of my rehearsal schedules.

Strength Training for the Dancer

Over the past twenty years or so, I have studied and trained in the area of muscle conditioning and strength training, and I have found that I'm at my best and strongest when I am doing a good blend of light-weight training, low-impact aerobics, Yoga and Pilates. Years ago, it was thought that strength-training was bad for dancers, and that it went against our grain as dancers. I asked Dr. Baron what his thoughts were about strength-training. He said "It is a fantastic way of keeping in shape, while strengthening your overall muscle tone and providing the body with additional resistance greater than your own body weight. As dancers, you have naturally trained yourselves over the years to endure your own body weight. Strength-training can only help to enhance what you do naturally, by adding that additional resistance.

"Your body is an amazing mechanism; its accommodative reflexes are so cool, and we totally take them for granted. Think of calluses on your feet. They are due to repetitive trauma, which is just enough stress to the superficial tissues to make the body go 'Hey, I need some more skin cells down here,' so what does the body do? It thickens that area and makes it more durable. When you stop doing what caused the irritation in the first place, the calluses go away. That is exactly what is happening to your body when you stress it just enough over a long period of time. The accommodative reflexes add increases of minerals to the bone, ligaments, tendons, and muscles. This strengthens them, so now you become more tolerant of the stresses that you're going to encumber in your performances."

As dancers, we tend to use the same muscle groups over and over again. Think about what happens when you change your routine by starting rehearsals for a new show. How often do you come in the following day stiff and aching, suddenly feeling muscles that you never knew existed? I remember one particular show that I was doing; it was the summer production revue at the Royal York Hotel in Toronto. The first day of rehearsals was so exciting—meeting the new cast, learning the choreography, and getting an overall flavor of what the show was going to be like. Day two, I woke up feeling like a Mac truck had run over me. I was so stiff, it hurt to get out of bed, let alone move my head. My friend and roommate at the time, who was also doing the show with me, woke up feeling pretty much the same. I remember both of us moaning and groaning all the way to rehearsals and lamenting about what horrible shape we must be in, only to arrive at rehearsal and find the entire cast with leg warmers and scarves wrapped around their necks. No one was moving too quickly that day! On the other hand, imagine when you are in the same routine day in and day out. Your body adjusts to the routine, so when you are performing the same show, or in class executing the same or similar exercises, certain muscles are not getting any attention, and, therefore, may not be getting strengthened, or even maintained. I personally believe from my own experience, that strength-training is a great way to develop muscle groups that may not get adequate work in your dance training. Years ago, I was that dancer who wouldn't dare enter a gym or take an aerobics class; today, I could not imagine my life without my workouts. As a dancer, strength-training helped to improve my physical strength overall, and it especially helped me to rehabilitate when I was injured and brought me back even stronger.

> ### Encore:
> *Strength-training is a great way to develop muscle groups that may not get adequate work in your dance training.*

Exercise Do's and Don'ts

I asked Dr. Baron which exercises, if any, he would not advocate for dancers. "I will sum it up this way: you want to stay away from the activities that are first and foremost pounding. As I mentioned earlier, like jogging or running on a treadmill; this is the last thing you want to do. The upper body bicycle known as an Ergo Meter would be an excellent exercise for dancers to do; this is the only activity where you can gain a sensational amount of activity without using your legs. So no pounding activities, and most importantly for the dancer would be no one-sided sports. I hate to say it, but activities like golf, tennis or pitching are not good for you. If you spent all summer at tennis camp, then you could be doomed. Think about it—balance is crucial to a dancer. The last thing you want is one-sided activities that could create any imbalances and possibly interfere in any way with the symmetry necessary for your dancer physique and for the execution of your dance."

Social and Peer Pressures—the Do's and Don'ts

Unfortunately, in the entertainment industry, there is sometimes a natural association with drinking, smoking, and social drugs. Aside from the fact that drugs are illegal, the physical complications that can occur are absolutely detrimental to your health and career. I am a huge advocate of health and nutrition and the tremendous role that they play in keeping you fit and on top of your game. Social drugs simply do not have any place in your life, and I can't say this strongly enough. No curiosity or peer pressure is worth losing yourself to or compromising your integrity for. I have witnessed some extremely talented artists lose themselves to social drugs, and some to serious drinking problems. In the end, it cost some of them their jobs, while it costs others their careers. This is a small business and word gets around. When it comes to your reputation, you want it clean and untarnished. There are a few things that will get you fired with immediate dismissal, and drugs are certainly at the top of the list. Although having a couple of drinks may not get you fired, an addiction to alcohol is a problem that will often interfere with your work, and eventually cost you your job. Do not compromise yourself or your integrity ever, not to any addiction, especially drugs or alcohol. Just stay away from them period! Choose a healthy path for all the wonderful reasons we're talking about in this chapter. After all, you are an athlete, so why not be a fine-tuned athlete, in mind, body, and spirit. Trust yourself—you know what's best, and making the right choices makes for a much better experience and overall performance. You haven't spent your life preparing for and dreaming about this career only to throw it all away.

Here's what Dr. Baron has to say: "With alcohol, moderation is everything. Now you may have those days where you put the pedal to the metal and party a little too much; inevitably, you will have to pay. When you overindulge, whether it is drugs or alcohol, you are depleting something in your system, so if you understand this, maybe you'll make better choices. Don't think that you can overindulge, then simply fortify yourself with all the proper nutrients; this is not how it works. You don't simply get to replenish with some supplements and make all the damage disappear. No, you must understand that what you've done has taken away from your system, and this oftentimes produces injuries. As an example, alcohol is a dehydrator; that being the case, consider how you have depleted your system of its essential nutrients."

Dehydration is the loss of water and salts that are essential for normal body function.

"Here's what is really important. I am not just talking about the immediate pain that you may feel from a hangover. I am talking about the depletion and potential for injury you have caused your body. Once the damage is done, you had better take extra care of yourself, because you don't want to, and you can't afford to, end up injured. In other words, you play, you pay, and no, you don't just get to suffer quietly through your hangover. Now you have to be responsible and make sure that you get yourself back in shape with a lot of TLC. This means extra work on your part."

During rehearsals, I will forewarn cast members of the intense demands on them during this period, and I will ask them to be intelligent and keep the use of alcohol to a minimum. I understand that some people like to relax with a glass of wine or beer at the end of a long day, and that's fine with me as long as they are not reckless and it does not interfere with their ability to perform the next day. It is very important to the team that you are responsible and there for each other 100 percent.

As an ex-smoker, someone who speaks from having been there and done that, I would love nothing more than to not see anyone smoke ever again. I always said that I would not be "one of those ex-smokers" who drove others crazy about it. And, therefore, I will try not to go on too much; I will simply point out the obvious. Today we know more and more about the terrible effects of smoking, not to mention that it is far less socially acceptable now than it was in the past, yet so many continue the habit, and still too many pick it up. I smoked for years so I can attest to how addictive it is. I add to that the fact that one who smokes must make the firm decision and have the desire to quit, in order to be successful. When I finally decided with a firm conviction that I wanted to be a non-smoker, it was so much easier than I had ever imagined. That's not to say it's easy for everyone, but merely to say that it *can* be done, and possibly, with less difficulty than you might think.

On December 27th, 1999 a very dear friend suffered a stroke and I spent the following week at the hospital. Every four hours or so when the cravings got to be too much, I would slip away to have a cigarette, and as I stood in front of the hospital smoking, I thought to myself, *Something is really wrong with this picture. Here I am slowly throwing away my life while my friend is up there in his hospital bed fighting for his.* As the millennium was approaching, I had been talking about quitting and planned to pick up some nicotine patches on New Year's Eve. My best girlfriend from home flew into Miami to celebrate the New Year with me. The nurses at Mount Sinai Hospital were kind enough to allow us to bring in the millennium with our very dear friend who was doing much better, but unfortunately, still laid up in bed. That night before going to bed, my friend who was visiting took my cigarettes and flushed them down the toilet, even though I had not picked up any patches yet. As far as she was concerned, a deal was still a deal. I am thrilled to say that I am still smoke-free all these years later, and that was doing it cold-turkey.

I do believe that dancers today are better educated in the area of health, even if only for the simple reason that in general, people are better educated. However, as a reminder, and for those who may not be aware of the dangers associated, I will quote a few facts and statistics. According to the American Cancer Society, "About half of all Americans who continue to smoke will die because of the habit. Each year about 443,600 people die in the United States from illnesses related to cigarette smoking. Cigarettes kill more Americans than alcohol, car accidents, suicide, AIDS, homicide, and illegal drugs combined."

Nicotine is a drug found naturally in tobacco. It is highly addictive—as addictive as heroin or cocaine. Over time, the body becomes both physically and psychologically dependent on nicotine. Nearly everyone knows that smoking can cause lung cancer, but few people realize it is also a risk factor for many other kinds of cancer, including cancer of the mouth, voice box (larynx), throat (pharynx), esophagus, bladder, kidney, pancreas, cervix, stomach, and some forms of leukemia. Smoking increases the risk of lung diseases, such as emphysema and chronic bronchitis, and for the first time, the U.S. Surgeon General has added pneumonia to the list.

Smokers are twice as likely to die from heart attacks as are nonsmokers. According to the American Heart Association, "Cigarette and tobacco smoke is one of six major independent risk factors for coronary heart disease that you can modify or control. Cigarette smoking is so widespread and significant as a risk factor that the Surgeon General has called it 'the leading preventable cause of disease and deaths in the United States.' Cigarette smoking increases the risk of coronary heart disease by itself. When it acts with other factors, it greatly increases risk."

There are over four thousand chemicals in tobacco smoke and at least sixty-nine of those chemicals are known to cause cancer. As I did promise to be brief, I would like to share one final personal story with you. I lost my father at a young age; I was only twenty. He was relatively young, only sixty-nine when he died after a long illness with both coronary disease, and cancer of the lungs and throat. As you can imagine, his final years were not merely as pleasant and peaceful as they should have been. He was in an out of hospitals and underwent radiation therapy that left him each time, feeling and looking much worse for it. If you've ever been through such a loss, you know how difficult and heartbreaking it is to watch someone you love suffer. God bless my mother who never left his side and took care of him until his last breath. My father, of course, always wanted me to quit smoking. As a matter of fact, when he first found out that I was smoking, he asked me to promise him that I would quit. My mother, who never smoked a day in her life, could not understand how I could continue smoking after watching what my father went through. I, being young and foolish, thought I was invincible; but lucky for me, I eventually smartened up. It might have taken me a while, but I did it and it means a lot to me that I did keep my promise to my dad.

Getting back to alcohol and drugs, as I mentioned earlier, I have seen a few unfortunate situations where both alcohol and drugs have cost people their jobs and careers. I want you to be extremely clear and understand the severity of such actions. So, in an effort to drive this home, I asked Dr. Baron to point out some of the physical complications you can suffer from a few bad choices. "Here's the thing," he said. "I hate to keep dwelling on the nutrition issue, but I want you to realize and recognize what not taking care of yourself from the onslaught does to you. There is a whole cascade of things that can go on, and that you subject yourself to as a liability for the way in which you think and the way you feel. I will give you an example; let's say that you did not eat well (the way we've suggested in this chapter) and you are exhausted, having given an exerting and dynamite performance. After the show, your friends want to go for a drink. You would like to join them, but you know that you shouldn't because you need to rest. Due to the fact that you are so tired and depleted from your day, you lose your sense of rational thinking and your discrimination as to what would be the right thing to do or not. Since you did not give your body the proper fuel that it needs to function optimally, you have depleted your system of all nutrients and neuro-chemicals—those required for proper nerve transmission and thought. Hence, you make poor decisions.

"Our decision-making is handicapped when we're tired or exhausted, even when there is just a remote shift in our state of mind; this is the worst time to make a decision. The best time is when we are fresh and sharp; this is when things fire off properly. You cannot push yourself physically and expect to give a pinpoint performance, when your body is depleted of its nutrients and basic needs. This is why I cannot emphasize enough as a preventative measure that you absolutely need a good, sound nutritional orientation and meal plan for each day."

The bottom line is, it all comes down to how you take care of yourself, and nutrition is an extremely important factor. Over the years, I have had the opportunity to work with dancers and artists of various backgrounds, and it is the conscientious dancer—"the new athlete or dancer," as Spencer refers to them, who have the edge. Dr. Baron and I discussed the fact that we have both seen in our respective lines of work the differences between those athletes and dancers who are much more conscientious and those who are not. Those who choose to lead a healthier lifestyle sustain much greater longevity in their careers. They avoid cigarettes and drugs completely and moderate their alcohol intake. They ensure optimum health by eating a nutritious and balanced diet, by keeping their fitness at the best possible level, and by working at keeping emotionally balanced. Those who unfortunately are not as conscientious and do not take care of themselves generally pay for it; they are often the ones who end up injured. In the end, it often costs them in time off, which can result in the loss of their job, or can sometimes interfere with them getting the next one.

Commit to yourself and your career by opting to make healthier, wiser, more informed choices. Let me remind you that it is never too late to get started on the road to a healthier lifestyle. If you are quite young and first starting out, you shouldn't have acquired many bad habits yet, thus it should be very easy for you to implement some good ones from the get-go. As Dr. Baron says, "You are to be commended on your interest in taking this preventive approach. When we are young, we tend to have the illusion that we are invincible; unfortunately, we don't learn how untrue that is until it is sometimes too late." And so I say it again: it is so absolutely important to be aware.

Dr. Baron gives the example of the new young professional athletes. "They don't take advantage of all that is available to them, not like the senior guys do. The new young ones often have that invincible attitude, and it's usually not until after their second or third year that they start succumbing to the thought that maybe they should be taking better care of themselves. As they start to get hit pretty hard, they begin to realize what is being demanded and expected of them. When the realization of all those long practices and having to be at peak performance all the time sets in, that's when they start to wonder, 'How do I duplicate this every day?' When you're young, you can get away with a lot, but it almost certainly catches up with you."

Once more, I will remind you of the analogy of our health pyramid and the importance of homeostasis—the perfect balance of our mental, nutritional and physical health. From the mixed examples that we gave, you can see the intimacy of all three areas. You see how easily our emotional state can be affected by stress, or a lack of proper nutrition, or proper rest. Or, how our physical strength can be affected, often weakened or depleted from the same things: stress, no rest, or a bad diet. Last, but certainly not least, our nutritional plan can be interrupted when we are emotionally stressed, physically exhausted, injured or ill. No matter which way you look at it, it's all the same, and the bottom line is that your nutritional, physical, and mental health must all be in proper balance.

Encore:
*When we are young we tend to have the illusion that
we are invincible; unfortunately, we don't learn how
untrue that is until it is sometimes too late.*

Dr. Baron Shares a Favorite Memory

I asked Dr. Baron, with all the various cast members from different Broadway shows, dance companies and musical revues that he has treated, if there was any one favorite story that stood out. Here is what he shared with me: "The story that I cherish the most was during *Cats*. It was funny because I had treated several of the actors before they put their costumes on. Then, during the show, this cat came running up to me. 'Doc, Doc, you need to check me. My throat is closing up on me and I can't reach my note.' I had no idea who this was under the costume. I asked her if I had already treated her and she said yes. Even though I was unable to diagnose as aggressively as I normally would, I went ahead and used what expertise I could. Meanwhile she was saying 'I have to get on stage; I have to sing. This is my main number.' I went ahead and adjusted her, and made sure that the mechanics of the spine were all adequate. I adjusted her further here and there to help loosen up some muscles. I worked on the lymph nodes of the neck and I made sure that all her ranges of motion were free. Once I was done she said 'Thanks Doc thanks, I'm feeling better already. Are you going to come out and watch me?' I said, I'd like to, so she runs me over to the stage manager and asks him if he can get me out to watch her number. He was on the phone and quickly said no, so I walked back to the green room with my tail between my legs. She darted off saying 'I'm so sorry but I have to go. I'm on.' Next, I feel a tap on my shoulder and it's the stage manager and he says 'I'm sorry. I was on the phone with the big wigs; I didn't mean to do that to you. Follow me,' and he takes off in a sprint. I'm running after him, and we're up and down stairs, through corridors and finally, we busted through the front doors. Next thing I know, I find myself at the very back of the house and I see the stage. With my wonderful vision, I see little tiny people on the stage, and all of a sudden, I recognize the cat that I just treated and would you believe, she goes on to sing "*the*" song *Memories*! I actually had tears in my eyes. Because I helped her, these people were able to have this beautiful emotional experience. It was absolutely breathtaking for me. I sat there quietly at the back of the house and a tear rolled down my face. I said to myself, 'This is what it's all about.' Afterwards, when I saw her and congratulated her on her performance, she was so thrilled she gave me a great big hug and said 'Thank you so much.' I had no clue whom I was treating at the time."

CHAPTER TWELVE

IN PERFECT BALANCE—MIND OVER MATTER

*Everything old is new again! Celebrity Cruise Lines' Century
dancers perform "I Get A Kick Out Of You."*

> *"The single most effective relaxation technique I know
> is conscious regulation of breath. Breath is the key to
> health and wellness, a function we can learn to regulate
> and develop in order to improve our physical, mental,
> and spiritual well-being." —Dr. Andrew Weil*

Much of the topic of mental/emotional health has been addressed in the
previous two chapters, through the intimate roll that it plays with both
our nutritional and physical areas. In this next section, I will address how
stress affects our daily lives and what we can do to help reduce it. In this
incredibly fast-paced world that we live in, where the demands of everyday
life seem to continuously become more and more kinetic, it is no wonder

that stress is so prevalent. There is good stress and bad stress. The truth is that what makes one tick and absolutely thrive could be the exact thing that drives another over the edge. Some people cannot exist without a certain amount of chaos in their lives; in fact, they can even thrive on it. What could be a thrill for one person could be an absolutely terrifying experience for another. For example, even something like a roller coaster ride, which, of course is intended to be fun, can be total exhilaration for one and complete terror for another. How about the stress of an audition? Absolute excitement, or physical illness from the anticipation?

If you weren't already, I am sure that by now, you are well aware that our mental and emotional health plays a huge roll in our overall well-being. Therefore, it is obvious that stress can be a huge contributing factor. Since everyone handles stress so differently, there is no one set way to control it. A great starting point is as simple as having a positive attitude over a negative one. Sometimes, all the best intentions cannot help us from feeling the negative affects of stress. If this is the case, then it will be paramount for you to find ways in which to reduce your stress. The following are twelve simple suggestions for natural alternatives to relaxation and stress reduction.

Exercise

Whether you want to burn some serious calories or do a long slow relaxing stretch, exercise is an excellent stress buster. From high energy and more intense aerobic-style workouts and gym sessions to the more relaxing Pilates, Yoga or Tai-Chi, it is simply a matter of taste and what works most effectively in helping you to relax and take a load off your mind.

Meditation and Breathing

Meditation has been around for thousands of years, and more recent scientific research in the United States has proven it to have many health benefits. It is a wonderful way to quiet and calm your mind. Properly done, it produces a deep state of relaxation. There are many forms of meditation; one should consider learning the practice from a professional. However, there are many simple ways to get started and reap the benefits of this state of mind, from focusing on a body part to focusing on your breath or a specific sound. It may not be easy initially to quiet your mind for long periods, but, as with anything, practice makes perfect, or in this case, practice makes *peace*. If you find your mind wandering, go back to your focus and do this as many times as necessary.

Take a Walk

Sometimes all you need is a little fresh air and a change of scenery. Take your pet for a walk through the neighborhood or go exploring some new territory. If you live by the ocean or near a beach, this can be a lovely and peaceful walk, when not too crowded. Invite a friend along, or go it alone if you prefer to just get lost in your own thoughts. This could be an opportune time to practice quieting that busy mind.

Laughter

Watch some re-runs of your favorite sit-com, rent a great funny movie, or find a comedy club. Laughter is one of the best forms of therapy! It has even been known to heal serious illness in some.

Spa Day

You can create your own home spa, or head off to your favorite retreat for a day of complete pampering. If you prefer the idea of the home spa, there's nothing quite like a hot bubble bath. Light some scented candles, add a few drops of your favorite aromatherapy oil, turn down the lights, close the door for a little privacy, and simply relax. You may want to get out the nail files, buffers, and polish, and add a manicure and pedicure. If you opt for heading off to the spa, then you should have a long list of treatments to choose from. How about a massage, a facial, or a body wrap? Set a budget, choose your favorites, and lavish in the indulgence.

Play with Your Pet

There is no greater way to de-stress than sitting and stroking a pet. Stroking a pet can actually help lower blood pressure. Playtime can be relaxing for you and fun for your pet. Therapy pets, or visiting pets, as they are sometimes referred to, are used for visiting patients in health-care facilities. These visits can help people feel less lonely and can heighten their spirits.

Hobbies

Hobbies are a great way to escape, and sometimes all we need is that distraction long enough to turn off our busy minds. Some people prefer quiet hobbies like painting or gardening, sorting through old photo albums, while others prefer more active hobbies like video games or sports. The idea here is to unwind, so any activity that helps you accomplish this is perfect.

Listen to Music

Why not make an evening of it? Choose some of your favorite music and kick back and chill to some cool tunes. You might want to check out some new artists, or some already familiar, to add to your IPod collection. If getting out sounds better, head over to one of your favorite music stores (that's if there are any left, unfortunately they are a dying breed) or check out the music department at your local library. Either way you can get lost in the endless selections, guaranteed for a few hours of entertainment.

Write in a Journal

Writing can be extremely therapeutic and relaxing, so how about setting aside a quiet hour, either weekly or several times a week if you can, to put some thoughts down on paper? There is no set way to keep a journal. You can keep a diary, you can use it for creative writing: poetry, song writing or story telling, or you might want to use it as a way of simply airing some thoughts that you want to get off your chest.

Read a Great Book

Try setting aside an entire afternoon or evening to escape with a good book. Chances are there's one that you've wanted to read. You may have some magazines piling up; why not settle in with a few of your favorites? Once again, if the idea of getting out is more appealing, head to your favorite bookstore or library.

Dinner and a Movie

Head off to your local Blockbuster or choose a few movies from home and make it a movie marathon. Invite a few friends if you like, or relax on your own. Either way, you can serve some popcorn and your favorite drinks, or create a full-on menu if you want to get lost in the kitchen for a while. Some people love to cook and use it as a wonderful way to just get away from it all. And, if you have that someone special in your life, bring out the gourmet in you and prepare a romantic candlelight dinner for two; then snuggle up for that movie.

Retail Therapy

I'm not sure how this one ended up last on my list, because it is by far one of my very favorite things to do, and ways to relax. Now I am not suggesting that you should break the bank or anything; what I am suggesting, however, is that if you like to shop, this can be a great way to truly forget about all your problems and get a natural high. The best news of all is that window-shopping can be just as effective. If you can afford to give yourself a budget for a purchase or two that's great, but it's not necessary. Studies have shown that shopping activates key areas of the brain, and releases a chemical known as dopamine which boosts our mood and makes us feel better. Just remember, you can have as much enjoyment from browsing and window shopping. No need to break the bank. After all, it's suggested for pleasure; we don't want any buyer's remorse when the high wears off.

Encore:
In order for us to have stability and balance in our health, we need all three areas—nutritional, physical, and mental—to be in balance.

CHAPTER THIRTEEN

No More Starving Artist—The Business of Being in "the Biz"

Style! "Smooth," Celebrity Cruise Lines' Mercury opening night

"Opportunity dances with those already on the dance floor."
—H. Jackson Brown, Jr.

I'm sure you've heard the age old question "What happens when you can't dance anymore?" Or how about those notorious opinions: "Dancers are a dime a dozen," "that's not a real career—you can't make a living at it," or "why don't you get a real job?" It's been said that there is a little truth in everything, so I'd like to take a moment and evaluate these "words of wisdom."

(1) Of course, there could come a day when you may not be able to dance anymore; this may be by choice or by necessity; however, whatever preparation you have done to plan your future will be a huge determining factor in where you find yourself at that time. Then would be a good time to put your other talents, education, or big savings account to work for you. (2) Dancers may not necessarily be a dime a dozen, but there

certainly isn't a shortage; at least not a shortage of female dancers. Male dancers will almost always find work. (3) Contrary to popular belief, this is a real career with oftentimes many more years of study than the average profession. It's not the easiest of professions, as we already know, but, yes, you *can* make a living at it; you can even make a very good living at it. You may not necessarily make millions, but then again, you could be the next Madonna. Although a legendary Recording Artist, Madonna started out like so many of you, as a dancer. She attended the University of Michigan on a dance scholarship for two years. She then moved to New York City to become a dancer, where she continued her studies with the world famous Alvin Ailey American Dance Theatre. One never knows what the future holds!

Encore:
Dancing isn't the easiest of professions, as we already know, but, yes, you can make a living at it; you can even make a very good living at it.

The "Business" of Being in Show Business

I'm sure that the concept of "starving artist" is not one that you aspire to. So let's get right down to business—the business of being in *show business*. I personally have never bought into that whole "starving artist" concept. Don't get me wrong—we have already established that you may not make a ton of money at it, and we've established that it is greatly about passion, and without passion, one shouldn't bother.

Are those not the perfect ingredients for the so-called "starving artist" role? Maybe, but not necessarily so? "For the love of the art" is huge in my books (I don't know of any other way); however, there is no reason why it can't be for the love of the art while earning a decent living at it. I made a decision when I was a young dancer first starting out that I was not going to live like a starving artist. I love the business, always have, and I have been very fortunate to have a great career doing what I love. But let's face it—at the end of the day, if you really couldn't earn a living at it, wouldn't you get another job or create a secondary means to earn a living, thereby negating the whole "starving artist" syndrome?

After all, wouldn't you be better equipped to truly do it for the love of the art if you created some financial stability? The truth is, there are different approaches one can take to do what they love. Is it really possible to have the best of both worlds: to work at what you love and create financial stability? Yes! By simply planning ahead, being intelligent about your business choices, and *dotting your i's and crossing your t's*, you can do just that, regardless of how much you earn. Just because you might not make huge amounts of money doesn't mean that you can't be financially savvy and create financial stability. And for the record, just because you love and enjoy what you do doesn't mean it's not a real job. If anything, this is the most envied position of all, and in my opinion, the only way to work. The most successful entrepreneurs of all, business moguls like Bill Gates (Microsoft Corp.) and Richard Branson (founder of Virgin) will tell you that first and foremost, you have to do something you love. Unfortunately, those who are not always supportive are often people who are not doing what they love and don't have the belief that it is even possible.

Encore:
I made a decision when I was a young dancer first starting out that I was not going to live like a starving artist.

You as a Business!

Your talent and the work that you get from having this talent are essentially your business. Just as you would when opening any new business, set yourself up with all that you need to properly operate your business. A good first consideration would be to have two separate bank accounts. Now I do understand that this may sound a bit over the top to you, but don't panic; it's simple and this will save you a lot of headaches later on. One bank account should be for your earnings (income from your business). From this account, you could pay yourself a salary and pay for your business expenses, such as marketing and training etc; your second account would be for personal expenses. If you learn to keep things separate early on, you will save yourself a great deal of stress, in general, but especially come income tax time. Getting advice from a good CPA (certified public accountant) who deals with entertainers or independent contractors predominantly can be of great value to you. In the meantime, a simple filing system can help keep you organized with your deductible expenses and save you the embarrassment of turning up at an accountant's office with shoe boxes or grocery bags full of receipts.

Although tax laws do change (hence the need for a good CPA), certain expenses that you incur for your business are allowable deductions against your earnings. For example: show make-up, rehearsal wear, training and education, transportation to and from classes and auditions, as well as memberships in industry-related organizations and show business or dance periodicals, are just a few of the deductions that may be available to you when earning a living as a performer. So make it a first rule of business to find out all of the various deductions available to you. Just a little groundwork and organization can go a long way.

Encore:
*Your talent and the work that you get from having
this talent are essentially your business.*

Be organized in all areas

Why stop at receipts and tax deductions? A simple filing system for all important documents will help keep you prepared for just about any situation or question that could come up. This system can be as simple as an accordion folder, a small filing cabinet or file box with individual folders in alphabetical order; no need to get complicated. Take into consideration all important documents that you might need to refer back to at a later date. Very important will be your bank account statements and artist engagement contracts, any union or association information, and, of course, all legal documents and any insurance policies.

Some monthly bills will fall into your tax deductible items and, therefore, should be filed under business expenses. Some accountants may even suggest a specific filing system that will simplify their process; thereby saving you money on those year-end accountant fees. If you like to keep a record of all your monthly expenses, even those non-deductible bills, I would suggest that you keep them separate, with other personal documents; this, of course, is entirely a matter of preference. Once again, these are merely suggestions to help you get organized; the sooner you start to create good habits, the easier it will be to stick to them and subsequently implement them in all aspects of your business.

In a survey conducted with twenty working performers, I asked what area of show business they would like to have known more about prior to getting into the business; 80 percent said they would like to have known more about the *business* of *being in the business*. Unfortunately, this is an area that is not usually taught in school or at dance classes. Although this material may not be quite as much fun or interesting, or for that matter even seem necessary to you, I assure you that if you read through it all and take in even just a few suggestions, you will be grateful later on. One of the biggest mistakes performers make is not to treat their careers as a business. Even worse, because we believe we are indestructible when we are young, and retirement seems a lifetime away, we tend to not worry about the future. The latter applies to the general public, not just performers. In order to be successful at what you do, you absolutely must treat your talent and yourself as a business. I hate to sound cheesy but, bottom line is this, if you don't take care of business, your business won't take care of you.

Aside from that file box, you will want a day timer/organizer so that you can keep track of all appointments, phone calls, auditions, classes, and any notes on contacts or upcoming events. Within your day-timer you should have a contact database, which can either be on your computer or in good old reliable written form. When soliciting agents or work, it's always a good idea to keep notes on every phone call you make. A quick note in the memo section of the individual's contact details, on the back of a Rolodex card or in your day-timer will help remind you of whom you spoke to on what date and any requests they may have made for promotional material. When sending out promotional material, keep a simple note as well with the date sent out and to whose attention. The next call you make to that person or company, you will be able to remind them of your last conversation and of any promotional material that you sent out.

> **Encore:**
> *The bottom line is this, if you don't take care of*
> *business, your business won't take care of you.*

Self-promotion a Necessary Evil

As for promotional materials, here are a few ideas to implement in addition to the standard photo and resume.

Promo DVDs

As mentioned in Chapter Six: Markets and Venues, some production companies and choreographers today will preview talent from a promotional DVD. In the event that you do not already have a promo DVD of yourself or your work, following are a few tips to assist you in creating one.

Promo videos should be kept short, somewhere between three to five minutes in length, and should show off your talent with the best possible footage. The quality of the footage is most important; you want it to be clear and you want to be easily identified. When it comes to hiring talent, everyone has different needs and specifics they are looking for. On rare occasions, you may be asked for something very definite; i.e., a particular style or technique, at which point you would send in only that which they are asking for. However, in general, it is a good idea to have a well-rounded compilation of your talent. Try to show as much versatility, as well as any special talents; i.e., tumbling, ethnic dance etc. Some performers find themselves in that frustrating situation of not being able to get good-quality footage of their performances. If this is the case, request permission from the producers and the choreographer to video tape small sections of your performance for editing and promotional purposes; otherwise, go into a studio and video tape yourself doing some of your own choreography. Keep in mind that you want to keep these pieces short, offer variety, and show off your versatility, and any of those special talents. This should be easy to accomplish. There is no need for it to be an extremely expensive ordeal. A good personal video camera can give you first-rate clear-quality footage, which is what you need, plus a good editor. Do your preparation in advance so that you know exactly what sections you want edited and save some time and money on the hours you spend in the studio with the professional editor. Ask around—you may have a friend with videography and editing abilities who is willing to help you out. Like many young talented people first starting out, you may have great footage of your recital or competition pieces. This is an excellent starting point. Simply have these pieces edited down so as to show your ability in a condensed presentation. Don't forget to ask your dance teacher or choreographer's permission, especially if this footage was from your personal recording and not sold to you by the studio. Many studios today make copies of year-end presentations available to their students, however, you should still obtain permission to use the footage for your own promotional use.

If you are a seasoned professional with a full library of videos to choose from, these same rules apply. Keep in mind that no one wants to receive or has time to view a half-hour or more of footage, and if they have to fast-forward and rewind, you can be almost certain they will lose interest or not bother at all. Some companies, due to copyright laws, will not accept full pieces; they will only accept edited versions. FYI, simply put, a choreographer owns the copyright to his or her work unless the work was created for another party as a work-for-hire. A work-for-hire means that the employer is paying for and intending to own all rights to the material created and the choreographer consents to give up his or her rights and ownership of the choreography. If a work is commissioned as a work-for-hire, it will be clearly stated in their contract. Otherwise, the choreographer owns all rights to their creation. Having said that, the copyright to the work will belong to someone (whether the choreographer or the producer), so make sure to get the proper permission to use it for your purposes.

Thank You Notes, Postcards and Announcements

Simple yet memorable ways to keep yourself in the auditioner's thoughts is to send out thank you notes after an audition or meeting, a simple email or even better yet, a thank you card via snail mail with a brief personalized note will do the trick. If you want to show a bit more "flash", you can have thank you cards or postcards printed with your photo to have handy for such occasions. Postcards can be multi-purpose: you can use them for thank you notes, and reminders or announcements of a special performance or showcase. Don't forget to include the name of the production, venue, date, and time. You may want to go the extra mile and print up special announcements which you can send out as a mass mailing for a specific event. These announcements could be for the purpose of publicizing a new gig, a special feature or an ongoing engagement. These are all relatively inexpensive ways to promote yourself and keep reminding people of who you are. Once again, I wish to remind you that if you want to have a long and prosperous career, you must treat this as a business. If *you're* not going to promote yourself, who is? As you already know, yes all of this can be done via email; and although some people may prefer to receive promotional materials this way, I think it just never hurts to add that personal touch with a short handwritten greeting. Due to the overwhelming amount of *spam*, more and more people are filtering and many have strong controls against unknown email addresses, so you really have no guarantee that your material will get to them. Good old snail mail is a sure way to make it to their desk. Getting a little creative with your mailer could also help you stand out. Remember, your potential employer probably receives a great deal of solicitation every day. Something different and eye-catching can keep you from ending up on the bottom of a pile.

Photo and Resume Updates

Of course, this one should go without saying, but it never ceases to amaze me how many people send out or turn up at auditions with old photos and resumes that have not been updated. With so many people today having access to personal computers and printers, there is no excuse at all for resumes not to be updated as needed. Yet another opportunity to initiate a great and easy habit, just that little organization can make the difference in presenting yourself in a professional manner. As for photos, make sure to keep them current; if you change your look, then you should change your photos. Turning up at an audition with short, dark, curly hair and a photo that shows a blonde with long straight hair wouldn't be very wise. A photo that looks nothing like you can be a mark against you. First of all, it can put someone off when they can't even recognize you by your photo, and secondly, it could give someone the impression that you don't care enough to stay on top of your business.

The Internet

The World Wide Web is without a doubt the Number One resource for so many people today. I will not go into specific details, as this is an ever-changing environment, but it's clear to see that it is a very important means of communication and marketing. In fact, according to "Internet World Stats" www.Internetworldstats.com as of March 31, 2009, 1.6 billion people use the internet.

Although we've talked about the internet sporadically throughout the book, at this point, I want to emphasize a few new ways in which you can utilize it, as well as re-iterate some of what we've already discussed. The Internet may be an old familiar friend or you may first be getting to know each other. Either way, you must not allow its overwhelming options to intimidate you in any way. You may want to consider taking an Internet course to help you along. Just take it one step at a time and remember that when it comes to self-promotion, all of the standard rules apply. Take in all that we have discussed throughout the book on presentation and professionalism and apply it to how you promote yourself on line.

One of the beauties of the internet is the ability to get yourself out there and reach a much greater audience in a quicker period of time. Here are a few ideas to help you promote yourself. Get to know your way around the Internet, and as with everything, check things out thoroughly. There are plenty of industry sites offering different resources so determine what your main objectives are and who your audience is; then start researching the various sites and what they have to offer you. You will want to check out the many casting and audition websites. Some offer free basic memberships with the opportunity to upgrade for a fee, while others are only available for a monthly or yearly fee. Some will allow you to post your resume and photo and video; others will post auditions and events, and some will do both. There are many dance organizations and publications that have been around for countless numbers of years that are now providing much of their information and services online. Every day there are new dance-related web sites and blogs being created and many of them are very reputable. What's hot today may not be the trend in a year's time, so as with everything, keep current, stay on top of what is happening and what is available to you on the Web, just as you would in the dance industry. When it comes to *social networks* such as *Facebook*, *Twitter*, and *My Space*, be intelligent about what you post. You may want to consider having a separate site for business purposes, and taking the time to educate yourself about ways to best protect your privacy.

Aside from promoting yourself on some of these established sites, you also have the opportunity to create a website of your own. Although this can be a costly endeavor, it doesn't need to be; again, know whom you are dealing with. Ask around to get some recommendations and then make sure that you have a contract which clearly states what you are getting for your money. A simple website with a few well-designed pages is all you need. Focus on your objective, which should be to promote your talent in the most professional presentation. Your headshot, resume, and biography should be standard pages. In addition, you should consider having a page for your promotional DVD, and if you have a good collection of performance and or portfolio photos, you can create a photo gallery. Regardless of whether you create your own website or simply a few promo pieces to send out, put on your public relations hat and use your imagination. The key here is to market and sell yourself, so get creative and have some fun. It's never been easier!

One final reminder—follow up is very important, so whether emailing a link to your website or attaching promotional pieces, it's always a good idea to follow up to make sure that they received your material. Today, we live in a much faster-paced world, and many business people are more prone to use email than telephones. However, some may still favor the old-fashioned way of doing things and prefer to speak to a live person. Either way, keep this in mind when making contact, and respect their preferred form of communication. If you choose to make a phone call, and if the person is not available, you can always leave a message. Just don't necessarily expect a return call. Although I will touch on agents a little later, I will mention that when dealing with agencies specifically, they will most likely have submission instructions on their website, and will often state if they do not take phone-calls. If so, please respect their instructions. You don't want to get off on the wrong foot (definitely not a smart move for a dancer) or be perceived as annoying.

Encore:
You are your own best promotion; promote yourself in a good light!

Contracts and Agreements

I have on many occasions sat down with entire casts and read through their contracts as a group. Believe it or not, for some, this was the first time they were actually reading what they had signed. I remember years ago when opening my first bank account in Los Angeles, the bank manager was shocked that I had read the paperwork before signing it. He commented that in all his many years in the banking industry, he often witnessed people sign their name without reading a single word. Okay, now that might be a bit extreme, but the point that I want to make is simple. If you don't read what you sign, you don't have a clue as to what is in the document, so what recourse could you possibly have after the fact? I'm sure you've heard "read the fine print." To begin with, read the entire document thoroughly, and make a note of anything you do not understand. You will want to question and have these points clarified for you. It is always an excellent idea to have someone well-versed in legal jargon read through it with you, or for you. This could be a parent, your agent, a mentor, a family friend, or business acquaintance. Of course the best case scenario would be if you had access to a lawyer.

If there is anything at all that needs clarifying by the producers or employers, make sure to have your list ready and go over it with them. As I've said throughout this book, always be respectful and courteous; any legitimate business person should respect you for your attention to detail and desire to understand fully what you are signing. Never sign a contract that you do not understand fully. Once you are clear on all the clauses you must then decide, if you haven't already, whether or not this contract is right for you. If there is anything that you are absolutely not willing to accept or live by, you must give this serious thought and consideration prior to agreeing. Some situations have room for negotiation while others don't. Be intelligent and diplomatic about your approach and you will quickly be able to determine whether you are on friendly ground or not. If there is no negotiation to be had, then once again I reiterate: Determine what you will or will not accept and either sign on the dotted line and uphold your end of the agreement or graciously decline. Don't get caught up in the excitement of landing the gig and lose sight of the details of the contract. Don't waste a potential employer's time. The worst thing you can do is walk into what you feel to be a compromising situation and then not fulfill your end of the deal. You will not only upset a few people and possibly leave yourself labeled; you could cause a great deal of expense for your producers and an enormous amount of work for your entire cast and production team if you were to leave your contract early. I stand behind integrity: if you are not going to be happy, be honest with yourself up front. Don't compromise yourself, the show, or make someone else's experience less than ideal. Once you have signed, you're in for the long haul. Your main objective should be to fulfill your end of the deal with an outstanding performance and a great attitude, and most importantly, to be that talent that your producers would want to hire again. It should go without saying that the same goes for the hiring party; the employer must also hold up their end of the deal.

My number one reason for ensuring that all my cast members have read through and understand their contracts fully is simple: it is to both of our benefits. When I am hiring talent, I expect that if you sign your name to something, you will stand by your word. I want to ensure that you know what you are getting yourself into and you know what will be expected of you. This way, I have the comfort of knowing that we are all on the same page and I can expect great things from you.

Encore:
*I stand behind integrity: if you are not going to be
happy, be honest with yourself up front.*

Representation—Agents and Managers

Artist representation, talent agents, and managers have been around forever. "Dance Agents," however, really came onto the dance scene back in the mid 80s and have been growing in popularity ever since. Today's dancers most likely don't even know of pre-agent days. Having an agent can introduce you to an area of the market and producers that you may otherwise never get to know. Many production companies like the ease and efficiency of going through dance agents for their casting calls as the agents can pre-screen and take all the guess work out of who might turn up at such auditions. This is a real comfort for a production company and can also be a huge savings in time, money, and frustration. The cost to the producer is a simple 10 percent or 15 percent commission added on to the dancer's salary. There may be certain occasions where the commission could come directly from you, if the producer and agent do not have a special agreement or working relationship.

There are many benefits to having such representation working on your behalf. As previously mentioned, many auditions and castings will be closed to agents' lists only, and short of successfully crashing an audition, if you are not on an agent's list, you will not get past the sign-in. Agents pre-screen so you will get called for parts for which you are the right look and fit. Agents can be very instrumental in helping to groom you for the business, as they can point out strengths and weaknesses, often offering advice on how to best prepare for auditions, as well as your career, in general. Agents negotiate your contracts, ensure you get paid, and stay on top of working conditions.

There are, of course, some production companies who still prefer to go it alone, preferring the old-fashioned way of handling their auditions and casting needs. These companies will post their notices and hold their own open calls, as I discussed earlier in Chapter Six: Markets and Venues. So although you may have greater exposure with an agent, don't fret if you haven't landed one yet. While you do not have representation, you will still have plenty of resources for finding work. I outlined earlier the many ways in which you can find work. Now I will discuss how to find an agent.

Not unlike finding work, dancers seeking representation should submit photos and resumes with a cover letter, and demo reels when requested, to the various agents. Agencies hold auditions on a scheduled and regular basis. Talent having submitted their photo and resume might get an invitation to a set audition being held by the agency or to a class at which their agents will be scouting. There may or may not be a callback, and you could be signed on the spot or called at a later date. Either way, once approved, you will be called in for orientation. Most important, I re-iterate to you be courteous, respectful, and professional. Just as an employer doesn't want to deal with a diva or "problem child," nor does an agent. Ultimately, they need to know how you will perform for their client. You want to put your best foot forward and be viewed as a positive addition to the agency and any production company they introduce you to.

Los Angeles, and more recently New York City, are home to the majority of dance agents. You will find that some are bicoastal and some have offices in other major cities in the United States. Following is a list of such agents that you may want to investigate further and consider when you are ready to submit. Most agencies prefer submissions by mail or email and many will clearly state no telephone calls. Most have websites where you can go to learn more about their requirements for submissions. They will give detailed information, sometimes with a specific contact, pay close attention to their requirements. If there is no contact name listed, write on your package Attention: Dance Dept. and you may want to add "New Talent Submission." You want to ensure that your package gets into the right hands. Other major cities that are not necessarily known for their dance agencies will still have a long list of talent agencies that you can investigate. You will want to determine if these agencies have a performing arts or theatrical division that handles dancers. If so, as with all the above recommendations make sure to submit a cover letter with your photo and resume. It seems redundant to say, but make sure that all your contact details are on your cover letter, your resume, and on your photo. In the event that your photo was to get separated from your resume, it is a good idea to have a label on the back of your photo with contact details. The following is a list of some of the most well known agencies.

Los Angeles

ACME Talent and Literary Agency
www.acmetalentandliterary.com
Main Tel: 323-524-0001

> Adult Commercial and Dance Dept.
> Talent Works
> 3500 West Olive Ave., Ste. 1400
> Burbank, CA 91505
> Tel: 818-953-7850

> Youth Commercial and Theatrical Division
> Michael Greene & Associates
> 190 N. Canon Dr., Ste. 200
> Beverly Hills, CA 90210
> Tel: 310-550-9333
> For other depts., please visit their website.

Bloc
www.blocagency.com
5651 Wilshire Blvd., Ste. C
Los Angeles, CA 90036
Tel: 323-954-7730

CESD Talent Agency
www.cesdtalent.com
10635 Santa Monica Blvd., Ste. 130
Los Angeles, CA 90025
Tel: 310-475-2111

Clear Talent Group
www.cleartalentgroup.com
10950 Ventura Blvd.
Studio City, CA 91604
Tel: 818-509-0121

DDO Artists Agency
www.ddoagency.com
6725 Sunset Blvd., Ste. 230
Los Angeles, CA 90028
Tel: 323 462-8000

Kazarian/Spencer/Ruskin & Associates
www.ksawest.com
11969 Ventura Blvd, 3rd floor
Box 7409
Studio City, CA 91604
Tel: 818-769-9111

McDonald/Selznick Associates Inc. (MSA)
www.msaagency.com
MSA Los Angeles
953 Cole Ave.
Hollywood, CA 90038
Tel: 323-957-6680

Schiowitz Connor Ankrum Wolf Inc.
1680 N. Vine St., Ste. 1016
Hollywood, CA 90028
Tel: 323-463-8355

Trio Talent Agency
www.TrioTalentAgency.com
1502 Gardner St.
Los Angeles, CA 90046
Tel: 323-851-6886

New York

Bloc NYC
www.blocnyc.com
Attn: NEW TALENT
137 Varick St., 6th floor
New York, NY 10013
Tel: 212-924-6200

CESD Talent Agency
www.cesdtalent.com
257 Park Ave. S., Ste. 900
New York, NY 10010
Tel: 212-477-1666

Clear Talent Group NYC
www.cleartalentgroup.com
325 W. Thirty-eighth St., Ste. 1203
New York, NY 10018
Tel: 212-840-4100

DDO Artists Agency NYC
www.ddoagency.com
224 W. Fourth St., Ste. 200
New York, NY 10014
Tel: 212-379-6314

Kazarian/Spencer/Ruskin & Associates
www.ksawest.com
Media Arts Building
311 W. Forty-third St., Ste. 1107
New York, NY 10036
Tel: 212-582-7572

McDonald/Selznick Associates Inc. (MSA)
www.msaagency.com
MSA New York
140 Broadway, 46th floor
New York, NY 10005
Tel: 212-858-7549

Schiowitz Connor Ankrum Wolf Inc.
165 W. Forty-sixth St., Ste. 1210
New York, NY 10036
Tel: 212-840-6787

South East

Bloc South
www.blocsouth.com
749 Moreland Ave. SE, Bldg. C-201
Atlanta, GA 30316
Tel: 404-622-4116

XCEL Talent Agency: Atlanta
www.xceltalent.com
PO Box 191731
Atlanta, GA 31119
Tel: 404-808-6546

South West

DDO Las Vegas
www.ddoagency.com
DDO Artists Agency Las Vegas,
5015 W. Sahara, #125–221
Las Vegas, NV 89146

Encore:
*Not unlike finding work, dancers seeking representation
should submit photos and resumes with a cover letter, and
demo reels when requested, to the various agents.*

UNITED WE STAND—UNION OR NON UNION?

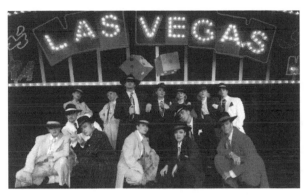

Meet the family. "Rock This Town," Las Vegas Then and Now, Celebrity Cruise Lines' Century

"I grew up with six brothers. That's how I learned to dance—waiting for the bathroom." —Bob Hope

One's career can often begin with non-union work; undeniably, there is a lot to be said for our hometown training ground—the many dance recitals, showcases, fashion shows, local cabarets, night club performances, or dinner theatre. Where you are living, and what entertainment markets are strongest in that area, can determine the type of work you do. Some dancers will make entire careers out of non-union work, while others will never know what it means to work non-union. I believe that becoming "union" is an ultimate goal of most aspiring professional dancers. Much of the best work is union. Broadway, film and television, many trade shows, industrials and conventions, as well as many community and regional theatres fall under union jurisdiction. Even some theme parks and specific cruise contracts may fall under union jurisdiction. Now, that's not to say that there isn't any great non-union work out there. There is plenty, much of which I spoke about in Chapter Six: Markets and Venues. There are many great producers and production companies whose work happens to be mostly in non-union circles and venues.

It really comes down to where you ultimately want to work, and in what capacity. When I say *in what capacity*, I mean that some of you may choose careers in different areas of the industry, such as stage management, costume or scenic design, make-up artists, stylists, etc. There are unions and associations for performers, directors, writers, stage hands, and designers alike. Answering two questions—(1) Where do you want to work? and (2) What capacity do you want to work in?—will help you determine your ultimate goal, and, therefore, will help you determine the smaller goals necessary along the way.

Following are unions in the United States as well as the Canadian and British Actors' Equity. First, I will list unions that pertain to you as a performing artist—dancer, actor, and singer. Next, I will list unions that relate to other career paths, within the entertainment industry; i.e. the technical, production and/or creative areas. I suggest that you visit their websites and learn more about them. Even if these are not your chosen career paths, you can learn a great deal about the industry, and some of the people you will be working with, and working for. Their websites will teach you about their history, who their members are, what they offer, and so much more. The following descriptive information is information gathered from the unions' respective websites and approved by a representative from each of the unions described below, the information is reprinted with their permission. I have not written about those unions which I was unable to contact directly. However, I have listed them with website addresses to further assist you in your own research.

Encore:
Some dancers will make entire careers out of non-union work, while others will never know what it means to work non-union.

Actors' Equity Association (AEA)

AEA or "Equity," as it is known, was formed in 1913. It is the labor union that represents more than 47,000 Actors and Stage Managers in live theatre in the United States. Equity has offices on the East Coast (in New York City and in Orlando), on the West Coast (in Hollywood), and a central office in Chicago. Equity negotiates wages and working conditions and provides a wide range of benefits, including health and pension plans, for its members. Actors' Equity Association is a member of the AFL-CIO, (The American Federation of Labor and Congress of Industrial Organizations), which is a voluntary federation of 56 national and international labor unions, and is affiliated with FIA (The International Federation of Actors), an international organization of performing arts unions. To learn more about Equity or how to become a member, you can visit their website at: www.actorsequity.org.

Actors' Equity Association
National Headquarters
165 W. Forty-sixth St.
New York, NY 10036
Tel: 212-869-8530
Fax: 212-719-9815

Canadian Actors' Equity Association

Canadian Actors' Equity Association (Equity) is the professional association of performers, directors, choreographers, fight directors (one who coordinates stage violence, he works directly with the director) and stage managers in English Canada who are engaged in live performance in theatre, opera and dance. Equity supports the creative efforts of its members by seeking to improve their working conditions and opportunities. The business of Equity is to negotiate and administer collective agreements, provide benefit plans, information and support, and act as an advocate for its membership. To learn more about Equity or how to become a member, visit their website at: www.caea.com.

Canadian Actors' Equity Association
National Office
44 Victoria St., 12th Floor
Toronto, Ontario, Canada
M5C 3C4
Tel: 416-867-9165
Fax: 416-867-9246

British Equity

British Equity is the only Trade Union to represent artists from across the entire spectrum of arts and entertainment. Formed in 1930 by a group of West End of London performers, Equity's membership includes actors, singers, dancers, choreographers, stage managers, theatre directors and designers, variety and circus artists, television and radio presenters, walk-on and supporting artists, stunt performers and directors, and theatre fight directors.

The main function of Equity is to negotiate minimum terms and conditions of employment throughout the entire world of entertainment. Looking to the future, they also negotiate agreements to embrace the new and emerging technologies. Satellite, digital television, new media and so on are all covered, as are the more traditional areas. In addition, they also operate at an international level through the Federation of International Artists, the International Committee for Artistic Freedom, and through agreements with sister unions overseas. To learn more about Equity or how to become a member, visit their website at: www.equity.org.uk.

British Equity
Head Office
Guild House
Upper St Martins Lane
London, England, UK
WC2H 9EG
Tel: + 020 7379 6000
Email: info@equity.org.uk
Fax: + 020 7379 7001

The American Federation of Television and Radio Artists (AFTRA)

The American Federation of Television and Radio Artists (AFTRA) is a national labor union representing over 70,000 performers, including dancers, journalists and other artists working in the entertainment and news media. AFTRA's membership includes an array of talent—sound recording membership includes artists who bring pop, rock, country, classical, folk, jazz, comedy, Latin, hip hop, rap, and R&B to the world. AFTRA members perform in television and radio advertising, nonbroadcast video, audio books and messaging, and provide their skills for developing technologies such as interactive games and Internet material.

The union negotiates and enforces over 300 collective bargaining agreements that guarantee minimum (but never maximum) salaries, safe working conditions, and health and retirement benefits. AFTRA was the first industry union to establish employer-paid health and retirement plans for members and their dependents that qualify. With more than 30 local chapters across the country, AFTRA promotes the success and welfare of members in a variety of ways, including contract negotiation and enforcement, advocating on legislative and public policy issues, supporting equal employment opportunities, and sponsoring or supporting health and retirement benefits and programs. For more information, visit www.aftra.com.

AFTRA
New York National Office
260 Madison Ave.
New York, NY 10016
Tel: 212-532-0800
Fax: 212-532-2242

AFTRA
Los Angeles National Office
5757 Wilshire Blvd. 9th Floor
Los Angeles, CA 90036
Tel: 323 634-8100
Fax: 323-634-8194

American Guild of Musical Artists (AGMA)

American Guild of Musical Artists, founded in the 1930s, is the labor organization that represents musical artists in opera, concert, and dance. Soloists and choristers, dancers, choreographers, stage managers, and stage directors are all part of AGMA.

AGMA is in business to protect performing artists. They negotiate contracts, called collective bargaining agreements, which provide guaranteed wages, standardized working conditions, rehearsal and overtime pay, regulated work hours, vacation and sick pay, resolution of disputes, and protection against discrimination and abuse in any form.

They enforce the contracts and assure that their collective bargaining agreements provide for health insurance, pension coverage, and protection against unreasonable working conditions and unsafe work places. For more information and to learn how to become a member of AGMA you can visit their website at: www.musicalartists.org.

AGMA
Head office
1430 Broadway, 14th Floor
New York, NY 10018
Tel: (212) 265-3687
Fax: (212) 262-9088

Screen Actors Guild (SAG)

Screen Actors Guild is the nation's largest labor union, representing working actors. Established in 1933, SAG has a rich history in the American labor movement, from standing up to studios to break long-term engagement contracts in the 1940s, to fighting for artists' rights amid the digital revolution sweeping the entertainment industry in the 21st century. The Guild exists to enhance actors' working conditions, compensation and benefits, and to be a powerful, unified voice on behalf of artists' rights.

With 20 branches nationwide, SAG represents nearly 120,000 actors who work in motion pictures, television, commercials, industrials, video games, Internet and all new media formats. SAG is a proud affiliate of the AFL-CIO. To learn more about SAG or how to become a member, please visit their website at: www.sag.org.

SAG
Hollywood - National Headquarters
5757 Wilshire Blvd., 7th Floor
Los Angeles, CA 90036
Main Switchboard 323-954-1600
for Deaf Performers Only: TTY/TTD 323-549-6648
for SAG Members outside Los Angeles 1-800-SAG-0767
For information on the SAG contract involving dancers, please contact:
SAG National Dancers Department
Tel: 323-549-6864
Fax: 323-549-6460

Society of Stage Directors and Choreographers (SSDC)

The Society of Stage Directors and Choreographers is a national independent labor union representing members throughout the United States and abroad. SSDC has jurisdiction over the employment of Directors and Choreographers working in the following areas: Broadway and National tours, Off-Broadway, The Association of Non-Profit Theatre Companies, New York City (ANTC), League of Resident Theatres (LORT), Council of Resident Stock Theatres (CORST), Dinner Theatre (DTA), Regional Music Theatre (RMT), Outdoor Musical Stock (OMS) and Non-Equity Tours. For more information on SSDC or to learn how to become a member, visit their website at: www.ssdc.org.

SSDC
1501 Broadway, Ste. 1701
New York, NY 10036
Toll free: 800-541-5204
Tel: 212-391-1070
Fax: 212-302-6195

Directors Guild of America (DGA)

The Directors Guild of America represents nearly 14,000 members working in U.S. cities and abroad. The DGA represents Directors, Unit Production Managers, First Assistant Directors, Second Assistant Directors, Technical Coordinators and Tape Associate Directors, Stage Managers, and Production Associates working in film, television, commercials, and new media. The Guild seeks to protect directorial teams' legal and artistic rights, contend for their creative freedom, and strengthen their ability to develop meaningful and credible careers. For more information, visit their website at: www.dga.org.

The National Writers Union (NWU)

The National Writers Union is the trade union for freelance and contract writers: journalists, book authors, business and technical writers, web content providers, and poets. It has approximately 1,700 members in sixteen chapters nationwide. The NWU works to defend the rights and improve the economic and working conditions of all writers. For more information, visit their website at: www.nwu.org.

International Association of Theatrical Stage Employes, Moving Picture Technicians, Artists and Allied Crafts of the United States, Its Territories and Canada (IATSE)

IATSE was originally chartered by the American Federation of Labor as the National Alliance of Theatrical Stage Employes in 1893. They still, to this day, keep the Old English spelling of Employes, not Employees, as you see in their title. Since its birth, it has grown to include not only the original stage hands and projectionists, but a great variety of other crafts persons in the numerous branches of the entertainment industry, including motion picture and television production, product demonstration and industrial shows, conventions, facility maintenance, casinos, audio-visual, and computer graphics. It is the largest labor union in the entertainment and related industries, boasting over 110,000 members. For more information, visit their website at: www.iatse-intl.org.

IATSE General Office
1430 Broadway, 20th Floor
New York, NY 10018
Tel: 212-730-1770
Office of the International President
Fax: 212-730-7809
Office of the General Secretary-Treasurer
Fax: 212-921-7699
www.iatse-intl.org

United Scenic Artists Local USA 829
(Affiliated with IATSE since 1999)

United Scenic Artists, Local USA 829, is a labor union and professional association of Designers, Artists and Craftspeople, many whom are world famous, organized to protect craft standards, working conditions and wages for the entertainment and decorative arts industries. The members of Local USA 829 are Artists and Designers working in film, theatre, opera, ballet, television, industrial shows, commercials, and exhibitions. The current active membership totals over 3,300. For more information visit their website at: www.usa829.org.

United Scenic Artists
29 West 38th St., 15th Floor
New York, NY 10018
Phone: 212-581-0300
Fax: 212-977-2011

Writers Guild of America, West (WGAW)   www.wga.org

Songwriters Guild of America (SGA)   www.songwritersguild.com

American Federation of Musicians (AFM)   www.afm.org

As mentioned previously, not all these unions will be relevant to you specifically; however, there is a wealth of information to be had. I hope that you will take some time to peruse the various websites listed and take advantage of the opportunity to educate yourself further about these different aspects of the entertainment industry. By visiting these websites, you can learn a great deal about the entertainment industry's history, and the great strides that have been taken to secure some of the bylaws and standards that we enjoy today.

Artist and talent exploitation has always, and continues to be, an issue. Our industry, like so many others, needs protection, not just from the outside, but sometimes from within; from those who unfortunately lack principles and respect for their profession and their peers. Regrettably, they often make decisions that have an adverse affect on the entire industry. As I just spoke of in the last chapter, "No More Starving Artist," always remember integrity first and foremost. I implore you to consider very carefully every move you make along your career path, you never know how your actions and decisions will affect not only your own outcome, but that of others. If you are going to blaze a trail, let it be the high road!

Thanks to the courage and efforts of those who chose way-back-when to come together and stand united, and the many people who have joined the cause along the way, today we have unions that continue to work on our behalf, making their voices, *our voices*, *heard*, where it matters most.

Encore:
If you are going to blaze a trail, let it be the high road!

CHAPTER FIFTEEN

MONEY MAKES THE WORLD GO ROUND
—YOU ARE YOUR BUSINESS

Let me tell you a story. "Minnie the Moocher," Celebrity Cruise Lines' Mercury

"Money isn't everything—as long as you have enough of it."
—Anonymous

I will preface this next section by saying, I know that some of what you are about to read in this section can all seem a bit over the top, especially if you are first starting out in your career, making a pittance of a salary. I'm sure you are thinking, "Why on earth do I want or need to know about all of this finance stuff?" Perhaps you already know about it, in which case you don't need to read this chapter at all, but to those of you who, like most of us, no matter what age, can use some sound advice about money matters, there is much to learn in this chapter.

Although it can be a bit overwhelming, don't panic; this information is for your edification and simply to help you recognize the importance of securing your financial future starting *now*. This is one area you do not want to be clueless in!

The Big Scary F-word "Finances."

"While it's never too late to start financial planning, thinking ahead when you're in your 20s and 30s can pay you very large dividends in your 60s and 70s and probably beyond. The earlier you begin to put money away (even in small amounts), invest it for the long term, and know how to protect it, the more you'll have when you need it, or want it." Kenneth M. Morris, Virginia B. Morris, and Alan M. Siegel, *The Wall Street Journal Guide to Planning Your Financial Future.*

Terry Fay, Financial Strategist of Fay Financial Group, in Orlando, Florida, was kind enough to offer his expertise as a financial advisor and indulge me and allow me to pick his brain so that I could offer you some sound financial guidance. Terry walked me through a typical meeting with a first-time client. He calls it, "Three Steps for Rainy Days and Opportunities." Protection—Savings—Investments.

Encore:
The earlier you begin to put money away (even in small amounts), invest it for the long term, and know how to protect it, the more you'll have when you need it, or want it.

Step one – Protection

Protection is absolutely imperative to each and every one of us.

Terry says, "*Always protect first.*" Let's take a look at some of the ways in which you might protect yourself.

Renters' Insurance

For example, if somebody is renting, they will want to have renters insurance. Of course, if any of you are homeowners, then you will be familiar with and have a homeowner's insurance policy. You might be thinking that you can't afford this extra insurance or that you don't have anything worth insuring. Often, when someone is first starting out and may not have that many belongings, they put less importance on their need for such insurance. However, what Terry points out is that in the unfortunate event of a fire or burglary, you could lose everything. He reminds us, "These belongings are possessions that you have collected and accumulated over years—goods that you may have purchased as you could afford them. When we're young and first starting out, we don't always have the luxury of purchasing everything that we need all at once, so you may have purchased these items on sale or maybe even from a garage sale." Many of us have had family members help us out with a bedroom set from Uncle Lou, a sofa or a dinette from Mom and Dad—you get the idea. The point is very simple: if you were to lose all your belongings in such an unfortunate event, you would have to replace them all right away. You wouldn't have the great luxury of waiting for the "great deals" again. Having such an insurance policy is not only sensible, it should be a priority. First of all, it's very inexpensive and believe me, you will be thrilled that you did it, if God forbid you ever need to file a claim.

It will be very important for you to have an inventory of your belongings; you'll need this proof for your insurance company in the event of such a misfortune. You must have a detailed recording of all of your personal belongings and valuables; this can be in the form of a list on paper and photographs or on DVD/Video. Either way, you'll want to ensure its safe keeping by storing it in a safety deposit box or someplace other than your home. If there was a fire at your home, this would be the last place you would want your proof to be.

Assets and Liability

Terry goes on to say that "We want to protect our assets and we want to protect our earnings from liability in the event that you were ever to get sued by someone. You wouldn't want all that you've worked so hard for to be taken away in a lawsuit, and, of course, the more money you make, the bigger the target you could be. So initially, the struggling artist first starting out may not be a very big target if something were to happen. However, as you become more successful and assets are accumulated, then you need to protect yourself with an umbrella policy or some other protection strategy. A financial advisor can help you develop such a plan. Some products are protected completely or in part (depending on what state you live in) from lawsuits. Those include life insurance, annuities, and government retirement plans."

For those of you who are considering owning your own business such as a school, a production company, or an agency, you will want to incorporate.

Some specialty performers who book themselves out as individual acts may also prefer to work under a corporate entity. When you are ready to consider taking this step, you should speak to a financial advisor who can assist in devising a strategy that will be most relevant to your situation and for protecting your assets.

I would like to take a moment to address the young artist first starting out. The idea that we want to get across is the importance of sensible habits. Thinking ahead and educating yourself about the value of such protection is all a part of developing and instilling these habits. Let's face it, as an artist, you must have discipline. Just as you must be regimented in your training and performance, it is equally essential to have strong business acumen. Even if at this moment, you don't think that you need liability insurance, we simply want you to be aware of it so that when you do need to protect yourself, you will know what to do.

Auto Insurance

Terry gives a great example. He says "Imagine that you were the cause of a car accident and you're in a courtroom about to be sued for some undetermined amount of money. How much protection against a lawsuit would you want to have from your insurance company? Most people would want the maximum protection available because unfortunately, you just don't know how much you could be sued for. This is a good guideline to use when purchasing insurance. Often young drivers purchase the very minimum requirements, and the obvious problem with this is that in the unfortunate event of an accident, you could find yourself under-protected. Some required minimums are so low that they don't even cover the cost of replacing a vehicle." The amount of coverage you choose is certainly up to you in the end. "However, you absolutely should consider more than the state minimums. You will also want to make certain that you have proper protection in the event that the other party does not. For example, if you were hit by someone who did not have proper insurance, you would make a claim against your own insurance company through the uninsured and underinsured motorist coverage. This would replace any damages to you." As the laws can very from state to state in the United States, and certainly from country to country, you will want to seek proper counsel in this area. "A general rule of thumb in property and casualty coverage," says Terry "is one times your assets or twenty times your income. For example, if somebody makes fifty thousand dollars per year, twenty times their income would be one million dollars. If someone harms another and causes them to lose a job, they can be sued and in some states, their wages can be garnished. What you want to do is to protect yourself and your earnings against such a lawsuit."

Disability Insurance

"Disability insurance replaces your income in case you cannot work because of sickness or injury," Terry points out. "All athletes can, and the smart ones do, purchase disability insurance because unfortunately, all it takes is one accident or injury—a twisted ankle—and they are out of the game; a serious injury can cost them their career." As with athletes, disability insurance is equally as important to big-name entertainers. There are companies that specialize in underwriting entertainers. You can be certain that every big name singer has their voice insured, just as every big name dancer should have their legs insured. After all, this is the foundation of their business and without an able body, they have no business, and, therefore, no income.

Medical Insurance

There are many different types of policies available. If you are traveling a lot, you may want to consider an international policy where you are covered in any country in which you might be traveling and performing. Otherwise, a standard policy for your country of residence should suffice. Travel insurance may also be a way to cover your medical needs when traveling for a contract. Different countries will offer different policies, and there are many options available. Once again, seeking the correct counsel is always extremely important.

Wills and Trusts

This is an area that we naturally do not give consideration to when we are young as it is often unfamiliar and may seem unnecessary. I have said throughout the book that when we are young, we have a tendency to believe that we are invincible, and, therefore, why would we even be concerned with such needs?

Terry explains that Wills and Trusts are vitally important to you, the artist, especially if you have children. It is of equal value and will be very significant to any parents of young artists reading this material on their behalf. Terry is adamant in saying that, "It will be extremely important to have the guardianship for your children established." He stresses the importance of ensuring that you have Trusts and various other legal devices set up so that in the event that your children do make it big, and in the unforeseeable misfortune that something were to happen to you, the parents, your children would be protected from all of the vultures trying to get at the money. These legal documents are invaluable and must be set up by a good attorney and reviewed on a regular basis.

Life Insurance

Life insurance is designed to replace lost income. Terry uses the example of a runaway truck causing a fatal accident: "I guarantee that the survivor would look to sue the truck company. The purpose of such a lawsuit is to replace the income that has been taken away from the family. Let's look at a different scenario: If someone has a heart attack in the middle of the night and suddenly dies, the end result is the same for the family, but there's no truck company to sue. This is where life insurance comes into the picture; it should replace the full economic life value of the victim, roughly about twenty times their income. The purpose of life insurance is not to pay off the mortgage, although some people do; its real purpose is to replace lost income and the deceased person's economic value.

If the deceased was a stay-at-home parent, there may not be any lost income; however, there is economic value which needs to be replaced. Suddenly, there could be the need to hire a nanny or a housekeeper or both, to carry on the duties of the lost parent; this is an economic value that is often overlooked. To lose a parent or a loved one is a horrible tragedy, and it would be a travesty to also have the children's dreams vanish because of something that was not taken care of; something that is so simple and easy to obtain such as life insurance.

"Oftentimes, young and single people think that because they are not married or don't have children, they do not need life insurance, but the reason a young person needs to consider purchasing life insurance early is to lock in their future insurability. The truth is no one needs life insurance; people want it, but nobody needs it. There may come a day when you decide that you want life insurance, maybe once you are married. However, if somewhere along the way, you were diagnosed with an illness that rendered you uninsurable, you would then find yourself in the unfortunate situation of not being able to purchase this life insurance at a later date. Unfortunately, these are some of the things that we never think of until it's too late." If you are young and considering life insurance, Terry suggests that you also include a rider to your policy that allows you the option of purchasing more life insurance in the future on a guaranteed basis without the need for medical underwriting (this means without the need for further medical examination). For example, if you were to become ill with cancer, yet survive it, you would now have this illness on your record. Even though you went on to be healthy, without this rider, you would either be uninsurable or unable to get additional coverage, whereas with the rider, you could at certain intervals add more coverage without the need for any evidence of insurability. This is a wonderful feature to have.

Another critical rider to have is called waiver of premium. "Basically, what happens is this," explains Terry. "If the insured were to become disabled and no longer able to work, and therefore not able to pay the insurance premium, then the insurance company would pay the premium for them. Let's use the example of a whole-life insurance policy that builds equity in cash value. If the policy holder suddenly became disabled, the insurance company would make those premium payments on their behalf for the rest of their life. Thirty years down the road, they would have equity built up, the policy would have cash value, and the insured would still have a little bit of savings. Chances are that any retirement plans and savings accounts would probably have come to a screeching halt. And, of course, without working for all that time, their insurance policy with cash value would be their only asset that had continued to grow."

Encore:
Always protect first!

Step Two – Savings

"Once your protection has been analyzed, the next step is savings. You and your family are, in fact, and must be considered, your Number One priority and the most important bill you pay. Therefore, you should be trying to allocate 15% of your gross income to your own personal savings plan. In the beginning, most of that money should be going into a completely separate savings account for those rainy days and opportunities. This way, should a sudden unforeseen rainy day come along, you will have the money set aside, whatever the emergency. Whether the air conditioner goes or the car breaks down, there is no additional stress and there's no credit card payment at the end of the month with hefty interest to worry about. It is simply taken care of through your savings account."

Let's take a look at the opportunity side of having this savings account. What if the prospect of buying into a business or investing in a great piece of real estate came along? How about an associate who would like to open a theatre or start a new troop? You just never know what opportunities might be available, and as Terry points out, "Cash is always king in tragedy and opportunity. To have the cash in the bank is huge. How much cash? The ideal plan would be to have 50% of your gross income in liquid cash."

Terry says that people often react unfavorably at the thought of setting aside 15% or even 10%. They just don't see how it's possible. He then asks his clients how they would react if their boss were to come to them suddenly one day and explain that the company was downsizing, but that they could keep their job if they took a 10% decrease in salary. (This may not be completely foreign to performers. It has happened on occasion and sometimes with new works first trying to get off the ground, where a producer might ask a cast to help save the production by taking a little less salary and thereby helping to guarantee the longest run possible.) Inevitably, in Terry's example, the clients always reply that they would find a way. They would just have to make it work, so he suggests why wait until there's a down-size to figure it out? "Why not figure it out now and set aside that 10% or 15%, if possible, for your own needs? This way, if you ever were hit with a down-size or other emergency, you would be prepared for it."

We understand that to go from never having saved, to 10% or 15% in your first year of work or first attempt at saving, can seem rather overwhelming, so start small and move incrementally. After all, our ultimate goal here is to instill the habit of saving and be successful at it. So be realistic. What can you commit to and stick to? Terry suggests that "you can start out with as little as 1%, and then every six months, add another percent until you reach your ultimate goal. You will be surprised at how well you do and how quickly it adds up. The truth is that when you commit and make it a habit, you don't miss it and you don't spend it. Just keep it very simple. You can have a savings account attached to your checking account and have it automatically programmed to transfer a set amount over on a specific day every month. The key here is making the whole thing systematic, so it's easy and it happens all the time. All you have to do is write it in your checkbook register and you won't even notice it missing."

Encore:

Our ultimate goal here is to instill the habit of saving and to be successful at it. So be realistic. What can you commit to and stick to?

Step Three—Investments

"After you are in the habit of putting 15% into savings, (or whichever percentage you have determined feasible and realistic), and you have successfully set aside at least six months worth of savings, then the next step is investing. Obviously, the more you can save, the better off you'll be and the quicker you will get to your goal of 50% liquid cash. Liquid cash means those investments that do not go up and down in value; it means investments that are safe and guaranteed—cash that you can get to and access instantly when an opportunity comes along. As examples, your savings account and any cash values in life insurance policies. These are your more conservative investments; you know that your money will not fluctuate and it will be there when you need it. Money Market Accounts are also considered conservative; however, although marginal, it is possible for them to lose value. The next tier of risk would be Mutual Funds; these may be more attractive to some. The cash is liquid; however, they can lose value.

"If somebody is making one hundred thousand dollars per year, then 50% in liquid cash would mean that fifty thousand should be available in cash." Now, using this same example of a yearly income of one hundred thousand dollars, let's consider how long it could take you to reach your goal. If you were to save the ideal 15% per year, it would take you just over three years to have that 50% cash available, and that would be just from your savings alone. That wouldn't include any additional investments that you might have made along the way.

"Although the ideal plan is 50%, for some that could be more or less. Start by putting your 15% into your savings account and allow it to build until you reach your goal of 50% liquid cash; from there you can go into long-term investments. You see tragedies never happen tomorrow or ten years from now; they always happen today and, unfortunately, we're never ready for them. This is why cash and protection are very important. This simple plan allows us to protect against those unexpected things that happen suddenly."

Terry goes on to say that, "Most of the time, people have it backwards. They usually start by planning for things that may never happen thirty years from now, all the while leaving their families completely exposed in the present. So first and foremost, protect and save for *today*. Then you can start planning for thirty years from now for your long-term plan and investing strategy. At the point where you have reached a comfortable amount in your savings (remember the ideal goal is 50% liquid cash), then your 15% savings can start to go into other investments such as mutual funds, individual stocks, bonds, bond funds, and real estate."

Encore:
Liquid cash—investments that do not go up and down in value; it means investments that are safe and guaranteed—cash that you can get to and access instantly when an opportunity comes along.

Learning and Instilling *Good Habits* in Three Simple Steps:

The following information is based on a plan that Terry has laid out in order to help you identify the simplicity of creating good habits with these three easy steps.

Learning this information is not enough; it's putting it all into practice and then owning it (for the rest of your life) that will make the difference.

Knowing what good habits are and making them a part of your life are two completely different things. In order to learn these habits and make them work for you, we are going to suggest you follow these three steps: step one—create a budget; step two—consider your values, and step three—be willing to make changes.

> **Encore:**
> *Knowing what good habits are and making them a part*
> *of your life are two completely different things.*

Step One—Create Your Budget

First and foremost, identify how much money is coming in; it is essential to know how much you are making. Earlier we addressed how extremely important it is to treat yourself as a business and your earnings as your business income. Next, you should identify how much is going out. Pay yourself a salary to carry you through the ups and downs and live on that set amount of money just as you would if you had a regular job with a regular paycheck every week or two. From this salary, you will want to set aside your determined percent for savings. In addition to, or as a part of your overall savings, you may want to include a "Splurge Fund" and a "Long-Term Savings Fund." The Splurge Fund amount and frequency should be determined in advance, and then you must stick to it. The Splurge Fund could be for that little something special, while the Long-Term Savings could be for bigger, more extravagant purchases, such as new furniture, a vacation, or even a home.

The additional money, over and above expenses and savings, should remain in the business for those times when you are not earning a steady salary or don't have any business income. As you may have already experienced, or if you are first starting out, you will most likely soon learn that there are financial highs and lows that can come from the lack of steady gigs. In the entertainment business, you are sometimes employed in long-running gigs, while other times, you will find yourself doing "one-off's" or "one-nighters." These could be corporate engagements or television shoots, as an example. Then there could be the most dreaded time of all, when there is no work. Of course, an equally important consideration is the differences in the financial compensation you might be paid; sometimes you are making great amounts of money and sometimes you are earning much less. Because of such inconsistencies, this is all the more reason to get a grip on your spending and savings habits. It will be extremely important to be meticulous in the area of budgeting. If you take this advice, you will have secured a steady availability of cash when a low point comes along. The additional money from your more prosperous jobs will pay your bills during those leaner months. Essentially, what you will be doing is creating a stable situation for yourself from what could otherwise be unstable. Good habits are absolutely critical to securing finances, in general, let alone being a performer with sporadic work and pay. Remember, the point to all of this is *no* "starving artist."

Taxes

If you are not working as an employee, you may want to consider putting aside a separate savings for your taxes. In some cases, you'll be considered self-employed and in the United States, you will be issued a 1099 form at the end of the year. This is a tax form that you will receive from any company that pays you over a set amount for work performed within that tax year. This means that you'll be responsible for paying your own taxes. It is always a good idea to have that money set aside in the event that you owe the Internal Revenue Service come April 15th. This way, you are prepared; no surprises. A tax accountant and the IRS may advise you to pay the IRS in quarterly payments so that you do not get hit all in one go. This may or may not be necessary. If this applies to you, your accountant can give you an estimate based on your previous year's tax return. He or she will estimate what you might owe and break it down for you into four quarterly payments.

Rough Spots

There will be rough spots; there will be hiccups along the way, and it is absolutely to your advantage to be prepared for them and not be surprised by them. You must have a financial back-up plan in place so that when they do come (and trust me, they do come), you're not back to a mattress on the floor and eating *macaroni and cheese.*

Look ahead to your future. Wouldn't it be great to know that if you wanted to make a change—whether to change careers entirely or to reinvent yourself within the industry—you could be in a strong financial position to do so? Long-term savings can help you by affording you the opportunity to take a hiatus while you decide what it is you want to do. Or, it can be the funds which you invest in either retraining or educating yourself in a new field. Last, but not least, it might be the capital you need to start your own business. This could be something entirely new and different or it could be something dance-related, such as a dance company, a school, a theatre, an agency, or maybe a production company. If you decide that it is time for a change, but you are not prepared for this day, you could find yourself at a major and difficult crossroad.

Here are some tips and considerations when writing your budget:

There are four main categories to laying out a budget. Within each of these four categories, you will decide what is discretionary and what is not discretionary.

a) The first category is *fixed expenses*; these are the ones that don't change from month to month, like your rent, your mortgage payment, or your car insurance. These are your fixed expenses and they are fixed non-discretionary expenses.

b) The second category is *fixed discretionary expenses*. These are also our expenses that do not change from month to month, like a cable TV bill, or a housekeeper, but they are discretionary expenses you choose to have.

c) The third category is *variable expenses*. These are the ones that are probably going to be different every month, like the utility bill, gas bill, or groceries.

d) The fourth category is *savings*. What amount will you allocate to set aside regularly, commit to and stick to?

BUDGETING TIP

Here's a great tip when it comes to budgeting. Understand this: the goal of retail stores is to have you make a purchase once you are in the store, so advertising is designed to lure you into the store. If you find yourself considering a purchase, and in that very moment, you feel you have to have it, *don't buy it*! Wait forty-eight hours; this will serve as what we have called the cooling-off period. When you find yourself with credit card in hand justifying the purchase, then you know this is a good indication that you probably shouldn't make this purchase in the first place. First ask yourself, "Do I need this for my business? Is it absolutely necessary, or is it just a pride thing?" There's a fine balance between keeping up the image and satisfying your ego. Second, you will want to ask yourself, "Do I need this on a personal level or is it just for fun and something that I merely want, not that I really need?" There's nothing wrong with something just for fun or splurging once in a while, it would just be wiser to do so when you have the *Splurge Fund* saved up.

Set a goal of a certain dollar amount and when you reach it, you can reward yourself with a special purchase. This could be something you've had your eye on for some time or a special shopping spree. That way, when you walk into the store, you know you can afford it and you don't have to question or justify it. Best of all, there is no credit card statement and no interest on top of it. By keeping a Splurge account, these purchases become rewards instead of regrets.

Encore:
Set a goal of a certain dollar amount and
when you reach it, reward yourself.

Step Two—Considering Your Values

The approach you take to budgeting will be based on your priorities. Some will choose to go at it in baby steps, while others will want to jump in head-first and take a more aggressive position. Terry points out that "It all goes back to a person's values: what is in their heart, what is important to them in their life, and where they ultimately want their life to go." He says, "Identifying those values first is critical, because they define who you are, they motivate your financial goals and, in turn, they will be the catalyst for change." Changing your behaviors will be necessary if the lifestyle you desire is different from the one you are presently living. On the other hand, if it's not broken, don't fix it!

Consider what it is that you desire most and aspire to. Make a list of your values, and then choose the top three which are most important to you. Does the lifestyle you desire align itself with your values? From this, you will be able to determine the necessary changes. Don't be short sighted! Keep your eye on the prize.

Encore:
The approach you take to budgeting will be based on your priorities. Some will choose to go at it in baby steps, while others will want to jump in head-first and take a more aggressive position.

Step Three—Make That Change

Here are a few examples of how you might make some changes. Terry explains, "For example, if financial security is a value to you, then you may need to rethink your spending habits if they are keeping you from having the emergency fund that would give you the feeling of more security. You might choose not to have cable TV because although it may be fun at the time, it could be keeping you from saving and accomplishing your long-term goals."

Those little extras that you might be able to live without could make the difference between having that safety net or not. Remember those unforeseen situations like a show closing early, or down-time in between gigs. You might want to rethink purchasing a few discretionary items that you might not miss.

You should think of it like having a crystal ball. If you could see into your future, what would you want to see? Where do you want to be in one, ten, or thirty years from now? The answer to that question then becomes the motivating factor for choosing more carefully, creating better habits and making positive changes.

Encore:
Those little extras that you might be able to live without could make the difference between having that safety net or not.

Get a Grip

At the end of the day, we all know that we can talk ourselves into just about anything we want; we can be experts at the justifying game. And on that note, Terry says, "get a grip." The biggest problem is this, "Many people just don't get it! They don't have a handle on how much is going out, so when they get to the end of the month and they have more bills to pay and no money left, they wonder what happened to all the money. So first and foremost, create that budget, know what's coming in, and know what's going out.

"Secondly, identify what your values are. What is important to you and what are the expenses in your budget right now that are keeping you from living the life that you really want?

"Thirdly is change, and that is the hardest part of the whole process. 'Change is scary,' most people would say, but the truth is change can be great! And you must remind yourself that without change, you will not reach your ultimate goal. Ask yourself 'Who am I? Where is it that I want to be?' Then look at how you're spending your money, and if it doesn't match up with your ideal vision, you have to make a change. What if you have children and you want to make sure that they grow up with financial security, no matter what the circumstances are, whether you're here or not? If that is important to you, then you need to have life insurance plain and simple. So if the Movie of the Month Club membership is keeping you from paying fifteen dollars a month for a life insurance policy, then you need to ask yourself which is more important, the Movie of Month Club or life insurance?"

Terry reiterates: "There are only two ways to create financial security. One, you can either reduce your expenses, or two, increase your income." So you need to sharpen your pencil and cut back on a few extras, or if you like the lifestyle you have and do not want to cut back, then you need to work a little harder or smarter and create some additional income.

And so there you have it, the three steps to creating good habits. If you would like to, and think you can implement all the changes that you want to make in one shot, that would be great. However, if you would rather focus on one change per month, go ahead and do just that. For some that's easier. Remember, your goal is success, so implement the necessary change in a schedule and manner that you know you will commit to and stick to.

Sound financial advice is invaluable; talk to friends and family who use financial advisors and can share their experiences with you and check out Terry Fay's website at: www.FayFinancialGroup.com. (Securities & Investment Advice offered through G.A. Repple & Company, A Registered Broker/Dealer & Investment Advisor. Member FINRA & SIPC. 101 Normandy Road, Casselberry, FL 32707 407.339.9090.)

> *"Open your arms to change, but don't let go of your values"*
> **~ Dalai Lama**

THE GRAND FINALE—SUMMARY

Take a bow. La Cage, Blue Angel, New York City

"Dance like no one is watching." —*Mark Twain*

As I look back over all the years that I have spent in the entertainment industry, I can honestly say that I wouldn't change any of it. Let me explain: Who I am today is a culmination of all that I have experienced and the many people who have touched my life along the way. Some moments, as you've already heard me say, have been incredible, while others were tough lessons, but, nonetheless, all worth it, for without them, I might be headed down a different road entirely; one that might or might not have included some of my favorite moments and favorite people. Sometimes, we merely cross paths with people—sometimes we tag along for a while, and then other times, we find those few gems that we collect along the way. The ones that we hold onto, never to lose touch with; they are the precious few with whom we may be blessed to share a lifetime.

My intention for writing this book was to fill a void that I have felt and seen time and time again. Through my work and many of the talented people who have worked with me, I am constantly reminded of how tough and often times discouraging, even overwhelming, this business can be. For someone first starting out, for someone a little less confident or shy, or for someone who simply may not have had the encouragement along the way, it can be so very intimidating, even downright scary.

And yes, it can be all of that, but the key is to expect it, accept it, and move through it. Just as Susan Jeffers says in *Feel The Fear And Do It Anyway*, (one of my all time favorite reads) "Pushing through fear is far less frightening than living with the underlying fear that comes from a feeling of helplessness."

I do know from my own experiences in the entertainment industry that the material in this book can be absolutely invaluable to you. These words of wisdom and knowledge that I share with you are lessons that I have learned along the way, some through personal experiences and others from my mentors. Many are the exact lessons that countless dancers and other artists repeatedly tell me they wish they had known before starting out. So, I hope that you will refer to this book often. I hope that you will use this guide when you need to revisit a specific topic, such as preparing for your audition or signing a contract, and I hope that you will pick it up when you need a simple reminder. Most of all, though, I do hope that you will pick it up when you need a little encouragement.

I wanted more than anything for this book to be comprehensive and insightful, motivating and inspirational. I know that if you pay attention to the lessons in this book and put them into practice, you will be very well prepared for this sometimes scary, often crazy, but totally *amazing* business of show business.

Okay, let's recap:

Born to Dance

Why do you want to dance? Remember the question? I asked this of you at the beginning of the book. I believe that within you is the key to your own success—the road map to your future—and knowing this is half the battle. The next step is simply tapping into it.

First, there's introspection, the art of becoming in touch and in tune with oneself. Next, focus: you must have peace with your conviction so that nothing can deter you. You must be in complete harmony with your big picture. You must visualize it, own it, breathe it, and live it! When you want something so badly and you know *why*, then you will be truly empowered! Your path will become undoubtedly clear.

Encore:

I believe that within you is the key to your own success—the road map to your future—and knowing this is half the battle. The next step is simply tapping into it.

Goals, Dreams, and Commitments

Goals and dreams are the energy of life; and commitment is the outlet through which that electricity turns into reality. Our goals and dreams help fulfill us; they fuel us and drive us to great accomplishments. In other words, what moves you is what gets you there, and your passion is the fuel that propels and then keeps you going headed straight toward your ultimate goal.

When you have passion, everything else falls into place. Everything that is required seamlessly comes together. They all go hand in hand. Hard work, dedication, and commitment all come effortlessly when you know where you are going. Nothing is too difficult when you want something badly enough. When you know what you want and why you want it, then there is only one thing left to do, and that is to *just go for it*!

So, what is your ultimate destination? Be very clear about where you want to end up. Don't worry about how you are going to get there; just define what that final destination is, how it looks and how it feels. The clearer your picture is, the more specific each goal can be along the way. Are you prepared to do everything you possibly can, and then some, to get to where you want to go? Are you willing to break down walls to get to where you want to be? If you have talent and the kind of passion and conviction that it takes to persist, even when rejection is staring you in the face, then you *will* succeed.

You must never lose sight of your ultimate goal and you can never compromise your integrity. The road may sometimes be hard and long, but stay the course. You'll get there and it will be so much more gratifying when you do.

Our journey in dance is no different than the dance of life itself, and if you treat life like the great opportunity that it is, you will find so many moments worth celebrating, even those once believed to be wrong turns. The truth is that often a "wrong turn" is the exact turn you needed to take at that moment to get to where you ultimately needed to be. You just didn't know it at the time.

Take every opportunity in life to build a solid foundation, because you are going to need it. When the going gets rough, as it can, you will want that foundation to be strong enough to hold you up. As we all know, things don't always happen perfectly or exactly as planned, so when you take a left turn and you think you should have taken a right, or if you are somehow slowed down along the way, just remember that there is a reason for it all. Take each one of those stumbling blocks and turn them into building blocks.

Imagine if you turned every little upset into a positive step toward your end result. Wouldn't the road naturally seem shorter? Wouldn't it be brighter? Wouldn't you enjoy your journey so much more? Always stand firm in your convictions, especially in those moments when you feel a bit discouraged. Try to remember the old Japanese proverb "Fall down seven times; get up eight." The bottom line is, no matter how many times you fall down, the only way to make it is to get straight back up again—and again and again.

Encore:
Imagine if you turned every little upset into a positive step toward your end result. Wouldn't the road naturally seem shorter?

Mentors and Inspirations

Be grateful for those who touch and influence your life. Learn from others and their experiences. Be sure to recognize and acknowledge your mentors. Gratitude is food for your soul. When choosing a mentor, consider those qualities that you aspire to.

What do you admire in others? What do you want out of your career and life? Who in the business do you respect? What qualities of theirs do you most admire? Look for mentors with those similar characteristics—those that define who you want to be, and how you want to live your life. And most important, don't ever compromise your integrity.

Encore:
Be sure to recognize and acknowledge your mentors.

Attitude Spelled D.I.V.A.

Speaking of integrity, this would be a great time to remind you of that all too important attitude. It all comes down to this simple phrase—respect for yourself, respect for show business, and respect for the people within the business.

When you come from the right place, and by that, I don't mean where you grew up; I mean when you come from a good place in your heart, when you have the right intention, and you go about your business with integrity and respect, you *will* find your way. A friend and business acquaintance, a very talented songwriter, has a great but simple saying: "You will find your people." They're not all going to be *your* people. Not everyone fits together and that's okay. Don't worry about it; just move on. You will find your people—those who just make sense in your world. They understand you and your needs and you understand them and theirs. When you find them, you will know.

Let's face it—all the right attitude in the world isn't a foolproof guarantee that you won't any real jerks along the way. But the right attitude will help you bounce back when you do. It will make you more resilient and, therefore, hurt a little bit less. And besides, if we never met any jerks, how could we be sure we'd recognize the good guys when they came along?

The truth is that the right attitude is a key ingredient in all that you do, not only in your career, but in life. Attitude is at the very core of all decisions; it is often responsible for how we do things, and how we view what is done to us. So often, a simple shift in attitude is all we need to change the outcome of a less favorable situation or at the very least, our perception of it. Very important for you to remember, is that a fabulous look and all the technique in the world is not going to guarantee you work if you have the wrong attitude. It may initially get you the gig, but if your attitude spells Diva (and not the kind we often admire), then it's only a matter of time before you are found out, or you burn yourself. In the end, no one wants to work with a Prima Donna!

Encore:
Not everyone fits together and that's okay. Don't worry about it; just move on. You will find your people—those who just make sense in your world.

Triple Threat

Let's revisit training and the importance of being a triple threat. It goes without saying that technique is essential; however, versatility is such an important quality to possess—it is what often helps you seal the deal. The more versatile you are as a dancer and performer, the more you have to offer, the more work you will be suited for, and, therefore, the greater your chances for a full and well-rounded career. Proper training and technique will also help you to prevent injury and, thereby, ensure longevity in your career. Of course, accidents do happen, but a well-trained dancer will be in tune with his or her body and take all the necessary measures to ensure a healthy and able body.

On that note, I implore you to take your health seriously. Without your health, you cannot have longevity. If you don't take care of your health, it will come back to bite you, usually in the form of injury or illness. Proper nutrition for a healthy mind and body will help you to prevent such setbacks. A fine-tuned, healthy mind and body will also help you with early detection of any potential injuries or illness. When we are at our optimum health, we are much more in tune with what is going on inside our bodies and, therefore, we can feel the slightest of inconsistencies and/ or ailments. Remember Dr. Baron's health pyramid. A solid understanding of our nutritional, physical, and mental health, and the intimacy which they share, will save you a great deal of heartache down the road, not to mention other aches and pains.

> **Encore:**
> *The more versatile you are as a dancer and performer, the more you have to offer, and the more work you will be suited for, and, therefore, the greater your chances for a full and well-rounded career.*

Markets and Venues and the Business of it All

The dance world and the entertainment industry in general, cover a very large scope of possibilities, as I previously pointed out in Chapter Six: Markets and Venues. One of my intentions in writing this book was to help educate talented people about the many possibilities available to them, and to plant a seed about the importance of the business aspect of all that we do. As for the business side of our business, I will remind you simply of this: treat your talent and what you do with that talent as a business, plain and simple. And if you use the business chapters in this book as a constant refresher for yourself, then I can guarantee you that you will save yourself a headache or two.

As we all know, the truth of the matter is that not everyone can be, or necessarily wants to be, the next Broadway sensation or film star. So if this is not in the "stars" for you, then what is? This is where once again, you need to ask yourself a few key questions. If your dream is not ultimately to perform, yet you aspire to a career within the dance industry, there are many capacities in which you can work. You must first determine a few things. Here are some questions you might want to ponder. Are you a natural born teacher or leader? If so, maybe teaching dance or producing is what you are looking for. Are you the innovative type? Do you have your finger on the pulse? Do you know what is happening and hip before the rest of the world has even clued in? Are you the next trend setter? Trends come and go in dance as they do in everything else. Maybe you are extremely creative and have a natural-born talent for choreography. Maybe you envision yourself with your own dance company, or choreographing for stage and film. Do you have a great vision for the big picture? Do you see the story unfold in your mind's eye? As I asked earlier, do you prefer to be behind the scenes? The options are endless and it all comes right back down to tapping into your resources.

Who are you? What makes you who you are, what makes you tick, and what are your most important values? Now consider all that you aspire to in your career. Does it align with who you are and most importantly, does it align with your values? I believe that the key to living a good life and living it to the fullest, all begins with that list of values. At the end of the day, will you truly be happy if your integrity is compromised or your values are not supported by all that you do?

Encore:
As for the business side of our business, I will remind you simply of this: treat your talent and what you do with that talent as a business, plain and simple.

Audition & Performance

My last recap is a favorite topic—audition and performance—very simply because, *performance is what it's all about!* Why do you dance? You have got *to love it*, and so, if you love it, then you must always let your audience know. No matter who that audience is, whether at an audition, whether before a full house, or whether before two lonely ticket holders, they deserve your best performance and you should never cheat yourself or your audience of this. I say it again; *don't ever throw away a performance—not one single performance ever.*

Appreciation for the art of dance and the talent you've been given is a must. There is so much in life to be grateful for, and especially when, in life, you have been so privileged as to fulfill your dreams and have a career doing what you love. Always remember that to dance for a living, is a privilege like no other. Despite the many ups and downs you may encounter in the business, it is a *great* business, full of exciting moments and people.

We all have heard many times that life is what we make it. As I look back, I feel very fortunate for the life I've led, bumps and all! And as I look ahead, I know that I do not want to, nor will I leave, one stone that interests me unturned.

As I have said repeatedly, this is your journey. How do you want it to unfold? Shoot for the moon and land on the stars. With a bit of faith, a bit of luck, a lot of passion, hard work and determination, you can create the life that you want. And with the right attitude and plenty of gratitude, you can truly enjoy the process. So, as Mark Twain said,

"Dance like no one is watching."

Encore:
Shoot for the moon and land on the stars.

EPILOGUE

My inspiration, my strength, my mother

---

*"Scratch the skin of any artist and you'll find
a spiritual seeker; when artists resonate to that aspect
of themselves, they do their best work."*
—Shirley MacLaine, in her book <u>Out on a Leash</u>

I started out this book by sharing with you the gratitude that I feel toward my mother, who did all that she could so that I might have this life and career in dance. I'm sure that when I was nine years old, first starting out, she did not consider that this would be my career, but was merely a mother giving her daughter an opportunity to do something that I loved.

What she did was encourage me every *step*— and I do mean literally— of the way, and when she saw the talent that I had and how much I loved it all, she encouraged me more. She always taught me to do what I loved and to go for all that I wanted in life, truly supporting every dream and empowering me, whether she realized what she was doing or not.

My hope is that this book will inspire you to dance, and answer your questions while helping you on your journey. I hope that it will encourage *you* every step of the way. Cherish the process for there is so much wonder and knowledge to gather along the way. And, *break a leg*!

Encore:
*She always taught me to do what I loved and
to go for all that I wanted in life,
truly supporting every dream and empowering me,
whether she realized what she was doing or not.*

May your journey be rich with opportunity and experience! Whether you dance your way through it, choreograph it, write it, design it, arrange it, or produce it, give it everything you've got, do it with integrity, and do it with *Style*.

If you'd like to share your own inspiration, or if you have any questions or comments, I'd love to hear from you.

Please visit our website at www.inspiredtodancethebook.com or feel free to contact me at: info@inspiredtodancethebook.com.

References

Celebrity biographical information

Bio: www.biography.com

Internet Movie Database: www.imdb.com

People: www.people.com

Tune, Tommy. *Footnotes: a memoir.* New York, NY: Simon & Schuster, 1997

College research

Dance Magazine's College Guide 2006/07 New York, NY: Macfadden Communications Group LLC, 2006

Everett, Carole, J. *Peterson's College Guide for Performing Arts Majors 2009.* Lawrenceville, NJ: Peterson's a Nelnet company, 2008

Everett, Carole, J. *The Performing Arts College Guide 3rd Edition.* New York: Macmillan, 1998

FAFSA: www.studentaid.ed.gov

Finance information

Morris, Kenneth, M. *The Wall Street Journal Guide to Planning Your Financial Future.* New York, NY: Lightbulb Press, Inc. and Dow Jones & Co., Inc 1998

Health, fitness, and nutrition

2006. *British Journal of Sports Medicine;* 40:700-705 BMJ Publishing Group Ltd

American Heart Association: www.americanheart.org

American Lung Association: www.lungusa.org

Ban Trans Fats: www.bantransfats.com

Health, fitness, and nutrition (cont.)

British Association of Sport and Exercise Medicine: www.basem.co.uk

Dr. Andrew Weil: www.drweil.com

The National Fragile X Foundation: http://www.fragilex.org

The Mayo Clinic: www.mayoclinic.com

The Rader Eating Disorder Program: www.raderprograms.com

Miscellaneous

World Casino Directory: www.worldcasinodirectory.com

World Intellectual Property Organization: www.wipo.int

Internet World Stats: www.internetworldstats.com

U.S. Copyright Office: http://www.copyright.gov

New York

Gordon, A.L. 2007 To Live & Give In L.A., *The New York Sun*. NY vs. LA: Exploring the Differences. Page 11

Internet Broadway Database: www.ibdb.com

The Broadway League: www.broadwayleague.com and www.livebroadway.com

Theme Parks

Cedar Fair Entertainment Company: www.cedarfair.com

Six Flags Inc: www.sixflags.com

Valhouli, Christina. The World's Best Amusement Parks. *Forbes.com*

Unions

Actors' Equity Association: www.actorsequity.org

American Guild of Musical Artists: www.musicalartists.org

British Equity: www.equity.org.uk

Canadian Actors' Equity Association: www.caea.com

Directors Guild of America: www.dga.org

IATSE: www.iatse-intl.org

Screen Actors Guild: www.sag.org

The American Federation of Television and Radio Artists: www.aftra.org

The National Writers Union: www.nwu.org/nwu

United Scenic Artists Local USA 829: www.usa829.org

About the Author

Mande Dagenais

Synonymous with Style, Mande Dagenais' work as a Director/ Choreographer and Producer has been appreciated by millions of people around the world. Her career has spanned over twenty-five years, seventy production shows and four continents. Standing ovations from sell-out audiences and accolades from universal stars have been customary throughout Mande's tremendous career.

At age fifteen, she began working professionally as a teacher and choreographer. At nineteen years of age, she co-founded "The Dance Academy" in Northern Ontario where she further demonstrated her love for teaching and nurturing talent. Mande's professional show credits include twelve years as resident Director/Choreographer of the world famous musical revue, *La Cage Aux Folles*, Los Angeles, and *La Cage* productions worldwide. *The Tonight Show* starring Johnny Carson, *A Celebration of Legends* with Milton Berle and Tom Bosley, Caesar's Palace, The Fountainbleau Hilton, and three years as Choreographer for Deerhurst Resort, are some of Mande's early career credits.

As the owner of Mande Dagenais Productions and ADC Entertainment Inc., Mande has produced corporate events for clients such as: Amoco Corporation, Umbro International, Walt Disney Special Events Group, Ford Motor Company, Citibank, and IBM to name a few. To industry talent and peers, Mande is also well known for her production shows on Celebrity Cruises and Costa Cruise Lines. The *Costa Victoria* was voted "Best Production Shows & Entertainment" in the Fielding's Book of European Cruises in her first year with the company. Other credits include: Gaylord Entertainment and Opryland Productions in Nashville, the Alabama Theater in Myrtle Beach, Saban Entertainment in Los Angeles, Dick Foster Productions in Las Vegas, The Blue Angel in New York City, and the list goes on. Mande lives in

Miami Beach with her husband, Alex, and their two dogs, Sassy and Luigi. When not in production, Mande can be found writing in her library or at a local Starbucks, or designing jewelry in her home studio. She is a lot of right brain in perpetual motion, loving everything creative. Her passion runs deep and her compassion deeper; she loves to nurture and inspire talent, and to help others. Mande has created a line of jewelry called the "Forget Me Not Collection" as a tribute to her mother, and a way to help raise awareness for Alzheimer's. She is thrilled about the launching of this, her first book *Inspired to Dance*, and is already planning her next. She is currently in pre-production for two brand new, original musicals, one being, *Dog Show—The Musical,* which she is co-producing with her husband, Alex Marchant, and producer Lou Paciocco. Bound for Broadway, they have high aspirations for its final destination.

An honest and dedicated voice, a true teacher at heart, Mande tells it as it is, and hopes that her book, *Inspired to Dance* does just that: Inspires You to Dance!